Abolition Revolution

'A powerful analysis of the transformative potential of the abolitionist project. Day and McBean show why we must go beyond shifting a few dollars around to directly challenge the logics of capitalism, racism and patriarchy at the heart of the carceral state.'

—Alex S. Vitale, author of *The End of Policing*

'Not only does this superlative book expertly dismantle the dogmas of liberal anti-racism and carceral feminism which reproduce the systems of power, it also points the way forward to a post-abolitionist future in a meticulous, clear-headed way. Highly recommended.'

—Silvia Federici, author of *Caliban and the Witch*

'A thorough, engaging and important read – that held me through new information whilst never sacrificing depth. I'm so glad this book exists!'

—Travis Alabanza, award winning writer, performer and theatre maker

'Essential study for organisers and scholars across borders, *Abolition Revolution* vibrantly chronicles the cultural and political landscape of abolitionist practices in the UK. Day and McBean weave a powerful array of analysis, histories and voices – from organisers, scholars, unionists and/or incarcerated people – to offer profoundly necessary historical lessons that formulate the pathways that shape our abolition feminist revolutions.'

—Erica R. Meiners, co-author of *Abolition. Feminism. Now.*

'Aviah Sarah Day and Shanice Octavia McBean speak with such eloquence, conviction and passion that readers will want to join their struggle for abolition revolution. Their trenchant and concrete analysis of the criminalisation of Black and Asian youth, of carceral white bourgeois feminism, gentrification, and police and state violence, makes for essential reading. Let's heed their call for an abolitionist future.'

—Françoise Vergès, author of *A Decolonial Feminism*

T0150471

FireWorks

Series editors:

Gargi Bhattacharyya, Professor of Sociology,
University of East London

Anitra Nelson, Associate Professor, Honorary Principal Fellow,
Melbourne Sustainable Society Institute, University of
Melbourne

Also available

Empire's Endgame:
Racism and the British State
Gargi Bhattacharyya, Adam
Elliott-Cooper, Sita Balani,
Kerem Nisancioglu, Kojo
Koram, Dalia Gebrial, Nadine
El-Enany and Luke de Noronha

Settler Colonialism:
An Introduction
Sai Englert

Reinventing the Welfare State:
Digital Platforms and Public
Policies
Ursula Huws

The Politics of Permaculture
Terry Leahy

Exploring Degrowth:
A Critical Guide
Vincent Liegey and Anitra
Nelson

Pandemic Solidarity:
Mutual Aid during the
Covid-19 Crisis
Edited by Marina Sitrin and
Colectiva Sembrar

Abolition Revolution

Aviah Sarah Day and
Shanice Octavia McBean

PLUTO  PRESS

First published 2022 by Pluto Press
New Wing, Somerset House, Strand, London WC2R 1LA
and Pluto Press Inc.
1930 Village Center Circle, Ste. 3-384, Las Vegas, NV 89134

www.plutobooks.com

British Library Cataloguing in Publication Data
A catalogue record for this book is available from the British Library

ISBN 978 0 7453 4652 6   Hardback
ISBN 978 0 7453 4651 9   Paperback
ISBN 978 0 7453 4655 7   PDF
ISBN 978 0 7453 4653 3   EPUB

This book is printed on paper suitable for recycling and made from
fully managed and sustained forest sources. Logging, pulping and
manufacturing processes are expected to conform to the environmental
standards of the country of origin.

Typeset by Stanford DTP Services, Northampton, England

Simultaneously printed in the United Kingdom and United States of
America

This book is dedicated to Sarah Reed.

Contents

Part 2 – Roots In Empire: The History of Criminalisation and Resistance

Part 3 – Systems of Criminalisation Today

Part 4 – Abolitionist Futures

Part 5 – Symposium: Abolition in the UK

Series Preface

Addressing urgent questions about how to make a just and sustainable world, the FireWorks series throws a new light on contemporary movements, crises and challenges. Each book is written to extend the popular imagination and unmake dominant framings of key issues.

Launched in 2020, the series offers guides to matters of social equity, justice and environmental sustainability. FireWorks books provide short, accessible and authoritative commentaries that illuminate underground political currents or marginalised voices, and highlight political thought and writing that exists substantially in languages other than English. Their authors seek to ignite key debates for twenty-first-century politics, economics and society.

FireWorks books do not assume specialist knowledge, but offer up-to-date and well-researched overviews for a wide range of politically aware readers. They provide an opportunity to go deeper into a subject than is possible in current news and online media, but are still short enough to be read in a few hours.

In these fast-changing times, these books provide snappy and thought-provoking interventions on complex political issues. As times get dark, FireWorks offer a flash of light to reveal the broader social landscape and economic structures that form our political moment.

FireWorks

Acknowledgements

We have told the stories of many people throughout this book. Stories of struggle, stories of celebration, stories of grief and loss. We want to thank all those whose stories, experiences and organising have contributed to this book. We send solidarity and support to the families of those whose stories we tell, who due to the violence of carcerality or through the passage of time, are no longer with us. We are inspired by your strength and determination.

There are many people we want to thank for helping us make this book a reality. To the organisers, academics and thinkers who have offered their time, support and reflections – from the initial seeds of the proposal through to the manuscript – we are incredibly grateful: Sita Balani, Nadine El-Enany, Kojo Koram, Rees Arnott-Davies, Luke Wenman, Sarah Lamble, Kerem Nişancıoğlu, John M. Moore and Adam Elliott-Cooper.

To friends who offered their homes for writing retreats, provided fuel to keep us going and gave us their patience during our long periods of absence and frustration: Lucy Gaymer, Siân Robins-Grace, Hero Austin, Dennika Francis-Phillips, Nadia Vogel, Melissa Cespedes del Sur, Florence Dent and Bekah Sparrow.

We want to acknowledge our families who, over many years of wading through life together and in many different ways, made this book possible. A special thanks to Aviah's family: Fiona Day, Jourdan Thomas Alex Day,

Bisi Ogunjimi, Da'vid Tzadok. And a loving thank you to Shanice's family: P. Dyke and Shamar Tyrese Thompson.

Shout out to those who went the extra mile to contribute their thoughts and ideas by participating in the symposium, providing dope poetry and supporting us to navigate the publishing world: Kadeem Marshall-Oxley, Zahra Bei, Lydia Caradonna, Temi Mwale, Zara Manoehoetoe, Adam Elliott-Cooper (again!) and Andrew Franklin.

Thank you to our sisters, siblings and comrades in Sisters Uncut, CopWatch and the wider anti-racism and abolitionist movements, whose tenacity, fire and clarity are the backbone of this book, and everything in it.

Finally, thank you to Michael Etienne for his time and support with the finishing touches, and for his patient determination to sustain his partner Aviah, and friend Shanice, through this challenge. A special mention goes to Miriam Franklin who has been a rock of a partner to Shanice, and comrade to both of us, throughout the entire process. From doing the first (and most challenging!) edit of the symposium, to providing a critical and loving eye from start to finish: we couldn't have done it without you.

Introduction

A NOTE ON STRUCTURE

This book tells the story of carceral systems in Britain. To tell that story, we have structured the book into 16 theses. Each thesis is a self-contained argument that can be read on its own. This means they can be easily used for reading groups, activist meetings, skill shares, workshops, etc. That said, we hope you'll like them enough to read the whole book! The book ends with a conversation; where Aviah and Shanice take a step back to hear from other abolitionist organisers.

THESIS 1

A national abolitionist movement has erupted in Britain. Abolition is a tool to re-imagine revolutionary politics.

There wasn't a single moment when we became police and prison abolitionists. There wasn't one event, or a single officer or an individual incident that turned us entirely away from the status quo. Things that come in ones or twos often have sensible explanations, reasons why they're an aberration and not the norm. And we, like everyone, were convinced of these explanations for at least some of our lives. But we are Black, working class, queer women – the realisation was perhaps inevitable. Over time, the one or two bad experiences with police became threes, fours, tens. The incidents we experienced weren't just our own, but were the incidents of our moms, cousins, neighbours and friends. We both have younger brothers; working class boys born into a system where they are perceived as criminals-in-waiting. Thug. Chav. Drug dealer. Mugger. ASBO. Knife crime. Hoodie. All words aimed at communicating the line between evil and everyone else. Working class boys, especially when they're racialised, experience a viciousness with police that we were forced to learn about by watching it play out like a horror film in their lives. And we know how horror films go: the Black guy always dies first.

Over time individual incidents where police failed to keep us safe, or actively caused us harm, became a pattern and the pattern revealed itself to be a system. This system – of state violence, coercion and criminalisation – brought us back to our working class, city roots; even though both of us, at different points, had illusions of escaping our humble beginnings. It's this journey that not only made us abolitionists but brought us together as friends. And it's this friendship – grown over years of struggle, changed ideas, mundane and exciting organising, and moments of real political rupture – that underpins this book.

Abolitionism – the call to abolish institutions of state coercion such as police, prisons, detention centres, borders, arms and the military – didn't start with people like us, the new kids on the block who call ourselves 'abolitionists'. Abolition originated as the movement to end slavery. Resistance to policing and state violence is a common theme throughout working class history, and a defining struggle of Britain's Black and Asian communities. In many ways, abolition gives a name to a project that many have been working on from before we were born! We stand on the shoulders of giants, many giants – some of whom are still with us today, some of whom we've met and worked with. It's their work, their struggle, their perseverance that has given us the tools through which we analyse the world today, through an abolitionist lens. Our abolitionism is a homage to those who have struggled before us and our attempt to make real the vision they had for our futures. As we cast a revolutionary eye to the social relations inherent in capitalism that underpin the violent institutions we seek to abolish, we hope to provide a glimpse of the world we want to live in and are working towards.

ABOLITION IS THE PRE-DRINKS, REVOLUTION IS THE SESH

There is a new and burgeoning debate in the UK over what abolition as a radical political project is and could – or should – become. And while the siloed musings of left-leaning twittersphere can be exhausting, these debates reflect a broader contestation at a national level around just how far the state is allowed to reach into our lives. A crisis of legitimacy is playing out around policing, bordering and criminalisation in the UK today, as the myth that the police and state protect us continues to unravel at the seams. In very direct ways, this crisis was hurried along not just by the conflicts and contradictions inherent in the global capitalist system, but by years of social movement activity. Alongside abolitionists, family campaigners demanding justice for those killed by police, youth uprisings, student organising, Black Lives Matter (BLM), and environmental and feminist organisations have all been key protagonists in the story of the growing UK abolitionist movement. Many of the people who are part of this story wouldn't call themselves abolitionists, but they have all contributed to a deepening crisis around police and state violence. They have made visible the violence some try so hard to hide, mapped out routes to resistance in the heat of state repression and taken radical ideas out to people who have never heard them. And you best believe the last few years have been momentous.

The movement that erupted on to the global stage in the summer of 2020, following the grotesque murder of George Floyd in Minneapolis in the US, gave us the biggest anti-racism protests 'since the slave abolition movement',[1] even though they took place during the worst throes of a global pandemic. The world woke up, and rose up, to the fact that the system put down the whips and shackles, only to replace them with cuffs and cages. We lived through the statue of Bristolian slave-holder Edward Colston getting dashed into Bristol Harbour by anti-racist activists, and celebrated the court victory of the campaigners who put him there. Following the murder of Sarah Everard by a serving London Metropolitan Police officer, we participated in the sudden emergence of a national Kill the Bill movement against government plans to expand police powers. We've witnessed the confidence ordinary women have in the police in freefall, whilst organised feminists have taken a prominent role in the anti-police violence movement. Out of this web of resistance, an organised, national police and prison abolitionist movement has burst into the messy fray of British politics – a movement now reckoning with its history, searching for its identity, sharing its ideas and trialling its strategies. So what does all this talk of abolishing stuff mean?

In 2020, Patrisse Cullors, an abolitionist leader within the Black Lives Matter Global Network, wrote a letter to Joe Biden and Kamala Harris after their election victory against then US president Donald Trump. The aim was to secure a meeting with the new White House leaders, influence the highest levers of democratic power and convince them – fresh off the electoral support they received from anti-racist activists across the US – to implement the BLM policy agenda for law enforcement reform.[2] They made this appeal in the context of the transformational language around race and policing being used by US politicians in the months after George Floyd was murdered. There was some hope for change, despite the rigorous and unapologetic history both Biden and Harris had in defending the police and harming Black communities: Harris being the self-proclaimed 'Top Cop' and Biden ushering in the 1994 Violent Crime Control and Law Enforcement Act that accelerated the mass incarceration of Black Americans. But by November 2021, Biden had signed three new policing bills. And to really stick it to the BLM movement and signal his disdain for the abolitionist call to defund the police, Biden promised more funding for law enforcement: 'When you look at what our communities need, what our law enforcement is being asked to do, it's going to require more resources, not fewer resources.'[3]

This is the impossible and hostile landscape within which projects seeking policy change from governments have to operate – navigating a dynamic where systems of oppression need to flex their rhetoric just enough to absorb and quell popular anger, whilst leaving the foundations of violence and coercion either untouched, or displacing them elsewhere. For example, while many of the largest cities in the US now have policies against the types of pressure positions that killed George Floyd, in 2022 police budgets are once again on the rise.[4] Just a few weeks after he took the knee against anti-Black racism, Keir Starmer – leader of the British Labour Party – described the call to defund the police as 'nonsense'. He was unequivocal, claiming he would have 'no truck' with calls to reduce police funding, while he boasted about sending 'thousands of people to court' throughout his career.[5] In 2022, ahead of local elections, Labour pivoted to a tough on crime, law and order strategy, with Starmer demanding a nationwide injunction to ban climate protesters from demonstrating and taking direct action.[6] The role of 'top cop' is, evidently, transnational.

Alongside this reformist work and often at a less visible and more grassroots level of organising, abolitionists are developing a vision and practice for alternative ways of living in community with each other – rehearsals for the world we want to usher in. In these spaces, communities practice non-punitive ways of dealing with intra-community harm. In recognising state institutions as principal drivers of societal harm and cycles of violence, abolitionists reject police and prisons as a solution to community safety and are invested in developing alternative frameworks. These alternative community practices draw on radical thought past and present. They look back to societies – often indigenous – who organised their resources, decision making and relationships in communal ways and so were able to develop responses to harm that centred the needs of people, not the needs of power. They also look back to movements and activists who were never explicitly abolitionist – such as Claudia Jones and rebels in the British colonies – who nevertheless have important things to offer those of us looking to build a future without police and prisons. And finally they draw on the organisers amongst us today, doing time-consuming and emotionally difficult work to create, test and re-create models of community safety outside of calling 999. This is the abolitionist work that centres creation, not ruin: it visualises the world we want to live in, not just the one we want to leave behind.

But none of these ways of conceptualising abolition or building towards an abolitionist future can, on their own, give us a world without violence. They can certainly help make the present more liveable, but who wants to live just to survive? Abolition demands we change not just ourselves but everything. It demands a fundamental transformation and reorganisation of society – and that can only ever be a revolutionary project. Practicing alternative models of community safety, living abolition in the now, is vital but will always be limited by the capitalist, imperialist social relations that permeate every aspect of our lives – from the ideas we hold, to the resources we have. And while imagining, and even rehearsing for, an abolitionist future is an important part of re-conceptualising human relationships, rehearsal alone is not enough to usher in a new, global reality. In some spaces, the work of practising non-punitive approaches to harm and violence has fallen into the neoliberal trap of focusing entirely on the individual and interpersonal, forgetting that we are made in the world we inhabit: in order to truly change the individual, we have to change the world.

And what of abolitionists intervening in establishment politics? Appealing to system-architects as a singular or central strategy has often left radical movements demobilised and demoralised. Those in power have developed a deftness for absorbing radical movements into their systems of control and power, giving the illusion of change in the direction of equality, while in fact containing and neutralising the possibility for radical change. And as we learnt from the Corbyn parliamentary project, what the establishment cannot contain, it smashes. In the aftermath of the Civil Rights movement in the US, as part of the strategy to pacify the wave of unrest across society, those in power capitulated to anti-racist sentiment by putting Black faces in high places. They created room for a Black political and economic elite to emerge and take on some of the grunt work for the system, whilst leaving the structure of white supremacist capitalism firmly in place. And while they gave Black people a seat at the table as mayors, governors and money-makers, the FBI was out murdering Black revolutionaries like Fred Hampton, caging Black radicals like Mumia Abu-Jamal, and using subterfuge to destroy revolutionary organisations that sought to fundamentally re-order US society. This strategy, waged against our elder comrades, was ultimately successful and it's one we see playing out in different guises wherever there have been powerful social movements that fight not just against the reality of oppression, but the *systems* that give rise to that oppression.

Let us cross the Atlantic back to Britain, where this book will be largely focused. The core architects of *authoritarian* Tory Britain also double up as poster children for *inclusive* Tory Britain. But the melanin didn't just pop its way to the top: the diversity and inclusion industry champions representation, and is leaned on by power brokers, in order to avoid the question of radical social transformation. Diversity and inclusion is used to sanitise systems that harm us, by making the person delivering the message a symbol of progress. Think about senior management in your own workplace: we bet they want more Black people in senior roles, but won't be paying their lower-paid Black staff more because *insert reason why systemic change isn't possible here* – and in general, most bosses don't feel the need to offer a reason. The Windrush Scandal, the 'Go home or face arrest' van,[7] the hostile environment, the Nationality and Borders Act 2022, the Police, Crime, Sentencing and Courts (PCSC) Act 2022 – these were all orchestrated by Home Secretaries who were women and, in Priti Patel's case, from a migrant-descended family. Black faces have been used to release reports claiming structural racism is a figment of our imagination, to run mayoral campaigns claiming knife crime comes from broken Black families, and to attack critical race theory in Parliament. The establishment is well practised in absorbing anti-racist demands – such as those for greater representation in politics – and using them against those of us in the anti-racist and abolitionist movements looking for more systemic change.

And this isn't new. The 1965 Race Relations Act was one of the first pieces of legislation that criminalised racism in Britain, but it was rarely enforced and when it was, it often ended up being used to criminalise radical Black political activity. Michael X, for example, was swiftly prosecuted under the Race Relations Act for speaking out against white supremacy.[8] Yet, when fascist leader Kingsley Read celebrated the racist 1976 murder of Gurdip Singh Chaggar by proclaiming 'One down, one million to go', a judge, citing free speech, claimed that this wasn't incitement to racial hatred. In the words of Sivanandan, a prominent activist and intellectual of the time, the 1968

Community Relations Commission (CRC) 'took up the Black cause and killed it': expanding the status quo just enough to allow some Black integration, whilst diluting and subduing Black radicals and revolutionaries. He went further, arguing the CRC created a layer of Black leaders ready to 'teach white power structures to accept the Blacks and the Blacks to accept the white power structure'.[9]

In response to the uprisings in Black communities like Tottenham, Toxteth, Brixton and Handsworth in the 1980s, the government responded to the 'canker [of Black radicalism and counter-hegemony] in the body politic'[10] by expanding its dilution and containment strategies: government reports that led to nowhere, equalities legislation that changed little, police and community liaison groups that created the illusion of accountability but had no material impact on racist policing, funding schemes that created new ethnic categories, where ethnic groups had to compete to fund community projects, but where that funding bound them to the politics of the system. All this alongside the usual tools of violent suppression and mass criminalisation after the uprisings succeeded in demobilising anti-racism in Britain for a generation – often obscured by the celebratory media around multiculturalism and diversity. How do we appeal to an establishment hell-bent on protecting its own power? How do we demand they strip themselves of the very power they need to survive? The short answer is we can't. The longer answer is revolutionary, abolitionist praxis.

Okay let us stop you there – because this doesn't mean never engaging in establishment politics or demanding reforms! In its short life, the Kill The Bill movement has had some minor wins, including forcing delays to the policing bill in Parliament and winning crucial defeats for the government in the House of Lords. This same movement expanded the scope for reform in Britain by setting the context within which a group of feminists – Reclaim These Streets – took the Metropolitan Police to court for contravening their right to protest violence against women. And they won. Both these wins occurred when taking the state on at its own game, forcing change from within. Abolitionists also have a concept of non-reformist reforms: pushing for system change that, in the words of Sarah Lamble, 'challenges the assumptions that underpin and sustain the system',[11] thus bringing us closer to abolition.

Harm-reduction approaches to substance use are a brilliant example. Evidence suggests consumption rooms, where people can safely inject drugs in the presence of trained professionals who have access to overdose inhibitors like Naloxone, can reduce overdose deaths, reduce the spread of blood-borne viruses, reduce anti-social behaviour and increase engagement with support services.[12] Despite this evidence, Peter Krykant, a former user who set up a life-saving mobile consumption room in Glasgow, was sacked from his job and criminalised by police.[13] Contrast this to a criminal-justice approach, where research from King's College London showed UK prisoners are 7.5 times more likely to die from heroin overdoses in the first two weeks of their release from prison.[14] This is likely due to a myriad of factors, including forced abstinence due to time in prison and therefore reduced tolerance when they come out, lack of access to healthcare whilst in prison, and absence of support on release. But also, more fundamentally, prisons are inherently harmful: they reproduce cycles of destitution and hopelessness. When we win non-reformist reforms – that is, reforms that reduce police and carceral power, so taking us closer to abolition – we also win the case against criminalisation, making police and criminal-justice approaches obsolete.

Choosing strategic places of weakness to leverage power during moments of rupture – like the Kill The Bill movement did in the House of Lords, or possibilities for non-reformist reform campaigns – can produce the meaningful victories needed to sustain and build an abolitionist movement. But police, prisons and detention centres are the ever far-reaching tendrils of the capitalist state, institutions designed to maintain power in the hands of a few, control the working class and protect capitalism. The final victory for abolitionists, or anyone who wishes to see a world without state violence, can never come from appealing to the conscience of our jail masters. There is a reason why they lock us in cages, and this reason emanates from the very soul of a society structured by class and race. Simply asking to be let out, or asking to be put in a slightly nicer cage, won't cut it.

One of our aims in writing this book is to contribute to a growing body of work carving out a space for UK voices, ideas and strategies in what can otherwise be a US-centric movement. Some of the boldest rehearsals in revolutionary anti-racism began in the States: from the Black Panther Party, to the League of Revolutionary Black Workers, the Memphis sanitation strikes and the Attica Prison uprising. As slavery ended and capitalist wage labour emerged, criminalisation and law enforcement stepped up to re-structure race and class relations in the US, so it is no surprise those conditions birthed a movement to end policing and prisons. But right here in the UK we have our own rebellions, our own revolutionaries, our own uprisings that come out of the legacies of policing in the colonies, and bordering on the mainland. For UK abolitionist politics to continue to mature, we have to grapple with the lessons of our specific histories and contexts. It's this desire that places both empire and neoliberalism at the core of our analysis: two systems that have fundamentally defined the boundaries of police and state violence across the British Isles today.

But this book isn't just an exercise in contextualisation. We want to contribute to a growing understanding of abolition that grounds abolitionist politics in a *revolutionary* vision – a vision that requires us to change nothing short of everything. We are not content with posturing on the sidelines of history; we don't mean a vague, undefined, almost romantic notion of 'revolution' where you don't know if the revolution is being made on the barricades or in the boardroom. We mean a steadfastly proletarian project where those on whose back this world was built are the ones who make the future. We are done with academics and influencers who use the language of abolition to give themselves a marketable edginess, lining their pockets with corporate deals, whilst refusing to call themselves anti-capitalists; talking about abolition, whilst walking the system. Our abolitionism is to be judged by the extent to which it weakens the state's monopoly on violence and coercion against the global working and under classes. We are judged by whether our work is oriented towards an internationalist revolution of ordinary folk, who re-make the world in the interests of themselves, not the interests of their masters.

We are not proposing to know *the* road to revolution. We are not even convinced an answer to that question can be written, though we hope that it will one day be lived. But we do know that if we are to get there, state violence and repression would be one of the biggest obstacles to our success. Revolutionary abolitionism can help us direct our activism towards chipping away at the systems of power, violence, control and coercion that help maintain the status quo exactly as it is. Some think abolitionism is the articulation of revolutionary politics in the language of the youth today. We don't think this is true. But we think it *could* be true. Abolition could be the window through which we imagine a completely different world, one that inspires hope across the world that we can choose life not destruction, but we have yet to dust off the junk obscuring that vision. You might think that an ideology underpinned by abolishing key institutions of capitalist and imperial power would naturally be more resistant to having its radical edges softened. But even amongst abolitionists, the allure of establishment politics and individualism can be blinding.

We need revolutionary abolitionism, but what might this mean in practice? Let's look at the recent call from the US abolitionist movement to defund the police. Defunding the police and allowing policymakers to simply delegate existing policing functions to other organisations – such as social services or schools – does not weaken the state's monopoly on violence and coercion. If the job of a cop is being done by a person in a different uniform or with a different role, then there is still a cop. And if we're not careful, here again lies the potential for radical demands to be absorbed into the status quo, allowing the state to hide coercive power behind guard labour,[15] performed by outwardly benevolent institutions: social work, schools, hospitals, even charities. This is exactly what the British state has done by bringing the war on terror into schools through the Prevent strategy, bringing borders into hospitals with citizenship checks and turning paramedics into cops-with-oxygen, pairing them with police to direct mental health patients away from A&E. A revolutionary abolitionist approach to defunding the police would demand we democratise public funding allocation at the community level, redefine the parameters and definitions of crime, design institutions that exist solely to respond to the needs of ordinary people and redistribute funds not just at the level of public services, but from the wealthy to the global poor in order to tackle the root causes of harm. Abolition must orientate our work towards a future run by people, for people, and not by profit, for profit: this is revolutionary abolitionism.

THESIS 2

Our Journey to Abolition in Sisters Uncut was Long and Bumpy: Abolition is a Road, Not a Destination!

Sisters Uncut (Sisters) held its first meeting at Crossroads Women's Centre in Kentish Town on 20 November 2014. Aviah was present at this meeting, with Shanice joining the group shortly afterwards in 2015. Our collective experience as survivors, service users and sector workers motivated a determination to protect the national network of domestic violence services from closure, due to the government's onslaught of funding cuts. In the wake of Sarah Everard's murder by one of the Met's own officers, by 2021 Sisters' organising had intensified a political and reputational crisis within the Metropolitan Police. Here we reflect on the group's political journey; from a politics of anti-austerity to that of police and prison abolition. The longevity and growth of Sisters Uncut provides a window into the shifting political trajectory of British social justice movements over the past decade.[1]

In the 1970s, the domestic violence sector started off as a network of self-sufficient feminist squats, laying outside of state structures and funding.[2] By the time Sisters Uncut was founded, this autonomous, grassroots network had become a professionalised service sector:[3] relying on state funding that then made it vulnerable to the sweeping cuts of the 2010 Tory/Liberal Democrat coalition government's austerity programme. In the early days of Sisters Uncut, most of us were under 30 and unfamiliar with the history of state funding and charity modelling being used to undercut and co-opt radical movements. Back then, we located the domestic violence sector's problems solely in measly state funding. The early rallying cry of our 'feministo' demanded ring-fenced funding to secure the sector's future, with an intersectional feminist influence appearing in the call to halt the closure of services for women of colour.[4]

Our largely uncritical support for state-based solutions to social problems reflected the politics of the wider movements for social justice at this time – movements that had been re-ignited to defend public services and the welfare state. Though we saw ourselves as radicals, our political horizons had been severely limited by the context in which most of us were raised. We were brought up – many of us dragged up – in the post-Thatcherite landscape which had seen worker and liberation movements annihilated. As our consciousness of the world around us grew, from our childhood through to adulthood, the memory of powerful mass-organised resistance was fading. After the 2010 election, the state looked to capitalise on our limited movement memory by making youth the first target of its austerity agenda, with sweeping cuts to further and higher education.[5]

Over the first few decades of neoliberalism's rise, the elite had cultivated our ignorance, engineered our movement's dependency through state co-optation, and severed us from our histories of radical resistance. The movement infrastructure and networks of mutual aid which had secured major victories – such as scrapping the Poll Tax only a generation earlier – had largely been smashed, demobilised, or incorporated into state structures.[6] The feminist anti-violence movement followed this same grim trajectory. This much-diminished organisational and infrastructural support magnified Sisters' political shortcomings: we developed patchy and sometimes uncoordinated connections to our movement elders, to histories of resistance and to the wider movements around us.

When the coalition government came to power, bringing with it an ideological commitment to shift money away from the public sector and into private coffers, the anti-austerity resistance that emanated from this context was a largely defensive campaign to protect the welfare state. UK Uncut, a predecessor of Sisters Uncut, was one example of the diverse shape this resistance took on. Taking headline-grabbing direct action against tax-avoiding corporations such as Vodafone and Starbucks,[7] UK Uncut sought to highlight boosting tax revenue through clamping down on tax avoidance schemes as a viable alternative to austerity – an act capable of bringing billions, they argued, into the treasury.[8] It was in this way that Sisters understood that domestic violence wasn't simply private or interpersonal; in a reversal of the famous second-wave slogan we knew that, in fact, the political was personal. The state plays a decisive role in reproducing patriarchal social relations and creating the conditions that make gendered violence more, or less, likely: that is, the state can choose to open or close doors to women's safety. In these early days, we understood the state made choices – always ideological – about how it approached the perpetration of violence against women. What we hadn't yet collectively clocked was that the state *itself* was a perpetrator.

Early Sisters Uncut actions made use of the spectacle of symbolic protest, such as the Valentine's Day blockade of Oxford Circus and dyeing the fountains of Trafalgar Square blood-red to chants of 'they cut we bleed.'[9] Plumes of purple and green smoke billowing from pyrotechnic flares has become a signature of Sisters Uncut actions: an homage to the militant suffragettes who took action under the same colours.[10] In 2015, when the film *Suffragette* was announced, a proposal was put forward to stage a 'die in' on the red carpet of the premiere.[11] Our aim was to force media attention on the deadly consequences of the government closing life-saving domestic violence services. On 7 October 2015, we jumped the barriers at Leicester Square's Odeon, landing at the feet of bemused Hollywood starlets. 'Dead women can't vote' was our clarion call, highlighting the contradiction between glorifying suffragette history in a context where austerity was shattering women's lives.[12] We interrupted the celebratory atmosphere on the advancement for women's rights – our liberation was not complete with the vote, we cried, with two women a week being killed by a current or ex-partner.[13] We expected only a handful of articles to feature in the more sympathetic media outlets, but were overwhelmed by the national and international attention generated by our storming the red carpet. With hundreds across the country wanting to join our collective, we grew from a single London group to establishing chapters in North, South-east and the East

End of London; soon followed by groups in Portsmouth, Bristol, Gloucester, Doncaster, Glasgow, Manchester, Leeds, Brighton, Liverpool, Newcastle, Birmingham, Cardiff and more.[14]

As our movement expanded, the diversity of our members did too. Doncaster Sisters Uncut was established by a group of women older than the London contingent, from migrant survivors of domestic violence, to those who had organised women's solidarity groups during the miners' strike of 1984–85.[15] Movement elders from Doncaster quipped that the relative security of a state pension bolstered their militancy, allowing them to wage an unrelenting campaign that, in 2016, succeeded in securing funding for Doncaster Women's Aid, after it faced imminent closure.[16] Despite initial victories in Doncaster, the celebrations were short-lived. The local authority initiated attacks on the service providers who protested, using their militant action as an excuse to victimise them out of their jobs. Despite this, the impact of groups like Doncaster on the wider Sisters network was significant: through struggle and political education, our horizons were shifting. Although the misery of the world around us was becoming entrenched by defeats – big and small – suffered across the wider anti-austerity movement, Sisters' defensive organising began to give way to a more confident and visionary politics. Our collective commitment to abolitionist and revolutionary politics had begun to emerge.

Between 2014 and 2016, as Sisters continued to grow, more working class, Black, trans and disabled women joined the collective. The growing diversity shifted the balance in favour of more radical organising – expanding the core anti-austerity politics towards a broader critique of how capitalist society is structured by class, race, gender and (dis)ability. The influence of these Sisters, and their politics, meant that alongside protests calling out cuts to domestic violence services were actions that spotlighted the particular realities of domestic and state violence as experienced by working class, migrant, trans, disabled and Black women. Sisters burnt copies of the *Daily Mail* outside the newspaper's headquarters, protesting the racist lies that led to women, often survivors of domestic violence, being locked up in immigration detention centres[17] – left to survive the compounded violence of the state. We joined migrant solidarity and Black women's organisations to call protests outside of the Yarl's Wood detention centre,[18] and supported groups like Black Lives Matter UK and United Families and Friends Campaign, as the global BLM movement shifted the dialogue around police and state violence.[19] It was through this work that Sisters began to understand the way in which violence against women was not simply incidental to the operation of the state, but built in to how it functions by design. The number of targets in our crosshairs grew from the chancellor of the exchequer and local authorities to the Home Office, the police, detention centres, prisons and the media that enabled them. Violence was no longer interpersonal: it was structural. The state was no longer a bystander, but a perpetrator.

Around this time, many of us working in the domestic and sexual violence sectors began noticing a shift in service provision. While local authority funding streams dwindled, new funds emerged through the criminal justice system and the Home Office. The US model of partnership working between domestic violence services and the police had been making its way to Britain for the two decades prior.[20] At Sisters meetings, service users and workers retold harrowing stories of cops arriving at domestic violence incidents only to cart survivors away in handcuffs – often for defending themselves against a perpetrator.[21] A US study found that survivors from Black, migrant and LGBT communities, and those on welfare, were most likely to be arrested instead of, or alongside, their perpetrator.[22] In England and Wales, half of all police forces have a policy of arresting those reporting domestic, sexual and other serious violence, if they are suspected of having insecure immigration status.[23] This has led to countless women who are survivors of domestic and sexual violence ending up in immigration detention centres like Yarl's Wood: hidden away and re-traumatised by the violence of immigration detention.[24] A 2015 report by Women Against Rape and Black Women's Rape Action Project documented 'a regime of predatory sexual abuse'[25] at Yarl's Wood since it opened in 2002.

At this time, Aviah was working in the domestic violence sector, whilst completing a PhD on the efficacy of Specialist Domestic Violence Courts (SDVCs) – founded during the Blair government – that many in the domestic violence sector championed.[26] As Sisters Uncut members became more critical of the state's role in the lives of domestic violence survivors, Aviah turned her research to understanding the processes behind the increasing criminalisation of women who report abuse. Her findings in turn helped to shape Sisters' political analysis. This research led her to critiques of 'carceral feminist' strategies, which advocate for more police powers, longer prison sentences and partnership working with police and prisons to deal with perpetrators – policies fast becoming the norm in Britain. This was increasing the contact already marginalised women had with police and prisons – therefore increasing their exposure to criminalisation. It's no surprise that these punitive strategies gripped the sector in the midst of frenzied austerity: locking people up is a long-practised strategy of ruling elites who need to be seen to be tackling social problems, whilst simultaneously refusing to fund the public infrastructure needed to address them. Abolitionist feminists had long identified the cause behind the huge increase in survivor arrests,[27] but these initiatives had been brought to the UK with minimal criticism outside of the BME service sector.[28]

Carceral feminist strategies have a long and rotten history in Britain, as they've been used to deepen the criminalisation of working class Black communities. In the US, from where these initiatives hailed, research has found evidence that white middle-class communities have been largely shielded from such law-and-order initiatives.[29] Of course, Britain followed suit: in 1985, after the Black communities rose up against relentless police harassment and brutality, the Metropolitan Police cynically established the country's first domestic violence units in Brixton and Tottenham –where the uprisings began[30] – giving them yet more powers and pretexts with which to target the Black community. Carceral feminism and state violence have been pals from day one.

The growth of Sisters, and their splitting into London regions, was closely followed by more localised community organising, confronting many in Sisters with the reality of state violence beyond the experience of women. This forced us to reassess what an 'intersectional' and 'safe'[31] space meant in practice: who wasn't safe, from what type of violence, in what spaces, and why? Answering these questions pushed us further towards an abolitionist feminism. In the summer of 2016, two political occupations took place in South and East London. Under our slogan 'how can she get away if she has nowhere to stay?',[32] we were fighting for more and better housing provision for survivors. By the entrance to the large uninhabited building that was the site of the Peckham occupation, cops set upon a group of young Black men, strip-searching them in the back of a police van. In a snap assessment of who needed protection from systemic sexual violence in that moment, the gender inclusion policy that usually excluded men was waived and they were invited into the occupation and off the streets.[33]

On an estate in Hackney, East End Sisters launched a three-month occupation of an empty council flat on Marian Court. A social centre and organising hub was established in the heart of Marian Court – which brought with it all the messy complexities of community organising, whilst nevertheless providing a space for political education. Homeless residents placed in temporary accommodation on the estate joined the campaign, and forced Mayor of Hackney Philip Glanville to the negotiating table – demanding safe, secure and accessible housing for all (which they all eventually secured).[34] The occupation's open door policy pushed group dynamics to the limit, and difficult conversations were common. White working class survivors from the area sought respite from beatings at home, whilst migrant survivors with no recourse to public funds stayed overnight with their children while simultaneously negotiating ongoing support. Muslim women who were new to political organising joined the campaign from the estate, alongside a number of trans Muslim Sisters.

The occupation created a place to talk collectively about how Islamophobic street attacks, harassment by transphobes, beatings by abusive partners, assaults by cops, and violent evictions had brought us all together in that space. This should not be romanticised: the relationships often played out in messy and confrontational ways. But the occupation birthed a political community that was able to carry these complexities. We acknowledged each other's struggles, made mutual commitments to work in solidarity and stood up for each other's right to live free from violence. Through local organising, collective action and mutual aid, we were developing non-punitive ways to address interpersonal grievances and harm. This inspiring atmosphere rubbed off on the children on the estate, who asked to speak with the Mayor at a negotiation meeting. A 12-year-old delegate presented a petition signed by the Marian Court children demanding the estate's caged playground be refurbished and unlocked, so they could play safely and avoid the busy roads. Their demand was met and their newly refurbished playground was reopened three weeks later.

As our political consciousness deepened, the shocking details of Sarah Reed's life and how she died in prison shook us to the core. Sarah, a 32-year-old Black woman, died in HMP Holloway in January 2016: she was in prison after being charged for defending herself against an abuser, who sexually assaulted her whilst she was detained under the Mental Health Act.[35] Four years earlier, she was viciously beaten by then Metropolitan Police officer James Kiddie, who was later found guilty of assault after CCTV captured his unprovoked attack, in which he can be seen punching Sarah multiple times in the head.[36] Later, an inquest into her death found the failure of prison staff to properly address Sarah's mental health needs and keep her safe contributed to her death.[37] As we threw ourselves into supporting the family justice campaign led by Sarah's mother Marilyn, our analysis of how police and prisons perpetuate cycles of violence against women matured. The police entered Sarah's life at two key moments: to beat her and to send her to prison, despite the fact she was a victim of sexual violence, and a grieving mother. They did not see a Black woman whose mental health had deteriorated after the death of her newborn baby[38] – a woman who needed love, support and care. They saw a danger that needed containing. Far from keeping Sarah safe, police involvement led to her being found dead in her cell with ligatures around her neck.[39]

Around this time, a proposal was put forward to the national Sister Uncut's network, arguing for a commitment to prison and police abolition. As a group that organises on the basis of consensus decision-making, this proposal didn't pass without difficulty. Some survivors found it difficult to envisage safety outside of a criminal justice framework. Others argued that the inherent violence of policing and prisons perpetuated violence against women – especially for poor communities of colour.[40] Through tender and careful discussions, we eventually established Sisters Uncut as an abolitionist collective: advocating for transformative justice based on community care and mutual aid, alongside state welfare, as a response to harm in our communities.[41]

In 2016, Western Europe's largest women's prison – HMP Holloway – was closed, and the site earmarked for development as a luxury apartment complex. Reclaim Holloway, a community coalition, had formed in early 2016 to wrest the site back for the collective good.[42] The abolitionists who formed Reclaim Holloway found inspiration in the 1970s prison abolitionist pressure group Radical Alternatives to Prison, whose pamphlet *Alternative to Holloway* argued for an end to incarceration. The pamphlet made the case for transforming the site into community provision – including housing, childcare and a community centre.[43] Reclaim Holloway argued that the land on which the prison stood should be used to permanently house the 20,000 households on the council waiting list,[44] and to establish a women's centre as a healing testimony to the trauma of 160 years of women's incarceration on the site.[45] Armed with a new and developing abolitionist praxis, the North London chapter of Sisters Uncut occupied the visitors' centre of HMP Holloway, aiming to prevent the corporate takeover of the site, whilst directing attention towards Reclaim Holloway's demands, which were put front and centre of the action.[46] The Holloway occupation – an 'abolitionist rehearsal' – built on their vision by transforming part of the prison into a temporary community centre for women and non-binary people.[47]

Reclaim Holloway's community campaign has been partially successful: London Mayor Sadiq Khan gave Peabody, a housing association, a loan to purchase the site.[48] This hugely expanded the number of 'genuinely affordable' housing units available,[49] compared to what would have happened had it ended up in the hands of greedy corporate property developers. Amazing though this victory is, it will remain a partial one while the exact number of units secured for social housing, versus those for private sale, remains contested.[50] There are further concerns that Peabody intends to turn the proposed women's building into a centre with a criminal justice focus.[51] The fight for 100 per cent social housing and a community-led women's building continues.

By early 2018, the #MeToo and #TimesUp movements – highlighting rampant sexual violence against women – had made its way to the British Bafta Awards. The #MeToo movement, originally founded by Black anti-violence activist Tarana Burke,[52] exploded on social media after movie star Alyssa Milano tweeted #MeToo, inviting survivors of sexual violence to join her. Milano's tweets built on the exposure of Hollywood producer Harvey Weinstein as a serial abuser; after that, #MeToo went viral. Bafta attendees announced their intention to support the #TimesUp campaign by inviting campaigners as their plus ones. Guests included Eileen Pullen and Gwen Davis, whose involvement in a Dagenham Ford women's strike of 1968 won equal pay; Marai Larasi, then-CEO of women of colour domestic violence charity IMKAAN, and Lady Phyll, founder of UK Black Pride.⁵³ As these conversations were happening, Sisters Uncut prepared to invade our second red carpet.

This action, which we called #TimesUpTheresa, was directed at then Prime Minister Theresa May's Domestic Violence and Abuse Bill. The bill proposed yet more police powers as the solution to gendered violence,⁵⁴ whilst papering over the decimated funding of life-saving domestic violence services. We argued that this would create a 'pro-arrest environment in which *everyone* involved will be more likely to be arrested';⁵⁵ more migrant women would be deported and criminalisation of working class Black communities would deepen.⁵⁶ In a context where the majority of women in prison – 57 per cent – have experienced domestic violence,⁵⁷ we were determined to disrupt the abuse-to-prison pipeline.

Our route to the red carpet was not as smooth sailing as the last. Exorbitantly high demand for viewing-pen wrist-bands meant that too few of us had got hold of them to safely carry out the action. A queer Black Sister took one for the team and spent the entire day flirting with the head of security. As his colleagues protested, slack jawed, he escorted the entire group past several security checkpoints and put us in prime position. Our true motives became clear when we jumped the barrier onto the red carpet, assiduously avoiding eye contact with the head security guard, who by now was red-faced with rage and incredu-lity, as he towered over us.

The press coverage for the #TimesUpTheresa's action was decent enough.⁵⁸ North London Sisters followed it up with an ad hack campaign replacing adverts on London's Underground with poems by survivors, some of which took aim at Theresa May's bill.[59] But successive delays in the bill, alongside burnout, meant that sustained action proved challenging. Sisters Uncut has never had paid organisers, and for many Sisters, jobs, studies and caring responsibilities had to be juggled alongside organising. By early 2021 – in the midst of both the global pandemic and Sisters' longest period of inaction – the bill was in the process of becoming an Act. Many of us wished we could have done more to resist the advancement of this carceral feminist legislation. We felt we had failed to stop any part of the bill becoming law, and failed to use the moment as a springboard to build an abolitionist feminist alternative.

All was to change just a couple of months later. In March 2021, Sarah Everard went missing while walking home in Clapham, London. The events that subsequently unfolded sparked a national movement against police powers: it was at this point that years of successful, less successful, burgeoning, yet interrupted, abolitionist organising within Sisters was harnessed. Those experiences gave us the speed and agility we needed to strategise and respond to the political moment before us. We churned out press releases and comment pieces advocating radical abolitionist politics, sustained mobilisations of thousands against incoming police powers, built coalitions between communities who had rarely, if ever, worked together before, and contributed alongside many other groups, to the police-critical environment that now exists across Britain.

On the shoulders of the many giants who came before us and the BLM movement of 2020, years of bumpy dress rehearsals suddenly saw us seamlessly outflanking police narratives and interrupting liberal attempts to turn Sarah's killer cop – PC Wayne Couzens – into a 'bad apple' anomaly. This movement refused to allow the establishment to scapegoat Cressida Dick – then head of the Metropolitan Police – to deflect criticism away from policing in its entirety. We were just one part of this story: groups like Reclaim Holloway, No More Exclusions, Cradle Community, 4Front and Abolitionist Futures had kept the embers of abolition burning on the margins of the British left. Years of abolitionist theorising and organising sprung into action, interpreting, analysing and agitating a way through what was, and continues to be, a significant political moment. In 2021, abolition in Britain took one step closer to becoming a reality: the atmosphere was electric.

This reaction to oppression isn't an act
I'm explicitly trapped,
let me explain,
poverty's deeply embedded,
our thoughts are estranged,
books and reports it's all for your gaze,
Self educate out of the racism maze.

We're Here to stay
Here to fight,
self proclaimed,
we'll state it twice,
we played the game,
we paved the way,
Through our thoughts the system changed,
Detained in cuffs,
we've seen disgust … but not discussed,
I've not succumbed, seen through disguise,
I'm not the one,
depict our aims in awful slums,
we're all for you,
you're all for one.

Still the target and you want to punish,
nothing worse … seems to me … like a curse
But we saw where your thoughts would lead
we'll prove you wrong by any means …
if that's a disability … I'll welcome it,
repressed emotions
We've held this in,
but if We speak it's … a certain win.
Grown Impoverished to my acknowledgement,
The only concern was safety,
institutes trying to take away mines to tame me?

Your view we're wild,
my view we're proud,
but if you're Black ... that's not allowed
not in this system,
we don't tell the stories of the victims,
why should I die for you to acknowledge the fault,
That's death without a probable cause,
Windrush!
Deport!
angers raging,
a tropical storm,
we can't express ourselves right,
we can't attend your hands are tied,
but ... if it's a battle of wills I'll enact mines,
if we were both at sea you'd capsize,
wait, we've been at sea,
we've been beneath a knee,
we've been a root,
we've been the seed,
we've been a tree,
left out to dry,
lost self esteem,
we should be fine,
this Crux is tight –
what's worth a fight
other than good times?

Kadeem Marshall-Oxley
No More Exclusions

PART 1

The Tools of Police Power

THESIS 3

Race is at the heart of policing; without race policing can't function. Dismantling the police means dismantling race.

'There is ... always something about race left unsaid ...'
Stuart Hall[1]

MARK AND SARAH

We live in a society founded on the principles of liberal, Enlightenment philosophers: all are equal, all are free, all have rights that must be protected. Yet capitalist liberal democracies hold within them a fundamental contradiction: in order for these capitalist liberal democracies to function, some people cannot be free. It's within this historical conflict that race emerges as a political tool, available to those in power to organise whose rights are protected – and whose are not. To begin to tell the story of how state violence is organised by race, we want to tell you the stories of two people: Mark Duggan and Sarah Everard, both killed by Metropolitan Police officers. The killings of Mark and Sarah happened ten years apart. In many ways, their deaths were very different. But they each illustrate the complex web of social relations that constitute British policing and state violence more broadly, each providing lessons for abolitionists looking to disrupt and dismantle police and state power.

Mark was a Black man who grew up in Tottenham, London. He was working class, with Irish and Caribbean heritage. He was part of the close-knit community of Broadwater Farm, a community with a long history of resistance to police violence. On 4 August 2011, Mark was gunned down by armed police in an operation led by a special unit of the Metropolitan Police: Trident. After his killing, the police were supported by several institutions – the Independent Police Complaints Commission (IPCC), the media, the political establishment – to surround his death in confusion – in some cases, lies. In what was a collective effort, they conjured up familiar tropes of violent Black masculinity to justify his murder to the public. Police sources fed lies to the media, and the media printed them without question, claiming he was part of a 'gang' that harboured 'violent' thugs, that he was a 'criminal' with imminent plans to cause harm.[2] Just days after the police killed him, the IPCC (Independent Police Complaints Commission) had to admit they misled journalists into believing there had been an exchange of shots between Mark and the cops.[3] There wasn't, yet it was this very idea that played a key role in portraying Mark as a threat so severe that the only option was extermination.

Many of these fraudulent distortions suppressed the key facts that cast major doubt on the police version of events. Here are some of those facts: Mark was unarmed when he was shot; Mark had no serious convictions; Mark was a worker, not a well-known criminal; the bullet that struck a police officer after Mark was apprehended came from a police officer's gun. One of the most frequently used images of Mark, portraying him as scowling aggressively at the camera, was actually a cropped picture of Mark mourning at the grave of his dead daughter, holding a tribute to her between his hands. At Mark's funeral, Archbishop Kwaku Frimpong-Mason asked people to 'stretch [their] hands towards the casket and thank God for Mark's life as he begins his heavenly journey'.[4] The *Daily Mail* and the *Express* reported this as mourners making 'gang salutes' for a 'fallen soldier' – the latter without correction.[5]

Mark was shot 1.50 seconds after leaving the minicab he was travelling in that day.[6] Not a single police officer at the scene of his killing saw him throw the gun that was later found seven metres away from his body, despite the fact the officer who shot him claimed to see it in his hand when he fired. The forensic pathologist originally commissioned by the IPCC claimed: 'I cannot conceive of how Mr Duggan might have thrown the gun to the place it was found, unobserved by the police.'[7] This chilling fact leaves open the possibility the gun was taken from the minicab and planted by officers so they could claim he was armed when shot – giving them a 'reasonably held belief' their lives were in imminent danger. But the coordinated campaign to suppress the truth and assassinate Mark's character means to this day police corruption is not the prominent image in the minds of the public when they hear the name Mark Duggan. A 2014 inquest found Mark had not been holding a gun when he was shot, but that regardless his killing was lawful. The slick – and sick – media machine that smeared Mark played a decisive role in creating a situation where it was legally acceptable for police to shoot dead an unarmed Black man.

Mark was murdered six years after police killed Jean Charles de Menezes, the Brazilian man travelling to work in South London when police fired seven bullets into his head, mistaking him for a terrorist. They smeared him too, claiming he wasn't wholly innocent because he 'jumped the train station barriers' and 'refused to stop' when police asked him to. Of course it was all lies and proven to be so, but only after the fact when it was too late, when the damage to a dead man's reputation had already been done.[8] Similarly, by the time the true circumstances surrounding Mark's murder became clear, the wounds to him and his family had already been deeply inflicted. Make no mistake: this was intentional. Discrediting the reputation of those they harm and kill – and mediating lies and distortions through commonly understood racial stereotypes – is a key instrument of police and state power. It's in this way abolition isn't just a struggle against the physical manifestation of violent institutions – the cuffing, the caging, the death – but also an ideological struggle to dismantle the narratives and ideas used to uphold them.

Sarah Everard's murder was different. Sarah was a white woman, a Durham University graduate, and a marketing executive. On 3 March 2021, a serving Metropolitan Police officer, using new powers granted to him under Covid-19 regulations, arrested, kidnapped, raped and murdered Sarah. Unlike the killing of Mark, Sarah's murder had politicians clambering over themselves to express shock at the capacity a serving police officer had for violence. Sarah's murder, and the events that unfolded afterwards, introduced many in Britain to the horrors of British policing for the very first time – horrors Black communities had been living like an unbroken nightmare for decades. During the sentencing of Sarah's killer, Lord Justice Fulford described her as a 'wholly blameless victim',[9] which contrasts dramatically with the character assassination that dominated portrayals of Mark. The difference in these responses tells us something fundamental about the philosophy of race operating within British policing, which we can grasp by looking at how police talk about race themselves.

Sir Kenneth Newman, the Met Police Commissioner from 1982 to 1987, described Jamaicans as 'constitutionally disorderly, it's simply in their make-up, they're constitutionally disposed to be anti-authority'.[10] Three decades later, little had changed. In 2020, then Met Police Commissioner Cressida Dick justified the disproportionate use of stop and search against young Black boys and men on the basis that 'In the past couple of years', police have 'considerably reduced the number of stabbings of young – I'm afraid I have to say black – boys in the streets of London'.[11] It's clear what's being said here: stop and search – and the police presence in Black communities more generally – exists to protect Black people from self-annihilation. In this, we find the loud echoes of colonial ideology: 'Take up the White Man's burden', Rudyard Kipling exhorted in 1899, 'to serve your captives' needs.' But instead of the colonies outside of Britain's borders, the Met operate internal colonies in places like Tottenham, Brixton, Handsworth and Toxteth. In 2021, a 14-year-old Black boy reported being stopped more than 30 times by Met police officers, leaving him afraid to leave the house.[12] In the first three months of lockdown in 2020, 22,000 searches were conducted on the bodies of Black boys and men in London

– a number equivalent to more than a quarter of the entire population of Black boys and men in the capital.[13] Eighty per cent of these searches led to no further action, but this is part of the point: police activity in working class and racialised communities is a form of organised harassment, intended to remind people of their place in the social hierarchy, and to maintain racial and class ordering.

Cressida Dick developed her justification for the disproportionate targeting of Black boys and men by police further, claiming the police are working 'among the drug markets and what it means is, overall, a higher proportion of young black lads being stopped than white lads'.[14] Here Dick is animating the old racial stereotype of Black men as 'constitutionally disorderly', in this case because they're drug-peddling hyper-criminals. Police leaders parade Black people, and Black masculinity particularly, as a symbol of urban threat and decay, where the only solution to protect Black people from themselves – and others from them – is containment through police coercion and violence.

The data available on drug use and ethnicity is scant, but 2010 UK Drug Policy Commission research suggests that Black people use drugs at a lower proportion than white people and this is particularly the case for Class A drugs.[15] But regardless of who uses drugs more, anyone who's been to a festival like Glastonbury, Download, Reading, or Leeds would have a sense that drug use in white and middle-class spaces is under-policed. The police presence at festivals like these is often minimal, despite the fact many people are high as a kite on Class As: creating what are essentially zones of drug decriminalisation for white people. So much for being 'among the drug markets'. Contrast this with Notting Hill Carnival, an event that comes out of Black community resistance to racism, yet is policed with a £7 million budget,[16] and high-end surveillance technology. Class A drugs are common on university campuses and, most recently, found in all but one of the toilet areas of Parliament, but you won't be seeing searches and raids on Members of Parliament any time soon.[17]

Contrary to what Dick claims, there is no straight line between where drugs are and over-policing in Black communities, and this is because drug policy is not intended to respond to the realities of drug use, but operates as a highly successful form of social control. If the police were serious about tackling social harm that comes from drug markets, you'd expect more than none of them to talk about the most decisive measure for solving drug violence: decriminalisation of drugs and a paradigm shift to a public health approach to substance use. But drug enforcement is central to the policing of working class communities: nearly 70 per cent of searches in 2020–21 were for drugs, with 77 per cent of all searches ending in no further action.[18] The stigmatisation of drug use is the pretext upon which over-policing in communities deemed deviant – racialised urban areas, council estates, traveller sites, homeless populations – is justified.

In this context, narratives around race and crime have a political function: to shift the responsibility for social problems – for example, youth violence – on the individual neuroses of racialised communities, allowing the state to dodge an honest assessment of the historical, political and economic conditions that give rise to violence

and harm. Creating the spectre of social threat emanat-
ing from a racialised 'enemy within' primes entire social
groups for scapegoating, ready to be leaned on at times
of political crisis and rupture. When Mark was killed,
there was a ready-baked narrative of gang violence and
drug dealing for the state to mobilise. When the 2011
riots erupted, sparked by Mark's murder and the disre-
spect police showed to his family by not informing them
of Mark's killing,[19] it was easy to trot out these same narratives of 'gangs', 'thugs' and 'criminals' – which served to
justify the draconian criminal justice response – instead of
grappling with the context of deprivation, police violence,
hopelessness and neglect experienced by the youth who
rioted. Since the 2008 financial crash, the establishment
has used the criminal threat of multiple racialised folk
devils – gangs, terrorists, economic migrants – to direct
popular frustration away from itself.

RACE

Abolitionists should understand race not as a biological
reality, but as a tool of control and domination: created to
justify and sustain state violence. Race is used to define
the boundaries of criminalisation and the subjects of state
coercion and control; in the process, race itself is constructed through notions of criminality. When Cressida
Dick justifies disproportionate policing in Black communities on the basis of Black people being more likely to be
involved in drug markets, whether or not she is correct
is irrelevant. Disproportionate policing in Black communities and disproportionate arrest of Black people feeds a

greater number of Black people into the Criminal Justice System (CJS).[20] And disproportionate treatment across the CJS feeds a greater number of Black people into prisons. The 2017 Lammy Review found unequal outcomes across the CJS, particularly regarding drug offences: 'within drug offences, the odds of receiving a prison sentence were around 240% higher for BAME offenders, compared to White offenders.'[21] In a perverse reversal of reality, the presence of a proportionally higher number of Black people in prisons is then pointed to as justification for why the police are right to target Black communities in the first place. This is how race is crafted: it is the *process of policing* racialised bodies that gives race its meaning.

In the tradition of thinkers like Frantz Fanon and Stuart Hall, abolitionists should be critical of the very notion of race and the ordering of people into racial hierarchies, as this hierarchy only serves to order state and police violence. We must be brave and re-imagine not just a future without the physical systems of state violence, but also the ideological systems created and recreated to sustain them. This doesn't mean abandoning a connection to people or place, or letting go of the histories and identities that give us as Black people a sense of self and pride. But it does mean challenging ourselves to let go of politics that replicate the racial logics of state violence. The idea that the correctness of a political position can be determined solely by race, or that solidarity begins and ends at racial boundaries, or even that there are irreconcilable conflicts between racial groups, are common positions that pop up again and again in progressive circles. But underneath these ideas is the assumption of race as immutable and inflexible, that race can fix people to a particular way of being in the world. This is known as 'racial essentialism' and it's exactly this logic the state and media relies on when it trots out narratives of the drill- and grime-performing, knife-carrying, hooded youth ready to cause chaos on our streets; this 'logic' expects you to understand drill means Black and Black means criminal and criminals are dealt with by police.

So when did race start being used in this way, as a tool of domination and power? Well, the beginning of race, and the beginning of race as a tool of social control, occurred at the same time. Race emerged in different ways in different places, but in all as a tool to legitimise the violent exploitation of labour and land in the context of colonialism and slavery. In Britain, race became a way of ideologically tying the working class to a nationalist, imperialist, colonial project. Cedric Robinson, summarising this historical process in his seminal text *Black Marxism*, argued: 'Race became largely the rationalisation for the domination, exploitation, and/or extermination of non-"Europeans" (including Slavs and Jews).'[22] Race is not to be understood as static and unchanging, but is instead a product of the context within which it operates. The context has fundamentally shifted from the seventeenth and eighteenth centuries that Robinson was theorising about, but the use of race as a technology of violence and domination continues.

Let's fast forward to the 1970s. 'Mugging', 'gangs', 'thugs', 'knife crime', 'drill music', 'drug dealer', 'smell of cannabis': you will recognise these as words the British state has used since we arrived on this island to say 'Black' without actually saying 'Black' and, specifically, to *criminalise* Blackness. In 1972–73, a moral panic spread through the courts, police, Parliament and the media, creating intense public anxiety around the alleged rapid rise in 'muggings', particularly in Black, working class, urban areas. This panic was used to increase repressive policing in Black and working class communities including mass, suspicionless stop and search using the Vagrancy Act 1824 (known as 'sus laws'), false arrests such as the Oval Four who were stitched up by anti-mugging squads, and the hyper-surveillance of Black activists, businesses and cultural establishments – such as The Mangrove restaurant. Yet as Stuart Hall and colleagues forensically argue in their seminal text *Policing the Crisis*,[23] crime had been rising year by year since 1915 – so the idea that underpinned this moral panic, of a sudden spike in 'muggings', was misleading. In the years leading up to 1972, crime had been rising at a *slower* rate than between 1955 and 1965. The statistical basis for the mugging moral panic didn't stand up to scrutiny; the establishment was responding to a symbolic, as opposed to actual, threat. The early 1970s was a time of intense crisis – strikes, Black power, rising inflation and unemployment – and there was talk in political circles of England becoming ungovernable.[24] Prime Minister Edward Heath was able to present himself as re-establishing law and order when in July 1973 he declared victory against the scourge of mugging.[25]

Today, there is a similar moral panic playing out around knife crime. The category of knife crime, as it's recorded by the police, is actually incredibly broad. It refers to all recorded crimes that involve a knife or sharp object: from threats, assault, robbery, homicide and sexual offences. In 2021, homicide involving a knife accounted for 224 of the 41,259 recorded knife offences in England and Wales. Yet 'knife crime' as it exists in the popular imagination centres the narrative of a rising epidemic of Black youth killing each other on the streets of urban areas, with drugs and gangs identified as the underlying causes. So like Stuart Hall did in *Policing the Crisis*, we want to ask to what extent the statistics support this narrative? Before we answer that question, it's worth raising an important caveat: as *Policing the Crisis* made clear, the production of crime statistics does not always represent an objective reality. In the 1970s, 'mugging' wasn't itself its own category of crime. Its 'rise' was statistically manufactured by police taking a pic 'n' mix approach to what counted as a mugging: bashing together different categories of crime and projecting a new crime – 'muggings' – into existence. Numbers are not gospel, but by looking at the knife crime statistics we hope to understand what is conveniently ignored, misrepresented and manipulated. This may help us understand how knife crime (which like mugging is not one, but many, different categories of crime rolled into one concept) operates as a political and ideological phenomena.

So, the first thing to say is that there has been a rise in offences involving knives – or sharp objects – including threats to kill, robbery, sexual violence and attempted murders. But interestingly, the exception to this trend is homicide. In 2010–11, homicides involving a knife stood at 221. They then decreased year on year until 2015–16, before reaching a peak of 265 in 2017–18. Since then, there has been year-on-year *decrease* in homicides, and in 2021 the figure was almost exactly the same as 2011 at 224.[26] Despite this, there were thousands of articles written about knife killings in 2021, with media headlines dominated by the idea of a rising wave of murder on London's streets. The *Sun* ran stories such as 'London gripped by bloodiest teen murder epidemic EVER' and 'Bloodbath Britain'. The *Daily Mail* spoke of a 'gang and stabbing epidemic sweeping the capital's streets'.[27]

The idea of a soaring number of 'gang murders' is usually underpinned by one of two narrative arcs. First, reality that non-fatal offences involving knives *have* increased is used to cultivate the idea that 'gang murders' are rapidly rising too. Second, the fact that 30 teenagers were killed in the capital in 2021 – the highest number since 29 in 2008 and 27 in 2017 – is isolated out of the general trend of *decreasing* knife homicides in order to build a narrative of a growing epidemic of gang murders. But the narrative of rising 'gang murder' does not stand up to scrutiny both because knife homicides have been falling since 2018–19, and also because there is no evidence the rise in non-fatal knife offences is being driven by the loosely defined, racialised notion of 'gang violence'. Indeed, the detailed government report that breaks down the statistics on knife crime over the last decade does not mention the word 'gang' once.[28]

Moral panics are never without political consequence. In 2019, Knife Crime Prevention Orders were introduced, which can be used to inhibit the civil liberties of any person above the age of 12 on the basis of police suspicion alone.[29] As Adam Elliott-Cooper argues in *Black Resistance to British Policing*, moral panics that rely on vague categories of crime like 'gang murders' allow 'the police ... to widen the net of young Black people they can punish'.[30] What is even more revealing is that recorded rapes involving a knife or sharp object more than doubled, from 240 in 2011 to 547 in 2021.[31] The same picture is true for sexual assaults involving a knife or sharp object. Yet in 2021, we could find only one article in *The Times*, and one in the *Bolton News*, mentioning this particularly stark rise in violence against women.[32]

Not all crimes are treated, or policed, equally. How knife crime is managed by the establishment in many ways mirrors the moral panic of muggings in the early '70s. But one of the key differences is where the mugging moral panic was acute but relatively short-lived – lasting from 1972 to the latter months of 1973 – the moral panic around knife crime is chronic. It diverges from how Stan Cohen defined a moral panic in *Folk Devils and Moral Panic* as, instead of being either 'quite novel', or 'suddenly appear[ing] in the limelight',[33] knife crime and its [mis] association with Blackness is a more permanent feature of political discourse around race, policing and crime – perhaps reflecting its more versatile and timeless political use as a tool to manage and police crises. 'Gangs' are regularly used to criminalise and scapegoat those who experience state violence; shift responsibility for social, political and economic problems onto racialised communities; expand police and state powers; justify the abandonment and neglect of racialised communities, and divide the masses of ordinary people along racial lines.

And the final thing to note is how criminalisation and police violence 'leak' beyond their racially defined boundaries. The riots of 2011 (and indeed the uprisings in the 1980s) were racially mixed in every city where they occurred, with working class young people from all backgrounds putting their differences aside to defend their communities against the police.[34] When working class people defy police and state power or otherwise become undesirable in the eyes of the state, they 'become Black', as David Starkey put it in 2011.[35] They are then free pickings for police and state violence. Robbie Shilliam discusses the way power brokers in nineteenth-century England made ideological distinctions between the 'deserving and undeserving' poor by associating the undeserving with African slaves and the deserving with English propriety.[36] The undeserving poor, largely wanderers and vagabonds, were seen as a threat to the moral and economic fabric of a swiftly changing class hierarchy. In behaviour, mentality and even physical appearance, they were 'blackened':[37] described in the newspapers and by the political establishment as being dark, dirty and of low moral character, 'like slaves'. This 'blackening' allowed them to be represented to the wider public as an internal threat, as opposed to what they really were, which was a new class of impoverished people created by the violence of industrial capitalism. Everything, from draconian legislation in the form of Poor Laws to police oppression, was justified in order to contain them. Race, in this sense, is porous: its boundaries can bend and flex, letting people in and out as a function of state coercion and control. This is seen throughout history, in the way shifting political, economic and social contexts force Jewish, Irish, Eastern European and Gypsy, Roma and Traveller folk to enter and exit whiteness.

THESIS 4
The police need public consent in order to exist. Withdrawing our consent brings us closer to abolition.

> *'This is serious and it is urgent. To lose public consent would be unthinkable. Action is needed now. Enough is enough.'*
>
> Cressida Dick, January 2022[1]

British policing is underpinned by the concept of policing by consent. This philosophy holds that effective policing requires building and maintaining public respect and approval; developing positive relationships with members of the public; and securing the willing participation of the public in the work of maintaining law and order. The nine Peelian principles of policing by consent, first articulated in writing by Charles Reith in 1948, argue: 'the police are the public and … the public are the police … .'[2] The principles that guide the notion of policing by consent aim to blur the distinction between officer and citizen, creating a form of state coercion that feels part of, not separate from, the community. Modern British policing is not built solely on the use of force, but is underpinned by many overlapping social, political and ideological processes of maintaining legitimacy and manufacturing consent. As Reith continues: police must 'recognise always that the power of the police to fulfil their functions and duties is dependent on public approval of their existence'.[3]

Some revisionist narratives of police history pluck the origins of policing by consent out of its historical context, reconceptualising it as an ethical code created by moral men, on a mission to create a well-behaved police force. In reality, policing by consent was a response from the English bourgeoisie, who were confronting the hard truth that policing the new industrial working classes purely by force was ineffective. When the lethal force of the army was deployed against working class rebels in the early decades of the 1800s – such as during the 1819 Peterloo Massacre – this led to more, not less, popular and insurrectionary resistance.[4] In a context where there were many more of us than them, policing based on legitimacy and public consent, performed by a force that felt less distant and oppressive than the army, originated as a tool for effectively maintaining social control – not as a compass for benevolence or morality.

This is why, when the police are in the midst of reputational crisis, they pivot immediately to the language of 'rebuilding trust'[5] and public confidence. After seven months of snowballing scandal, then Met Police Commissioner Cressida Dick pleaded, 'Every single one of us in the Met realise that it will take time to rebuild your trust.'[6] When she was forced to resign a few months later, Mayor of London Sadiq Khan vowed to 'restore trust in the police'.[7] In October 2021, the Met Police released their first ever Rebuilding Trust plan,[8] setting out twelve immediate priorities for restoring the 'precious bond' broken by the avalanche of revelations of police sexism and racism that year.[9] A 2022 report by the Police Foundation opens with a Foreword on the 'crisis of public confidence in our police institutions'.[10] It goes on to set out a comprehensive police reform agenda, aimed at rebuilding public trust by making policing institutions capable of addressing the 'challenges of the 21st century'. There is no doubt that public consent is the lifeblood of British policing.

As Abolitionist Futures have noted – from the 1981 Scarman Report (on the Brixton riots) and the 1999 Macpherson Report (which examined the murder of Stephen Lawrence), and right up to the present day – police emphasis during a crisis is never on how to eliminate racism or sexism from policing and society; but focuses squarely on how to placate public sentiment.[11] These generational cycles of crisis management – where our anger and energy are syphoned into the latest report into, and admission of, police failures – have made the police better able to protect their power by creating the illusion of change. Moreover, calling for improved policing to rebuild trust (as opposed to calling for *less* policing to reduce police violence) only ever leads to greater police powers and resources. The police often *do* change in response to crisis, but only ever in a direction that benefits them, never marginalised communities.

For example, despite the fact that Sarah Everard was murdered by a serving police officer, the state responded to her killing by hiring 650 more Met Police officers,[12] trialling new police GPS surveillance technology,[13] and providing additional funding for Project Vigilant[14] – a scheme that involves deploying plain-clothes officers into nightclubs.[15] Calls for improved policing are a central part of the machine that legitimises police power: to believe the police simply need to 'do better' is to still give your consent to the existence, and evolution, of police powers – but simply distributed in a different way.

The notion of policing by consent contains an inherent contradiction: policing exercises coercive force and control over the very public from which it demands legitimacy and consent. As the world moves closer to catastrophe, and society more regularly finds itself gripped by crisis, the number of people targeted by police powers, and the reach of state coercion into our lives, is growing. The balance between policing by consent and policing by force is tipping steadily towards force, as state coercion and control spreads beyond the racialised and working class communities it is usually bounded by. It is within this contradiction that British police have found themselves in repeating, and deepening, cycles of crisis. And it is also this contradiction that abolitionists should work to wrench open.

In March 2021, a vigil was called by Reclaim These Streets to mourn the disappearance of Sarah Everard, and to protest police misogyny and victim blaming: when Sarah's murderer was still at large, police had instructed women to stay indoors.[16] The police, citing Covid-19 regulations, claimed the vigil was illegal and threatened the organisers with £10K fines if they turned up.[17] It emerged after the vigil that Home Secretary Priti Patel had intervened before hand, making it clear she did not want the vigil to take place.[18] This revelation chimed with the fact the government and police had already been trying to use Covid-19 regulations to levy a wholesale attack on protest rights.[19] It's in this context that Sisters Uncut assumed leadership of the vigil and called for it to go ahead, despite the police ban, and despite the original organisers pulling out of hosting the event, fearing criminalisation.[20]

On 13 March 2021, hundreds of women and comrades defied the ban, ignored police diktats to stay home, turned up to the vigil and withdrew their consent to policing on a mass scale. Many of these people would not consider themselves abolitionists; yet, in that moment, they recognised that even the ordinary execution of police powers can be illegitimate. The decision to turn up to the banned vigil was an open challenge to the legitimacy of police power: it forced the state to choose between ignoring their own impositions by letting the vigil go ahead, or using force to break up a peaceful gathering of women and mourners. At the time, it felt implausible the police would choose violence and force. After all, the gathering was mostly women who had come together to mourn the death of a woman who was murdered by a serving police officer. But the state, on a mission to expand the reach of its authoritarianism, chose to violently break up the vigil; crisis engulfed the police thereafter.

In the context of ongoing debates around the utility of A-to-B marches and static demonstrations, abolitionists should approach the question of mass, street-based action strategically. As John Berger theorised in 1968, mass demonstrations have the potential to force the state to make undesirable choices, like they were made to at the Clapham Common vigil:

Either authority must abdicate and allow the crowd to do as it wishes: in which case ... the event demonstrates the weakness of authority. Or else authority must constrain and disperse the crowd with violence: in which case the undemocratic character of such authority is publicly displayed. The imposed dilemma is between displayed weakness and displayed authoritarianism.[21]

We need to let go of mass demonstrations that come and go, passively, without consequence. As the state escalates its coercive powers, we must escalate our resistance. Mass demonstrations should be radical opportunities, where we come together to proactively challenge state power and withdraw our consent. It's in this way that street-based action can evolve from being mere processions or spectacles, to becoming spaces where we collectively disrupt and stifle the state's capacity to manufacture consent. And this isn't just a tactical question: it's only by curbing police power that we can ensure another Sarah Everard, or any killing in police custody, never happens again.

Working class urban areas, particularly those with large racialised communities, make up the primary targets of police activity,[22] and their populations experience the sharpest end of police violence: Black people are five times more likely to have force used against them than white people.[23] The policing of the Covid-19 pandemic cemented once again the way coercive and punitive policing powers target working class and racialised communities. People in deprived neighbourhoods, or those who are Black or Asian, were significantly more likely to receive fixed penalty notices, or be arrested for breaching Covid-19 restrictions.[24] With George Floyd's murder at the forefront of public consciousness, racist pandemic policing led to a freefall in confidence within the Black community. The Mayor's Office for Policing and Crime (MOPAC) data revealed that Black Londoners in 2020 were less likely to report police do a 'good job' or 'treat everyone fairly' compared to 2019.[25] By 2022, this sentiment had not improved: Mile End Institute (MEI) research suggests 64 per cent of Londoners believe the Met Police is probably or definitely institutionally racist, rising to a stark 72 per cent for BME Londoners.[26]

The long history of racist policing has meant Black people have always had a comparatively poor view of policing. What is new about how the crisis of police legitimacy is playing out today is how it has spread to another marginalised group: women. The reality of patriarchal violence, and horrific scale of abuse against women and girls, is often used as a way of legitimising and expanding police powers. Despite this, women's trust in police has plummeted: YouGov data suggests 47 per cent of women have lost trust in the police following Sarah Everard's murder,[27] while the 2022 MEI poll goes on to show 63 per cent of Londoners believe the Met is institutionally sexist.[28] With public opinion of police so low, politicians have been trotting out well-rehearsed strategies of containment and pacification.

A 2020 City Hall report summarised the tactics for rebuilding public consent to policing as coming under five key areas: 'recruitment; retention; training; operational practices; [and] community engagement'.[29] In the year since Sarah Everard's murder, we have noticed a significant recruitment push, with advertisements targeting minoritised and marginalised groups springing up across London, calling for them to join the Met Police. In 2022, an advertisement in Seven Sisters Underground station featured a female officer acknowledging the fact 'the last year has been incredibly tough' for policing, but 'now more than ever, become a police officer' to 'support some of the most vulnerable people'. Because policing by consent requires policing duty to feel like an extension of civic duty, it has become increasingly important for police to look like the populations they exert force over. In October 2021, the Home Office celebrated the fact that it had recruited 'more women than ever before' into the police, with record numbers of people of colour being employed across UK police forces.[30] But abolitionists must be clear: demands to increase the number of Black or women officers ultimately serves to protect police legitimacy; it reframes police violence, and institutional oppression, as a product of a lack of representation and diversity. In reality, oppression and violence are a necessary function of police power under capitalism. Diversity in recruitment allows the police to claim they're addressing a particular community's concerns, whilst leaving the violence of their coercive powers intact. The issue has never been the colour, or gender, or sexuality of police power: the issue is the existence of police power itself.

Sitting alongside recruitment drives are more ominous strategies for manufacturing consent. According to 2021 government data, white people in managerial or professional roles report having more confidence in their local police, compared to white people who were unemployed or in traditionally working class jobs – and compared to all Black groups surveyed.[31] This reflects the material relationship between policing, race and class. White, middle-class communities and spaces, where wealth and strong social safety nets keep people afloat, are typically policed generously. These communities are far more likely to experience policing as protective, not threatening. But it also reflects the ideological role race and class play in maintaining police legitimacy. The media and political establishment play a decisive role in actively manufacturing public consent, often by whipping up middle-class anxieties around crime. These anxieties are then translated into calls for greater police powers and resourcing.

Take, for example, the way narratives around 'county lines drug gangs' have been used to fuel fear that crimes traditionally contained within urban, working class and racialised areas are spreading to the 'leafy suburbs' and 'shires'.[32] This narrative is contradicted by the fact that drug movement across the country isn't new, nor is drug use a new feature of middle-class life: a 2018 Social Metrics Commission report found 9 per cent more middle-class people report consuming illegal substances than their poorer counterparts.[33] But the story of imminent danger spreading from the working to the middle classes is a powerful one: the whole country is drawn into the drama of knife crime in big cities, like a sordid plot line in *Eastenders*. In reality, 'county lines' is a story about the exploitation of vulnerable young people – young people who need support, care and nurturing, not criminalisation and prisons.[34] Yet in January 2021, the Home Office announced an additional £40 million fund to go towards county-lines policing for the year 2021–22.[35]

Outside of the working class urban communities where policing is its most violent, views of policing tend to be more favourable, although by no means entirely so. For example, the Gypsy, Roma, Traveller (GRT) community – often situated in rural areas, and whose very existence is criminalised for being outside of so-called 'mainstream society' – are well versed in resisting oppressive policing.[36] But the image of the polite, plodding, country bobby who is embedded in the heart of a small village community is an important antidote to the reality of the metropolitan warrior cop, engaged in the daily work of coercing and controlling mostly working class sections of the population. Yet even this image is 'culturally bounded',[37] often coming from curated depictions of police in TV shows. Termed 'copaganda', cop shows create either glamorous, thrilling, and dramatic – or dim, clumsy and harmless – depictions of policing that mislead the public about the actuality of the job.[38] This pervasive police PR franchise plays a central role in shaping public opinion of police, masking the unfriendly truths they'd rather hide.[39]

One of these is the fact that, across the board, police are neither good at preventing crime, nor good at solving crime once it has happened.[40] In 2020, 98.4 per cent of reported rapes led to no charge, and this is before we factor in statistical drop-off due to unreported rapes, or consider unsuccessful prosecutions after charge.[41] People often ask abolitionists what we will do with rapists if we abolish prisons. Yet we already live in a society where rape is decriminalised and the overwhelming majority of perpetrators of sexual and domestic violence remain entirely unaccountable. Yet if you take the hype of cop shows at face value, even those like *Line of Duty* where police corruption is a central theme, you'd be forgiven for believing police are actually catching sexual predators.

In fact, police are solving the lowest proportions of crime ever, with just 6 per cent of recorded crimes in the year prior to September 2021 leading to charges.[42] And the blame for these abysmal clear-up rates cannot simply be put on successive Tory funding cuts. In 1992, Audrey Farrell critiqued the myth of investigative policing: her work demonstrated the fact that clear-up rates in the 1970s and '80s were abysmal – little better than they are today.[43] In order to present a more favourable image of detective work, police often distorted statistics[44] and engaged in oppressive, racist operations – like those of the infamous special 'anti-mugging' squads[45] – to create the false impression they were solving crime. The police are terrible at dealing with crime, despite this being their stated purpose, because the model of responding to events once they've happened is inherently deficient.

The best way to stop harm is to understand its root causes, and eliminate the conditions that give rise to it. Yet police play a fundamental role in protecting the state and the very political and economic conditions, in the context of a capitalist society, that give rise to crime. This is why manufacturing consent, and protecting police legitimacy, is so vital to them: it mystifies the role police play in sustaining cycles of harm and violence by presenting themselves as the only solution to these cycles. Abolition demands we equip ourselves with the tools to end harm and violence

by *re-organising* society: not just so that everyone's basic
needs are met, but so everyone has meaningful opportunities for fulfilment and happiness. Abolition demands we
understand and address the political, historical, economic
and social conditions that give rise to harm and violence.
Abolition is a project that can create the space needed to
truly address harm; meanwhile, policing simply attempts
to paper over it after the fact, with negligible success.

It's also a myth that certain police activities have a discernible impact on crime. Take, for example, stop and
search. The government tirelessly defends stop and search
as a key tool for stopping crime, with Prime Minister Boris
Johnson even describing it as 'kind and loving'.[46] In the
1970s and '80s, police used the Vagrancy Act of 1824 to
harass Black communities with suspicionless searches and
crimeless arrests. This was known as the 'sus law'. After
grassroots resistance and social unrest, sus laws were eventually ditched. But suspicionless searches returned through
the back door in the 1994 Criminal Justice and Public
Order Act, as Section 60.[47] Section 60, when approved by
a senior officer, empower police to stop and search anyone
for any reason in a given area for a limited amount of time.
In July 2021, the Home Secretary announced plans to permanently relax the conditions of Section 60 use, making
them more frequent and easier to use.[48] The 2022 Police,
Crime, Sentencing and Courts (PCSC) Act has increased
the use of suspicionless searches by introducing Serious
Violence Reduction Orders (SVROs),[49] enabling the
police to search individuals under a SVRO any time they
are in a public place.[50]

In the three years prior to the 2011 riots, police began Operation BLUNT 2, where Section 60 was used to drastically increase the number of suspicionless stop and searches across London boroughs. A 2016 Home Office report assessed the impact of the three-year operation and in their words: 'overall, analysis shows that there was no discernible crime-reducing effects from a large surge in stop and search activity at the borough level during the operation.'[51] Little has been heard of this report since, yet stop and search is often leaned on by politicians and police to placate the public, and to convince them that something is being done about crime – even when that 'something' doesn't work.

One of the measures of abolitionist – as opposed to reformist – practice is the extent to which our work challenges the legitimacy of police power. In 2021, this found expression in British abolitionists calling for the public to withdraw their consent from policing.[52] Conceptualised as an abolitionist approach to challenging the PCSC bill outside the trappings of parliamentary politics, Sisters Uncut advocated for a strategy of making new and existing police powers ungovernable by building class power – on a local and national level – to disrupt and disobey police activity.[53] Under this strategy, if the government passes new trespass laws that criminalise GRT life, we must hold mass trespasses in protest.[54] If they create new stop and search powers, we must disrupt and intervene in those searches.[55] In response to proposed legislation that criminalised noisy protest, Sisters Uncut set off 1,000 rape alarms outside Charing Cross police station,[56] after an Independent Office for Police Conduct (IOPC) investigation found that

– alongside racism, sexism and homophobia – multiple officers from this station joked about domestic violence, child abuse and rape.[57] Tactics like these are designed to collectivise the idea of withdrawing consent to policing, moving away from small direct actions towards mass radical disobedience. As part of this strategy, in September 2021, Sisters Uncut launched the national CopWatch network[58] – police intervention groups that provide an organising vehicle for the idea of withdrawing consent to policing.[59] Building on, yet diverging from, the traditional model of police monitoring groups, CopWatch groups don't just intervene in police work that falls short of legal standards, but intervene in all police activity; understanding police power *itself* as illegitimate.

The concept of withdrawing consent to policing can bridge the gap between reformist and abolitionist demands, as the act of withdrawing consent can be both pragmatic, whilst creating a gateway to more radical and revolutionary thinking. The nature of carcerality in the UK, and the way it is increasingly embedded in everyday life, provides ample opportunity to organise people who may not see themselves as abolitionists into campaigns organised around abolitionist politics and principles. For example, many schools in Hackney require parents to sign zero-tolerance behavioural contracts that include the use of police as part of student behavioural management. In the wake of Child Q – the teenage girl strip-searched at her school, in what was a horrific case of state-sanctioned sexual assault in 2022 – abolitionist activists in Hackney are asking parents to withdraw their consent from carcerality in schools, quite literally, by refusing to sign new behavioural contracts and tearing up existing ones.[60] The act of withdrawing consent at the community level is an empowering act of collective resistance that can be leveraged towards a revolutionary vision of withdrawing consent from police in more far-reaching ways.

Much of our discussion so far has centred the perspectives of working class communities in big cities. But abolitionists need to also be responsive to the realities of working class life outside of metropolitan areas, as the state often draws on hidden working class deprivation to justify expanding its coercive power. After decades of managed decline, the poorest communities in Britain have the worst social infrastructure,[61] and this makes them ripe for prison expansion projects. The New Prisons Programme is a multi-billion pound prison expansion scheme that the Ministry of Justice (MoJ) boasts is the 'biggest prison-building programme in more than 100 years'.[62] Alongside this, in February 2022 Deputy Prime Minister Dominic Raab announced an additional £4 billion to expand and refurbish several existing prisons.[63] A new 'green' prison is due to open in Leicestershire in 2023; meanwhile, consultations have taken place to build new prisons in towns such as Chorley, Buckinghamshire and Wethersfield.[64] In the first instance, we must wholesale reject the co-option of progressive language and ideas that are used to whitewash the reality of state violence. 'Environmentally friendly', or 'transgender inclusive' prisons[65] – often language mobilised during these consultations – are still prisons. Making a cage out of gold doesn't stop it from being a cage.

But crucially, one of the central ways the state sells these plans to local communities is by pushing the idea they provide jobs, both to construct the new buildings and run the new prison services once they're operational. Recent consultation documents show the MoJ work with local job centres to recruit poor and working class people into prisons, allowing the state to use deprivation they've created through austerity as a 'buy-in' factor to expand carceral systems.[66] Drawing local workers into prison expansion is one of the metrics of success for these new prison projects, with consultation documents often including key performance indicators that measure local recruitment.[67] In 2022, the MoJ claimed their plans to expand prisons 'are expected to offer over a thousand permanent jobs – providing a significant boost to the local economy'.[68]

Packaging new carceral institutions as benign, job creating opportunities allows the government to side-step interrogation into curious facts. Such as the fact that imprisonment rates in England and Wales are rising,[69] despite a general decline in imprisonment rates across the rest of Europe – a trend that began in 2013.[70] In this way, tying the economic interests of the working class to the growth of carceral systems is yet another process of manufacturing public consent. This elucidates a crucial fact: the social processes used to generate consent to police powers and carceral systems are not purely ideological ones. The material circumstances of life under capitalism create the conditions where people are compelled to consent. More and more jobs involve some kind of security, policing, or guard function – saturating workplaces and everyday working life in the logics of carcerality. Alongside state-organised programmes that turn public-sector workers into cops, such as the 2015 Prevent Duty, and the incoming Serious Violence Duty,[71] security companies are increasingly used to trial new policing and surveillance technologies in private workplaces. A 2020 collaboration – known as Project Zeal – between Nottinghamshire Police, the Co-operative Group and intelligence company Mitie, led to 25 convictions in six months, across nine Co-Op stores. In their own words, one of the key drivers of success was 'encourag[ing] engagement through the store colleagues involved in the trial'.[72]

Capitalism organises the means of survival around private property, tying our reproduction as human beings to the often violent defence of property relations. Capitalism ensures the vast majority of the global working class compete, under increasingly precarious conditions, for scarce resources. It is no surprise that people turn to carceral systems and police power to defend the meagre crumbs they have to sustain themselves and their families. Capitalism organises human relations in such a way that those who are the primary victims of coercive police powers – the exploited working classes who have the most to gain by shaking free of state control – are also forced to be committed to its existence. This is why abolition cannot be anything other than a revolutionary, anti-capitalist project. And it's also why, following in the tradition of revolutionaries like the Black Panthers, creating models for organising our lives collectively – such as mutual aid, workers' democracy, community funds and alternative public service infrastructure – is a vital part of building towards an abolitionist future.

THESIS 5

Coercion and control are the tactics of abusers, and coercing and controlling the working class is the job of the police. Abolition is class struggle!

Thinking about the origins of policing and prison systems often conjures up images of rampant crime sprees and untameable social disorder on the streets of Victorian England. These fit within a story that conceptualises the police as primarily a response to the harm experienced by ordinary people in society. Even within abolitionist circles, there is sometimes tacit acceptance of the idea that the police came out of the state's proposed solution – albeit a failed one – to harm and violence. We push back against this narrative, as the idea of policing institutions as a response to harm and violence between ordinary people is a powerful ideological fiction. Policing, in the first instance, is a response to the organised, collective power of the working class. It is only thereafter *naturalised* as a response to individualised harm, as part of legitimising the existence and function of police in society.

The rise of industrial capitalism brought exploited classes of people together, in workplaces and cities, like never before in history. The enclosure of land that people had lived and survived on forced them into wage labour in the smoky factories of expanding cities, to churn out huge profits for a developing bourgeoisie. And this, as Chris

Harman argues, 'provided [workers] with possibilities of resistance greater than those open to any previous exploited class – and it was resistance that could encourage the growth of ideas opposed to existing society in its entirety.'[1] The 1800s was a time of intense class and anti-colonial struggle. Mass demonstrations, direct action and strikes came in wave after relentless wave as the exploited classes struggled for parliamentary representation, better working and living conditions and an end to slavery. The cavalry, empowered to use lethal force, was still used to manage working class revolt and enforce public order. This was to have disastrous consequences in the 1819 Peterloo Massacre, when the cavalry charged into a crowd of 60,000 demonstrators, killing 15 of them. Far from subduing the protesters, the murders made their spirit more unwavering and ferocious: lethal force was clearly not a reliable weapon against working class resistance.[2]

In 1824, the government repealed legislation that banned strikes and picketing in the hopes this would quell the latest wave of workplace resistance and direct action. But it had the opposite effect, spurring on a fresh wave of strike action. The tools the state had been relying on to protect itself and capital were faltering. Revolution was in the air and as fear and anxiety bled through all sections of the ruling class, Robert Peel was finally successful in convincing the political establishment of the need for a domestic, state-funded police force. Having practised, developed and refined policing strategies in the Irish colonies, these tactics of coercion and control 'boomer-anged' back to the mainland:[3] Peel's Metropolitan Police Service was founded in 1829. From its very inception, the

Met has used coercive (but largely non-lethal) powers to control the organised collective potential of the working and exploited classes. This hasn't stopped being a core part of their function today: from Black radical activism in the 1970s and '80s, to the miners' strike, and environmental activism,[4] as well as the Stephen Lawrence justice campaign, and, most recently, the BLM movement,[5] police have worked to criminalise, destabilise and repress movements for social change, in a bid to protect and maintain the state and status quo.

The tools available to the police for the daily work of enforcing the law equips them with coercive powers. These powers allow them to exercise immense control over ordinary people: arrest, stop and search, detainment, raids, restraint, physical force, strip-search, dispersal, surveillance. It's in this way that the tools of policing differ from those of other emergency services: while the fire services, for example, centre preserving and protecting life, policing exerts coercive power over it. Yet while policing powers differ drastically from other emergency services, they are remarkably similar to the coercive and controlling tactics employed by domestic abusers. Where perpetrators search phones, police search pockets. Where perpetrators use their hands and feet, police use batons and tasers. Where perpetrators prevent their partners from leaving the house, police arrest, cuff and detain. Where perpetrators track their victims using mobile devices, police put people on tag. Even the narratives used to justify police power mirror those of abusers: 'We do it for your own good'; 'You make us do it'; 'We do it because we care, even if it hurts you.'

Detective Chief Constable Maggie Blyth believes, and we agree, that the power afforded to police to control others means 'there will be some attracted into working in policing, because of the powers that it offers them, the powers to exert and coerce other people, particularly vulnerable individuals.'[6] PC Frank Pulley, DS Derek Ridgewell, PC Joshua Savage, PC Wayne Couzens – these are the names of police officers now well known for enjoying the thrill of wielding coercive and controlling power over vulnerable people. But in each case, these officers were 'aided and abetted' by colleagues who not only enabled, but in many cases, actively facilitated their violence. Wayne Couzens, who killed Sarah Everard, was known by colleagues as 'The Rapist'.[7] Several colleagues were caught sharing racist and misogynistic messages with him.[8] Colleagues knew he exploited women, after a sex worker turned up to his station demanding he pay money he owed her.[9] In all cases, his colleagues did nothing. Relevant to this is the fact that policing is a permanent institution that employs permanent staff as part of a permanent state structure. This means it has a strong interest in protecting its own existence. It is also made up of employees who, since the 1918 Metropolitan Police strikes which shook the ruling class, have had their loyalty bought by successive dramatic wage hikes.[10] These facts create a push factor towards self-preservation and internal camaraderie, and a pull factor away from accountability.

It's for these reasons we go further than DCC Blyth, as it's not simply the case that policing attracts coercive and controlling people. The very foundation of policing is coercing and controlling the working class; policing culture is built on the legitimacy of exerting power over others and *all* officers act on the belief there are some whose status in society means they are deserving of it. Policing doesn't just attract, but *creates* coercive and controlling people, leaving its mark not only on the world but also on the officers who participate in it. When custody sergeant Kurtis Howard ordered the strip-search of Koshka Duff after she was arrested for handing a teenager a know-your-rights bust card, female officers jeered and laughed as they perpetrated state-sanctioned sexual assault against her.[11] Those women may not have entered the police force with the attitudes and behaviours of abusers, but they sure will come out of it with them.

And it's here we see that although Sarah Everard was not herself working class, her murder emerges out of the dynamics of coercion and control that underpin the maintenance of a class society, and the violent disciplining of working class people. And it's also here that Sarah's and Mark Duggan's murders converge: as police violence against Black people and police violence against women both come out of the violence needed to maintain the status quo exactly as it is – and this violence will always punch downwards along lines of gender, race, ability, sexuality and class. It's this historical analysis that grounds us in a politics of solidarity, a marked divergence from the politics of competition that has consumed many social justice movements today.

The domestic and sexual violence sectors have done important work over the years to spotlight the central role coercive and controlling behaviour plays in patterns of interpersonal violence. But the women's sector has viewed coercion and control through the largely *individual* lens of violence between a man and a woman. The transition from grassroots women's refuges to a complete reliance on state funding – which puts limits on how organisations can campaign – has made a systemic critique of wider political, economic and social dynamics impossible. Close partnership working with police and prisons in the women's sector has obstructed a structural critique of these very same institutions, and how they reproduce coercion and control at every level of society: in the home and on the streets. As the running and funding of women's services becomes increasingly tied in with the running and funding of police services, the critique that policing *itself* is coercion and control, that police *are* the perpetrators, seems a distant relic of the grassroots feminist organising that created refuges in a time long gone by.

This is why abolition of *state policing* does not mean replacing it by building up *community policing*. There have been new, grassroots, youth and Black-led community initiatives like Forever Family that sprung up after the 2020 BLM protests.[12] These groups, recognising the fact that policing is inherently violent and that police don't keep us safe, seek to address community safety by offering practical alternatives such as community-led patrols.[13] As a result of their grit and determination, groups like Forever Family have a lot of traction in working class Black communities. But we would go further, arguing the issue is not the *type* of policing but the practice of policing itself. In this, we find more seeds for a revolutionary approach to abolition. On the one hand abolitionists need to address, as Sarah Lamble argues, 'the conditions in which people feel that police are the only or best option for responding to harm in their lives.[14] Given these conditions, the pragmatic work of collectives like Cradle Community who are building responses to harm outside of violent institutions is vital. They are developing transformative, empathetic, community responses to harm, that encourage us to not just act beyond policing but *think* beyond policing. The work of groups like these provide a glimpse of our collective capacity to build an abolitionist future. But alongside this abolition must also be underpinned by an anti-capitalist, class analysis and practice. One that seeks to leverage class power in order to abolish the underlying conditions that give rise to a society that requires the control of the masses – the working and under classes – by the few in the ruling elite. This is the revolution in the abolition.

THESIS 6

Women have always experienced the sharp end of state violence: if your feminism is carceral, it's bullshit.

The twenty-first century was supposed to be ours. We came of age after the millennium, when the new dawn of equal opportunities was upon us: our gender, race, class, or sexuality wasn't going to stand in the way of success. The reality was crushing. Violence against women had not disappeared with the financial independence of a wage. We experienced workplace sexual harassment, misogynistic or homophobic attacks on the streets and racist policing, all navigated alongside the exploitation of our jobs. Simultaneously, 'Lean in' and 'girlboss' feminisms pushed a lock-'em-up agenda, arguing that domestic and sexual violence could be disappeared by cops and courts. But the 'carceral creep' of twenty-first century feminism felt like anything but liberation.[1]

The oppression of women particular to early industrial capitalism manifested as a gendered division of labour; forcing men out of the home and into the factories, to be productive for capitalists, while trapping women in the role of housewife, doing the domestic and emotional labour needed to reproduce the next generation of workers. When men and women resisted this dual system of capitalist exploitation, a hierarchy of violence that punched down was established to contain them. Men who organised for better working conditions in the workplace were met with police violence. In turn, the state gave men the authority to supervise the work of their wives in the domestic sphere: refusing to do domestic labour would result in coercive control, rape and domestic beatings, that faced little to no consequence from police.[2] Of course, it's a myth that women didn't work as well: working class and racialised women have always been an essential source of cheap labour. Exploited by bosses at work, and oppressed by men in the home, women have always been at the sharp end of violence. Naturally, equal pay for women was out of the question, as it would give women the option of leaving their violent and exploitative marriages – disrupting the nuclear family unit that was central to the development of early capitalism.[3]

The sexual violence that women faced in the street and workplace served to discipline working class women, and reinforce the message that safety and independence outside of a relationship with a man was impossible.[4] Historically, Black women faced even deeper exploitation as slaves, where the refusal to work would be met with torture or execution.[5] The rape of slave women was a brutal business imperative, which kept profits high by ensuring the reproduction of the next generation of slaves. Regardless of whether a woman's children were the result of rape by a slave master, or a consensual relationship with another slave, her children were not her own and could be sold off at any time.[6] Escape attempts were common, and as a result slave patrols were established. These patrols went on to form the basis of organised police forces in former slave colonies, after the abolition of slavery.[7] Since the early days of colonisation, capitalism has significantly changed – and so too has the position of women. But what has remained the same is the role of police in maintaining patriarchal and white supremacist oppression as tools to ensure the continued survival of capitalist exploitation.

By the 1970s, when feminist refuges had been established, and women were collectively organising against gendered oppression,[8] capitalism was no longer in the early stages of industrialisation, and workers were demanding more from life. Workers' unions sprung into action to utilise their class power; militant Black power and anti-imperialist revolts were threatening to overthrow white supremacy and colonialism across the globe, and women took radical action to smash the bonds of patriarchy. For women who could afford it, the growing availability of consumer goods, such as hoovers and electric washing machines, lessened the amount of time needed to be spent in the home.[9] Middle-class women seeking equal opportunity to men in the labour market dominated the women's movement, but working class women and women of colour fought for gender justice too. From the Ford machinists' success on equal pay, and the Grunwick strike for migrant women workers' right to unionise to the fight against virginity testing and other racist immigration controls; from campaigns for childcare provision, and campaigns against sexual violence in the street and the workplace, to the right to separate from violent and abusive husbands: women organised.[10] Though the women's liberation movement covered every aspect of women's lives, it was widely understood that freedom could not be secured without severing the violent and state-sanctioned hold that men had over women in the home.

In the 1970s, large parts of the grassroots feminist movement identified capitalist society and the state as the root of patriarchal oppression and violence. For this reason, many of the first refuges were set up in squats, and run by survivors and radical feminists in the community. They used consensus decision-making and mutual-aid models, whilst being independent of patriarchal structures – whether that was individual men in the home, or the authorities.[11] Many Sisters Uncut members had applied for jobs in the domestic violence sector looking for similar expressions of radical feminist collectivity. But it wasn't to be. The global financial crisis in the 1970s dramatically increased the cost of living, and made self-sufficient refuges much harder to sustain. Those living and working in these early refuges had grown up with the post-war welfare state, and so resigned themselves to pursuing local authority funding to sustain what had become a lifeline of national domestic violence provision.[12] But the state would only provide such funding on strict conditions, which limited the radical and political potential of these spaces. By the time Sisters Uncut members were working in and accessing the sector, the once-revolutionary movement had transformed into a highly professionalised, and often politically sterile, charity sector.[13]

Survivor-led consciousness raising was gone, and survivor-led refuges were nowhere to be found. Consensus decision-making, democratic structures and collectivism had been replaced by the strict separation of 'survivor' and 'worker', in deeply hierarchical and managerial structures.[14] Open door policies, committed to never turning away survivors, were scrapped to comply with local authority overcrowding rules, in the wider context of limited state funding for women's services. Today, two hundred women are turned away from refuges every day,[15] reflecting the grim, banal cruelty of women's lives under neoliberal capitalism. This disappointing entrance into the sector should not have surprised Aviah, whose family were evicted from a refuge because her mother had breached a rule that banned 'unaccompanied children on site'. Aviah was 14 years old, and would go on to spend a year of her GCSEs in a string of bed and breakfasts, some as far as 40 miles from her school. Local authority rules fuelled a punitive turn against refuge residents, but the punishment didn't stop at housing provision.

While large sections of the early refuge movement argued that the police should be treated as upholders of the patriarchal capitalist system,[16] others maintained that the police could be used to protect us. More recently branded as 'carceral feminism',[17] this branch of the women's movement argued that women's liberation could be achieved by reforming and partnering with the police, prisons and courts.[18] This is a strategy of containment and punishment, where arrest and detention is used to interrupt violence, and long prison sentences are used to neutralise any ongoing risks. According to carceral feminists, punishment will ensure perpetrators eventually come to understand that misogynistic violence is bad, and will change accordingly.[19] But in fact, the reverse is true, with data from the College of Policing's own think-tank showing that 'criminal justice sanctions for intimate partner violence have no consistent effect on subsequent offending', and that prison sentences in particular 'were associated with higher rates of recidivism 36 per cent of the time and had no effect in the remainder'.[20]

Returning to the late twentieth century, women were being recruited into the workforce as a reserve army of cheap labour to help manage the ebbs and flows of an unstable and crisis-ridden economic system. It was here the ruling elite saw an opportunity for compromise. Liberal and carceral feminists were co-opted to help shape the transformation of women's role in society, on the understanding that this transformation would subdue the women's movement – whilst keeping the capitalist system intact. The assimilation of the feminist movement was part of a crisis management response. Worker and anti-imperialist movements across the globe were rejecting colonial capitalism, and were threatening to destroy the labour hierarchies that capitalism was built on.[21] In a massive counterattack by the ruling elite, workers' unions were destroyed, a defeat cemented by the outsourcing of industry to the Global South, and a massive investment in law and order, which annihilated social movements.

It's in this context that the ruling elite seized the opportunity to make feminism work in its favour.[22] The state agreed to put meagre support in place for women to leave violent homes – creating greater opportunities for women to enter the workforce. But with the unions largely destroyed, women entered the labour market in low-paying, insecure jobs, juggling employment with unpaid child care.[23] The revolutionary wing of the feminist movement had been derailed. Capitalism compromised on women's demands for autonomy from the violent institution of marriage; however, where it was once the job of a man to maintain women's subordinate role, the state had taken over as the warden of gendered exploitation and oppression. The rapes and beatings once administered by a husband, may now instead be perpetrated by a cop, prison officer, or detention centre guard. This is compounded by a rapid growth in jobs that involve training in the use of surveillance, force, or arms in post-industrial service economies: security guards, bouncers, prison guards, soldiers, police officers, detention centre guards, immigration officers and many others.[24]

Britain's women's liberation movement was established while there was still a functioning and developed welfare state, providing avenues through which feminists could be recruited to do the state's bidding. Elite feminists agreed to champion the state's law-and-order regime on the understanding that the mainstreaming of gender equality would get them a seat at the table. It is no coincidence then that the staunchest advocates of carceral and trans-exclusive feminism are from the white bourgeoisie. These 'respectable' members of the feminist movement have built lucrative careers as CEOs of domestic violence charities and occupy senior positions in academia, the media, law, politics and the wider NGO sector. These glittering girlboss careers were built on the claim that they represent the best interests of women, whilst deliberately ignoring the Black, migrant, working class and sex-working women whose lives have been ruined by the carceral feminist strategies they advocate. Nancy Fraser scathingly calls them the 'handmaidens of capitalism'.[25]

Women attempting to cope in a deeply exploitative and crisis-ridden economy often turn to underground economies, such as sex work, to make ends meet. But anyone making a living outside the formal waged economy is seen as a threat to the ordinary functioning of the system, and is punished by the state. Carceral feminists have provided a 'legitimate' route of attack against sex workers. The Nordic Model of criminalisation, which they champion, has been used to facilitate the forced entry of sex workers into a version of exploitation they approve of: long hours, gruelling work and minimum wage.[26] This law-and-order agenda also increases the likelihood that child protection investigations are triggered, along with the threat, or actual removal, of children into foster care[27] – a form of criminalisation that ruptured Aviah's childhood. A lack of engagement with support services, or self-defence against a perpetrator, leaves survivors vulnerable to being held equally or more culpable for family violence than perpetrators, resulting in criminalisation and the removal of children.[28] Black and mixed-race children are amongst the most likely to be removed from their families, echoing the long legacy of family separation during slavery.[29]

Yet the 'feminism' in the carceral initiatives funded by the state has not been securely won. Despite attempts at reform, the state has stubbornly insisted that a recognition of gendered power relations have no place in criminal investigations on domestic violence.[30] Further, the men's rights lobby has launched a series of anti-feminist attacks on women-only domestic violence support, with 'vengeful equity' claims,[31] purporting women are equally as violent and abusive as men. Pressure from

men's rights activists chimed with the cost-saving mentality of local authorities, leading to council funding for
refuge support increasingly stipulating that men and
women fleeing abuse had to be housed under one roof.[32]
Yet rather than tackle this mainstreaming of misogyny,
elite feminists have retreated from an open fight with
the state and the men's rights lobby, instead mobilising
transphobia to secure their own gender-based rights. By
reinvesting in biological definitions of womanhood, elite
feminists are seeking to win the argument for the cisgen-
der women-only service provision that form the base of
their girlboss careers, whilst weeding out competition by
shutting down trans women's attempts to enter public life
on the same terms as cis women.

Pushing a disinformation campaign, elite feminists
have claimed that trans women in prisons and refuges
are actually men faking a trans status so they can rape
and harm women.[33] Yet when Black and abolitionist feminists pleaded with elite feminists to stop investing in the
carceral policies which were sending women to prison in
their droves, they ignored us.[34] When elite feminists give
their attention to incarcerated women, it's not to argue
for their release, but for their continued imprisonment
in strictly cis women-only prisons. In their panic over
the safety of incarcerated women, they've failed to cast
their eye on the long-established, and far more probable
issue, of rape by prison and detention centre guards,[35]
or the state-sanctioned sexual violence of routine strip-
searches.[36] A deluge of scandals exposing rape and
domestic violence perpetrated by police officers hit the
headlines after the murder of Sarah Everard, and yet

mainstream feminists have cynically attempted to pivot the conversation away from systemic explanations for gendered violence, instead preferring to focus on individual men and trans people.[37]

Sisters Uncut members employed in the domestic violence sector found that the staff on low-paid, insecure contracts often disagreed with the transphobic stance put out by their CEOs. But the hierarchies established when the sector went 'professional' meant there were no bottom-up democratic procedures for workers to influence their workplaces. Instead, many of us watched in horror as our employers unleashed a moral panic against trans women, perpetuating myths about their propensity for violence. To fight back, some members of Sisters Uncut, along with different sections of the social justice movement, have established a section of United Voice of the World (UVW) workers' union, to fight the injustices now embedded within the women's sector.[38]

In contrast with elite feminists, contentious rather than cosy relationships with the state can open up avenues for solidarity. In 2020, Sisters Uncut supported Sistah Space, Britain's only Black domestic violence service, by organising a protest against their eviction by Hackney Council.[39] During the protest, police attempted to grab and arrest a white trans woman from the protest. Speakers from Sistah Space invited demonstrators to block the road until the woman was released; as a crowd formed to de-arrest her – the roadblock prevented any prospect of a police pursuit. The de-arrest was successful. Our liberation will not be found in legislation designed to give cops more power to beat, rape and murder our sisters. Our liberation will be won by the growing movement of Black, trans, migrant, disabled and working class survivors and organisers, whose solidarity will dismantle the systems that exploit and oppress us.

PART 2

Roots In Empire: The History of Criminalisation and Resistance

THESIS 7

*Class struggle in the eighteenth century
sparked a prison abolitionist fire.
Abolition is nothing new.*

On 14 March 2022, four anarchists from the squatter group London Makhnovists entered an empty mansion owned by Russian billionaire oligarch Oleg Deripaska, who had been sanctioned by the British government for his ties to President Vladimir Putin, following Russia's invasion of Ukraine. The squatters wanted to turn the space into a refugee centre for displaced Ukrainians. The Metropolitan Police responded with a huge operation, out of all proportion to the 'threat', which involved – in total – 176 police officers, including riot cops. Alongside this were numerous police vehicles: squad cars, vans, a helicopter and a JCB cherry-picker – taking the total cost to over £80,000 of taxpayers' money. On social media, people naturally compared this heavily resourced police response with the indifference they had experienced when calling 999 for help during burglaries or hate crimes, or after having been raped.[1] Anarchist squatters had drawn the police into a conflict which exposed their role in society: to protect the interests and property of the rich elite. But scepticism about the function of punitive state systems has a long history: we turn now to an eighteenth-century insurrection – the Gordon Riots – within which an early prison abolitionist spirit came to the surface.

The first attempt to pass a policing bill in England came in 1785 and was a direct response to the Gordon Riots. The disturbances had taken place five years earlier, in circumstances remarkably similar to challenges we face today. Government legislation intended to ease some of the discrimination experienced by Catholics sparked unrest: expressions of anti-Catholic, anti-Irish and anti-immigrant rage ripped through London's streets.[2] However, some radical historians have argued that what began as a religious and ethnic conflict morphed into a generalised class conflict.[3] For us, what is interesting about how the uprising developed is the evidence that prison abolitionist sentiments became part of the emerging working class consciousness. By 1780, the cost of living had overtaken wages for the best part of a decade and the working classes were sinking into abject poverty,[4] much like the cost of living crisis that has deepened across the UK in 2022. Understanding the 1780 Gordon Riots as rooted in a toxic mix of racial prejudice and falling economic conditions maps onto similar debates today surrounding Brexit and immigration control. Regardless of whether the Gordon Riots are viewed as rooted primarily in economics or prejudice, the speed at which the rioters turned their focus on the political establishment – and then criminal justice targets – suggests that the divide-and-rule tactic of throwing marginalised groups under the bus to protect the political establishment can be undermined through struggle.

The first two days of rioting targeted the homes and chapels of London's Catholic community. Over the subsequent five days, the focus had shifted, with symbols of

Britain's political class and burgeoning criminal justice system becoming key targets. The Bow Street Runners – a group of magistrates and privately paid bounty hunters formed to protect private property from the working classes, and a forerunner to state policing – had their office raided and records burned.[5] The crowds set upon the homes of bailiffs, debtors, big business bosses and industrialists, as well as demolishing the homes of magistrates.[6] Rebels took aim at the Earl of Mansfield, William Murray – Lord Chief Justice, law reformer and the most powerful judge in England – notorious for the speed at which he concocted and then rushed through new laws facilitating the get-rich-quick schemes of the elite.[7]

These targets echo those of more recent riots and uprisings: during the 2011 riots, working class Londoners targeted wealthy areas in Ealing, West London; burnt police cars, and physically resisted police lines as they advanced into working class neighbourhoods.[8] In March 2021, protests in Bristol against the PCSC bill were met with brutality: maulings by police dogs, and indiscriminate beatings with batons and riot shields.[9] As both self-defence and retaliation against the police violence, protesters burned police vans and ransacked a police station. During the Gordon Riots, the Old Bailey and other courthouses were invaded and half a dozen prisons in the capital were smashed open, liberating the prisoners inside. As if to prevent the incarceration of another soul, the prisons were set ablaze in front of cheering crowds. Newgate Prison, which was one of those liberated, held 117 prisoners; most of whom were there for crimes against property.[10] In this respect, little has changed since Newgate

Prison was standing: overall, 50 per cent of those in prison today are incarcerated for non-violent offences,[11] with the number rising to 72 per cent for women in prison.[12] Most of the Newgate jailbreakers were made up of the property-less class of waged workers, many of whom had survived slavery and war overseas;[13] the freed Newgate prisoners joining the crowds included former slaves as well as pros-titutes – the offence terminology of the time.

Breaking through the dominant and sometimes narrow focus on prisons, calls to expand abolitionist organising to psychiatric wards have recently gained more atten-tion.[14] The story of Thomas 'Mad Tom' Haycock, as told by Marxist historian Peter Linebaugh and others, demon-strates that resistance to carceral systems has long been led by those with experience of mental health detention. The coffeehouse worker 'Mad Tom' had been given his nickname after being repeatedly detained and straight-jacketed for 'madness'.[15] The authorities accosted him after he was overheard gleefully recounting that he was the first to enter Newgate Prison during the rebellion, stating he had 'let out all the prisoners'.[16] At his trial, he was asked why he took part in the rebellion, to which he boldly and defiantly replied 'the cause'.[17] After being pressed for further explanation he proclaimed, 'there should not be a prison standing on the morrow in London.'[18] Detainment, criminalisation and physical restraint continue to be the primary responses to acute mental distress, exposing some of the most vulnerable people, disproportionately Black, to the extremes of state brutality.[19] Dame Elish Angiolini's 2017 report on deaths in police custody found 'many of those who die following the use of physical restraint suffer from mental ill health.'[20] Those with lived experience of mental health confinement, such as organisers in the Campaign for Psychiatric Abolition, keep the fire burning for Mad Tom's 'cause'.[21] Abolitionists today fight to rebuild community care and support whilst working to dismantle the system which makes us ill as they diagnose our resistance as 'madness'.[22]

By the time the army had brought the rebels of the Gordon Riots to heel, hundreds of people had been killed.[23] The Gordon Riots tested England's hitherto patchy and uncoordinated policing system, and it was found wanting. Prime Minister William Pitt drafted England's first policing bill in 1785. Pitt maintained that a professional police force would improve on the failed response of the informal systems, whilst providing a cheaper and less alarmist approach than resorting to the army.[24] The public press, which was by no means radical on questions of the state's use of force, protested passionately for the bill to be dropped.[25] Perhaps they feared the bill would be interpreted as a sinister power grab; sparking further rebellion, or even revolution. No matter: Pitt would simply do a 'cut and paste' job, with his policing bill passing the following year in Ireland.

The Gordon Riots were a spontaneous explosion of anti-Catholic rage that quickly gave way to an anti-establishment rebellion. How much more powerful might it have been if that anti-establishment spirit had developed into an anti-imperialist movement that welcomed Catholics, Irish and immigrants into the fight? Organising solidarity between different sections of the working classes by focusing on a common enemy can dismantle the influence of reactionary, racist and fascist ideology in our communities. In 1958, Oswald Mosley's fascist mobilisation of poor working class white youths sparked race riots in Notting Hill, resulting in the murder of carpenter Kelso Cochrane. Unlike more recent champions of hate crime legislation, communist Claudia Jones had no interest in appealing to the white suprema-cist state to address fascist violence in poor communities. Claudia founded a predecessor to the Notting Hill Carnival in 1959,[26] and invited Black and white working class com-munities to collectively heal through the vivid joy of Caribbean festivities, culture and talents.[27] The aboli-tionist spirit of the event shone through its programme, which stated that the proceeds would pay off the fines of the Black *and* white youths involved in the disturbances.[28]

Mosley's fascists had turned their attention towards West London's emerging Caribbean community after decades of anti-fascist organising had booted them out of the East End. The Battle of Cable Street is a much-cherished victory in our movement history, where 100,000 East-enders forced police lines to halt the advance of Mosley's anti-Semitic march in 1936.[29] Alongside this momentous street battle was longer-term organising by communist groups such as the Stepney Tenants' Defence League, who recruited Jewish and non-Jewish households to join rent strikes and housing struggles – as part of an anti-fascist strategy.[30] In 1937, a landmark victory by the League prevented the eviction of two fascist households who, prompted by weeks of solidarity eviction resistance by their Jewish neighbours, tore up their British Union of Fascist membership cards.[31] When fascists goad us with their violence and marches, we must defend our communities by physically confronting them through mass self-defence. This must happen alongside the longer-term work of dismantling fascist ideologies by building community solidarity through common cause.

Knowingly or not, the London Makhnovist squatters drew the police further into a crisis of contradictions. By entering the Russian oligarch's empty mansion, the squatters invited the police to reveal whether they would protect the interests of a sanctioned Russian oligarch, or go with public opinion and allow the mansion to be opened up for Ukrainian refugees. The public has grown increasingly sceptical of the government's claim that we are 'all in this together', and this scepticism can be mobilised for radical change. The modern-day British state has spent decades blaming falling living standards on migrants, and claiming that a lack of immigration controls were to blame for unemployment rates and poverty.[32] More people are in work than have been for decades,[33] and immigration controls are through the roof, yet people are facing the biggest drop in living standards since the 1950s.[34]

As abolitionists, we cannot wait complacently hoping that the public's rage will pivot towards justice. We must proactively pivot that anger to connect with those that might have previously been seen as competitors, or even enemies – whether they be migrants, Black working-class, or Gypsy, Roma and Traveller communities. Learning from the work of Claudia Jones and the Stepney Tenants' Defence League, we know that this will involve political education, door knocking, street stalls and phone calls – alongside a host of other activities. The next anti-establishment rebellion must combine rage over the cost of living, immigration enforcement, stop and search, and traveller evictions to build a united and powerful challenge to state power.

THESIS 8

The UK rehearsed its strategies of control and punishment in the colonies. Abolition continues anti-colonial and class struggle in Britain today.

Within just a few days, the face of another young white woman had joined Sarah Everard's on the front pages of British newspapers, both part of the same story of gendered police violence and brutality. As the shock of the news that Sarah had been murdered by a serving Metropolitan Police officer set in, images of Patsy Stevenson – an attendee at the Clapham Common vigil held in Sarah's name – being arrested, handcuffed and dragged along the ground by several male police officers, blew up on social media. As the news coverage surrounding these events turned from days to weeks to months, some concluded that the attention given to Sarah's murder, and the violent police response at the vigil, came down to the racial privilege of the white women involved. The column inches, chat-show segments, police resources and community vigils that were dedicated to Sarah, it was argued, should be re-allocated towards racialised victims who get no such airtime.[1] It is certainly the case that racial capitalism values the lives of some over others, and this drove the disproportionate media and police attention in Sarah's case. There is no doubt things would have played out differently had she been Black.[2] But it's a sign of how low the bar has sunk when visibility and representation in death sets the limit of our collective vision for liberation.

We could have focused our strategy on representation and visibility; we might have implored the media to report that it was Black survivors from Sisters Uncut who stepped in to lead the Clapham Common vigil, that representatives from Black domestic violence service Sistah Space were prevented by police from speaking, or that a woman of colour was amongst those snatched and arrested from the bandstand. We chose instead to organise the growing wave of popular resistance; people were waking up to the reality of police violence and we invited them to join our community's long fight against police brutality. Setting our sights beyond representation, we called for a coalition to fight the expansion of police powers. Out of this came the national Kill the Bill movement and the CopWatch police intervention network – we focused our energies on levying an open challenge to state violence.

This decision was a political one. As abolitionists, we understand the role the mainstream media and police play in protecting racial capitalism. Pleading with institutions to re-allocate resources, increase visibility, or prioritise representation for racialised victims of violence assumes they can solve the problems they collude in creating.[3] But as we've argued in earlier theses, both the media and police are fundamental actors involved in both creating and maintaining the conditions that lead to violence in our communities: there is no reforming this. Our liberation cannot begin or end with begging for leftovers from the very institutions complicit in our oppression. We do not want parity in mourning for another dead sister.

Ending gendered and racialised violence can only come from dismantling the systems of oppression that benefit from our abuse.

THE EMERGENCE OF RACE AS SOCIAL CONTROL

It often feels as if race and racism have always been part of the human experience. In reality, the roots of racism are complex: race is a historical phenomena that developed over hundreds of years as a tool to exploit labour and land.[4] Racial divisions that we take for granted today did not always exist: they are continually manufactured and have been fiercely resisted since their genesis.

One of England's earliest colonial ventures was the Virginia colony; so-called after the 'Virgin Queen' Elizabeth I. This was the dawn of England's shift from a feudal to a capitalist economy. What made capitalists' property relations different from those under feudalism was that they relied on seizing, privatising and enclosing common land – land that was previously free for all to wander, fish, hunt, or forage – so that the developing bourgeoisie could have total control over wealth accumulated from natural resources and wage labour.[5] Those who did not own land found that they were cut off from self-sufficient survival, and forced into waged labour in the growing capitalist industries.[6] Early capitalism relied on the constant accumulation of cheap land and labour in order to maximise profits, and this was achieved through aggressive territorial expansion and mass human servitude.[7]

While the Enclosure Acts affected Wales and Scotland, the greatest damage occurred in England, where landlords evicted peasants from the land their ancestors had worked for generations. To facilitate the rapid transition to waged labour, the state criminalised 'vagrancy' so that anyone found surviving outside of the 'legitimate' economy faced violence, surveillance and punishment.[8] Contemporary police harassment against Black, sex worker and homeless communities have their roots in these vagrancy laws. The Vagrancy Act has been used by police as a method of collective harassment all the way up until it was fully repealed in 2022.[9] While vagrancy laws helped put the growing class of paupers to work in the emerging capitalist industries, many were also transported to British colonies as indentured servants.[10] To sweeten what was a shit deal and to prevent rebellions, English indentured servants were promised a plot of land on completion of their term of indenture. But this promise was a swindle – harsh and brutal conditions killed most workers off long before their seven years of servitude were up.[11] When indentured workers developed strategies to survive, the ruling class scrambled to find ways to avoid making good on their promises.

In the early days, these indentured servants worked alongside small numbers of African slaves.[12] At this point, whilst still in an experimental phase of colonisation, the ruling class hadn't yet settled on the best techniques to control what was a growing and diverse labour force. You might therefore be surprised to learn that the status of slave in early colonial Virginia was not passed from parent to child: freed and even property-owning Africans were not uncommon; and in the 1660s, marriages between Africans and Europeans were routine – a quarter of all babies born over this period having European servant mothers and African fathers.[13] As it turned out, too much familiarity and commonality between European servants and African slaves would spell disaster for the ruling elite.

Throughout the 1660s, tensions were brewing, with multi-ethnic gatherings being held in protest against cruel and exploitative working conditions.[14] Resistance by the oppressed was mounting: physical violence, verbal protest, slowdowns and sabotage were common, and slaves and servants continuously ran away together to interrupt their exploitation.[15] Nathaniel Bacon, a disgruntled land-owner who'd been refused permission to invade Native American territories by the Virginia Governor William Berkeley, decided to make a play against him by launching a coup. He soon recognised his best chance of success was to recruit a combined army of European and African rebels. They provided military power on the condition that their victory would secure the abolition of slavery and servitude.[16] The rebel army entered the colonial capital Jamestown having proclaimed 'liberty to all servants and Negroes';[17] they burned the capital to the ground and looted the homes of the ruling elite. Groups of women, including sex workers,[18] joined the rebellion – choosing to die, for freedom, alongside the soldiers.[19]

Although Bacon's sudden death by dysentery brought an abrupt end to the rebellion, the governing classes were so shaken that the course of history changed forever.[20] That the ruling classes were still at the top was through sheer luck; next time they would not leave it up to chance. European and African rebels had launched a serious challenge as a unified class of exploited people. In order to cement their class position, the colonisers responded by sharpening their tools of social control. To break the power of the economically exploited classes, the ruling class manipulated ethnic difference by creating new *racial* categories, and codifying their status in the law books. African slaves, who had now become 'Black', were legally inferior to 'white' indentured workers. White loyalty was bought off, and whiteness aligned with the interests of the ruling class, by doling out better conditions and privileges for white workers based on their new racial status.[21] After Bacon's Rebellion, the colonisers began abandoning their reliance on European labour, instead investing heavily in the abduction and enslavement of West African people to fuel the transatlantic slave trade.[22] Slave labour produced a huge amount of surplus value. The immense wealth generated by slaves was seized and pocketed by the ruling class.[23] All the slaves got in return were minimal amounts of food, shelter and clothing – just enough to reproduce the next generation of slaves.[24] Even after slavery was abolished, the devaluation and dehumanisation of Black workers, and the hyper-exploitation of their labour, continued to feed immense riches into both the British empire and the capitalist industries of the US.

Even today, race creates contradictory interests within the working class, where many poor white people believe they have more in common with the wealthy bosses and landowners whose skin shade is closer to theirs, than they do their Black neighbour or colleague. The creation of race, locked into the law, was a clever manipulation designed to break the back of class solidarity; ensuring total control of the workforce, and establishing new technologies of social control. As the British expanded their empire, the list of 'races' only got longer, with more distinct racial categories emerging to demote the status of some and elevate the status of others. From its colonial origins to today, race is one of the central structures through which relations under capitalism are organised.

It often feels like united multi-racial resistance is a pipe dream. But occasionally, there are glimmers of hope. In the summer of 2014, when a group of single mothers in Newham's Focus E15 hostel were served with eviction notices, they decided to occupy two empty council flats on the nearby Carpenter's Estate.[25] Earmarked for regeneration, much of the estate's residents had been decanted, leaving huge numbers of perfectly decent properties sitting empty.[26] Aviah supported the Focus E15 mums and went door-knocking on the estate to rally support for the residents involved in the occupation. Some of the white residents asked why mosques were being established when there was no council housing being built for British people. Over that summer, the occupation became the focal point of the estate, with multi-racial, working class people working alongside each other to transform the empty council homes into a community centre. On the last night of the occupation, Bill, a working class white man from the estate, was feeling mournful that it had all come to an end. Reflecting on how much he had gained, both politically and socially, from being in such a rich and diverse political space he said 'I spent 20 years being a football hooligan. Maybe I should have joined a commune instead.'

THE EMERGENCE OF POLICE
AS SOCIAL CONTROL

Though race has been one of the strongest and most enduring tools used by the elite to divide and rule,[27] it was not by itself enough. The colonisers and capitalists still found themselves confronted with insurrections, riots, strikes, mass demonstrations, sabotage and direct action that challenged their authority.[28] In response, the ruling elite began experimenting with the idea of using a centralised repressive force to maintain their domination over the exploited classes. British experiments with a police force first began in Ireland, Britain's oldest settler colony.[29] Having first attempted, and failed, to establish a police force in England,[30] the ruling elite were anxious not to undermine their own legitimacy by overstepping the mark on their own doorstep, so they took the idea of policing to the Irish colony to test it there first. Throughout the 1760s, Ireland saw a wave of peasant uprisings against English colonisers who were evicting them through land enclosures and turning their land over to capitalists in the wool trade.[31] These rural rebellions involved small groups of peasants banding together and going on the offensive by attacking landlords and destroying livestock, with the aim of resisting eviction or wresting back seized land.[32]

A major influence behind the introduction of the police into Ireland was the authority's frustration with the wall of silence they met when attempting to investigate uprisings and actions.[33] Irish people 'informing' on other Irish folk was utterly despised, and would often lead to retaliatory violence from the wider community[34] – the working class code of 'snitches get stitches' has a very long history indeed. In addition, attempts to recruit colonised Catholics into the informal community guarding systems – for example, as night watchman – also fell flat: the colonisers doing the recruiting were not accepted as a legitimate authority.[35] Reports of the Irish rebellions made their way back to the English government, with greatly exaggerated and manipulated tales of violence.[36] Depictions of the Irish as violent – a trait which the British constructed as evidence of innate racial difference – helped to rally the English ruling class behind the need to bring in a centralised police force, outmanoeuvring the Irish strategy of non-compliance with force and violence.[37]

The Irish were cast as too dangerous *not* to be policed, and so a series of policing bills were instated, starting with the 1786 Dublin Police Act, followed by the Irish County Police Act and the Irish Riot Act, both established in 1787.[38] Rural economic rebellions led to the anti-colonial national liberation movement, followed by the insurgent Irish Rebellion of 1798. Enraged by the fierce resistance of the colonised Irish, Parliament removed full control from the settler colonialists, who could no longer be trusted to maintain control.[39] The Dublin Police Act of 1808 established the first modern police force, some 21 years before a much less militarised structure would be developed in London.[40] In the wake of all this, Sir Robert Peel would soon take over as Secretary for Ireland, continuing the tradition of ambitious politicians utilising Ireland as a stepping stone towards the role of Prime Minister back on the mainland. He would later become the brains behind the Metropolitan Police Service.

Colonised people do not usually accept the legitimacy of colonial rulers. As a result, a highly militarised police force was necessary in Ireland, one that emphasised brute force over the need to cultivate legitimacy.[41] Protestant settlers were recruited as officers, entrenching religious divisions in a context where Catholics were not trusted to enforce colonial laws against their own people. This divide-and-rule recruitment strategy of enlisting officers from ethnic and religious groups outside of the community being policed would be repeated across the empire, as Britain established police and military forces across the globe.[42] In parts of Nigeria, colonisers recruited Hausa officers to police Yoruba communities, explicitly identifying that the differences in language and customs should be exploited; the resulting hostility and polarisation between the groups was mobilised in service of the colonisers' interests.[43]

Once a police force had been established and tested in Ireland, trials in social control began to make their way back to the mainland, the most crucial example being in London's East End. Around the time of the Irish Rebellion, merchant and magistrate Patrick Colquhoun led a group of wealthy businessmen and slavers in establishing the Marine Police Office 'for the prevention of River Plunder', Colquhoun's initiative being the direct forerunner to the Metropolitan Police.[44] The empire was booming, and the docks – whether London, Bristol, Glasgow, or other British port cities – were the most important gateways into mainland Britain. For an unemployed Londoner looking for a day's work, the East End was the place to be. Despite this, life was still lived hand to mouth and wages paid to the dockers were not enough to live on. Acquiring 'perquisites' (perks) was a custom which allowed dockers to take home any cargo slippage as a recognised and accepted way of topping up their wages.[45] This was the case for many industrial workers, such as miners who would take gangue minerals – such as fluorite – from the lead mines of the North Pennines and sell them on the collector's market. In a city marked by great inequality, some enterprising dockers found ways to engineer the amount of 'slippage', rather than leave it to chance.[46] The Thames business class were determined to find ways to gain complete control over the spoils of empire and maximise their profits. When bosses attempted to remove the custom of perks, and 'persuade' workers to accept wage-only payment, it was fiercely resisted through strikes.

Through a sophisticated ideological and political campaign, Patrick Colquhoun successfully rebranded both the custom of perks, and workers' organised resistance, as 'criminal'. In 1796, he published *A Treatise on the Police of Metropolis*, launching a scathing attack on the working classes, casting them as an inherently criminal class who were diseased with the evils of laziness which could 'contaminate' and 'infect' others.[47] Colquhoun did not distinguish between the workers that played by the rules of slippage, those that took more than was agreed, and those that organised resistance to poor working conditions; to Colquhoun, and his eager bourgeois audience, these were all examples of an epidemic of working class criminality.[48] Colquhoun doesn't mention the Irish police force that had recently been established, but he makes use of remarkably similar ideological tactics to criminalise the English working class as those used to justify a centralised

policing system in Ireland. This proved hugely effective: he created a moral panic which, it was argued, could
only be 'solved' with repression and violence by a police
force. Perhaps learning from Ireland that fear-monger-
ing was a powerful tool in garnering consent for greater
coercive social control, Colquhoun massively exaggerated, and even fabricated, London's crime problem.[49] He
rebranded ordinary and accepted working class activities as 'crimes', painting working class life as dangerously
criminal in a calculated bid to lay the groundwork for
control through policing.

Colquhoun's writings were popular with the propertied
classes, garnering him enough respect to turn the London
Society of West India Planters and Merchants into a highly
influential political lobby, that protected the interests of
slavers in Britain's Caribbean colonies.[50] Colquhoun met
with his committee of slavers, having already met with the
Home Secretary to obtain political support for his plans,
and it was there they founded the Marine Police Office
in 1798. This private police gang set about bullying and
beating workers into giving up the old perks system, as
well as preventing workers from organising any resistance.
Robert Peel then used his colonial political education in
Ireland, and his association with Colquhoun, to establish the first centralised, state-controlled police force in
mainland Britain: the London Metropolitan Police was
established in 1829. Peel intended to maximise the gains
made by the Thames River Police by making the crackdown
on revolutionary potential, riots and collective resistance
by workers a state, rather than private, imperative.

Unlike the Irish police force and other forces established across the empire, policing by consent was a critical
and central part of policing on mainland Britain.[51] For
Peel, it was crucial that Metropolitan Police officers be
recruited from the communities they policed, giving
them an air of legitimacy and trust. This was the distinc-
tive aspect of policing in Britain: Peel understood that
a delicate balance had to be struck between the use of
violence and cultivating public approval.[52] Policing in the
colonies de-prioritised legitimacy, as the oppressive, dehu-
manising and exploitative nature of colonialism meant
control could only be secured through force. The ruling
elite understood that British workers' greatest strength
was their size: they massively outnumbered the bosses.
But unless the bosses wanted to spark a revolution, the
workers could not be subdued through extreme violence
or the threat of murder. When Peel established the Met
Police, he understood that the stability of the developing capitalist economic and political system relied on not
pushing the conditions of the English working class too
closely to those in the colonies; the use of violence had
to be balanced against the image of policing by consent.[53]

The tools that would prove most effective to the ruling
class – such as piloting new systems of policing in the
colonies before rolling them out on the mainland, and
manufacturing consent through narratives of criminally
dangerous and violent populations – would prove to be
some of the most powerful and enduring tools in the
utility belt of colonial capitalism. These techniques are
front and centre in today's political landscape. In contemporary multicultural Britain, the state refines its strategies

of control on communities of colour, before filtering those techniques it can get away with on to the remaining population. For example, CS gas, first used against anti-colonial resistance in Cyprus in the early 1960s,[54] was later trialled against uprisings in Toxteth, Liverpool, in response to Black communities across the country revolting against the racist use of vagrancy laws to conduct mass suspicionless stop and search.

In 1835, India, capitalising on reports that travellers had been robbed and murdered by groups of Indian natives,[55] the 'Thuggee and Dacoity Department' was set up by the East India Company to criminalise nomadic customs and wandering entertainers; both were seen as undermining the colonisers' monopoly on land control. Led by the racist theory that 'thug' criminality was inherent to particular tribes, and could be passed down the blood line, the authorities established the 1871 Criminal Tribes Act which would later give them the power to criminalise entire ethnic communities.[56] Similarly in modern-day Britain, the gangs matrix and joint enterprise laws, disproportionately used to target Black people, criminalise individuals even in cases where no crime has been committed, casting Black communities as inherently criminal and making Black people guilty by association.[57] These laws make loose affiliation enough to see you criminalised for life.[58]

THE INTERNATIONAL IMPERIAL BOOMERANG

When Ireland won independence in 1921, Royal Irish Constabulary officers, also known as 'black and tans', left to join other colonial forces, including those in Palestine.[59] As in Ireland, British colonial policing in Palestine was highly militarised, emphasising policing by threat of death, rather than by consent.[60] The term 'black and tan methods' was coined by Palestinians, in a nod to the brutal tactics brought over from Ireland – including collective punishment, widespread torture and shooting people down as they tried to escape.[61] Following the ethnic cleansing of Palestinians through violent military means by Zionists in 1948,[62] and the seizure of parts of the region to establish the settler colonial State of Israel, Israel retained the British 'state of emergency' – which has been renewed every year since, to this day. This has meant that internment, suspension of the right to a fair trial, home demolition, indefinite detention, mass displacement and the imposition of curfews are a daily part of Palestinian life.[63]

Building on the sordid history of imperial domination, the US has ensured its interests in the region are protected through more indirect arrangements, rather than the open colonial rule of the British empire. One aspect of age-old colonialism that has remained intact is the use of colonised regions as a social petri dish, testing grounds for new techniques of coercion and control.[64] Apartheid Israel uses Palestine as a laboratory and Palestinians as laboratory subjects: creating a 'try before you buy' window shop for nations looking for their next weapon or strategy of control.[65] This relationship in evident in the crowd-control training provided by Israel to US police officers.[66] We see it in the US-made tear gas canisters deployed against Palestinians, then used heavily against Black Lives Matter protesters.[67] Yet, the embers of internationalist, anti-colonial solidarity burnt brightly when Palestinians took to social media, offering practical solidarity to Black Lives Matter protesters injured by CS gas,[68] with advice on caring for injuries. Any serious challenge to the global, imperialist policing and military systems – that connect our struggles from Palestine to Toxteth – must be grounded in internationalist solidarity.

PART 3

Systems of Criminalisation Today

THESIS 9

From student revolt to urban rebellion, abolition must harness the radical energy of our youth!

When the Tory-Lib Dem coalition entered government in 2010, we both had a sense of what was coming. The 2008 financial crash had begun whittling away our hopes for a secure future. But the prospect of a Tory-led government spelled a deeper kind of pain for our communities. In 2010, Shanice was studying for her A Levels, while Aviah was working towards a (misguided and never practised) MA in Social Work. School, followed by university, was our only realistic route out of poverty: the £30 a week Education Maintenance Allowance (EMA) kept poor and aspirational kids like us in education. After coming to power, the coalition government immediately took aim at students and young people, tripling tuition fees, abolishing EMA, closing youth services and slashing funding to further education (FE). Austerity put the nail in the coffin of Tony Blair's 'education, education, education' promise of social mobility.[1] Today, the situation for young people is bleak. There are 600,000 more children living in poverty than in 2012; social mobility is declining, and is set to get worse due to the pandemic.[2] Vulnerable young people are being failed by the crisis in children's services, caused by funding cuts, and young people in the UK feel the most pessimistic about their life prospects of any age group.[3]

Neoliberal ideologues fervently categorise those of us that 'make it' into the category of 'worker' and 'striver', contrasting us with unemployed folk who are labelled as 'shirkers' or 'skivers'.[4] These distinctions supposedly create an ideological compass for the government, separating who is deserving of state support and who isn't. In reality, neoliberalism and over a decade of austerity has sent the conditions of the entire working class into freefall, regardless of whether you work or not: a 2021 Institute for Public Policy Research (IPPR) report found the majority of those living in poverty were in households with paid work.[5]

Disinvestment from working class life and the decimation of public services has ensured that for greater numbers of poor children – particularly those who are racialised or disabled – the school-to-profession pipeline has been replaced by a school-to-prison pipeline. Permanent and fixed-term exclusions have dramatically increased over recent years,[6] as academisation,[7] swelling class sizes, and cuts to youth, family, mental health and educational support services drive an authoritarian shift to punitive bootcamp models of education.[8] Successive governments have expanded alternative school provisions (AP) – which are increasingly situated in the private sector – and pupil referral units,[9] into which they funnel increasing numbers of excluded children failed by the system. These often disciplinarian and carceral institutions systematically fail children, with only 4 per cent of children in alternative provision coming out with English and Maths GCSEs.[10] As No More Exclusions, a pioneering grassroots campaign of abolitionist educators and students, have powerfully argued: 'Since the introduction of ESN ("Educationally Subnormal") schools in the 1970s, Black and minoritised children have been systematically removed from mainstream schools and funnelled into substandard alternative education settings. AP is the modern iteration of this.'[11] In a context where 63 per cent of prisoners had been suspended from school and 42 per cent had been expelled,[12] it is clear that rising exclusion rates only accelerate the conveyor belt between schools and prisons, with Black and mixed-heritage boys facing multiple and compounded disadvantages.[13]

The myth of social mobility has disintegrated, and with this, the material and ideological gap between poor, urban youth and socially mobile, working class students has closed. But young people haven't stood by, passively watching the state erode their futures: they have been central to every social movement that's erupted over the last 15 years. In the early years of austerity, youth on either side of the worker/shirker divide rose up in resistance to injustice and poured onto the streets with rage and fury. In 2010, FE students escalated action in response to the abolition of the EMA,[14] joining university students fighting a hike in tuition fees. In 2011, urban youth rioted and set our cities alight in response to police murder. In the minds of many, these are unrelated events, but this separation is a myth,[15] one that conceals the drivers behind these moments: the deprivation of increasing numbers of working class youth.

But crucially, this impoverishment took place in the context of escalating state repression, aimed at guaranteeing social control at a time of deep and enduring instability. Austerity hasn't just devastated the economic life chances of our youth – it has also brought increasing numbers of young people into the crosshairs of police violence. The last time Britain had seen mass, rebellious protest and direct action was against the Poll Tax in the early 1990s – before many of the young people impacted by cuts were born. But on 10 November 2010, a flame was lit. A student protest, which the police expected to pull in a mere 5,000 people, instead snowballed into a 50,000 strong revolt.[16] Determined to resist the proposed eye-watering £9,000 university fees and attacks on the EMA – the educational lifeline of working class youth – students overwhelmed the police and smashed their way into the Tory headquarters at Millbank Tower, establishing a political occupation.

We had them at Millbank. The occupation shot the starter-pistol for weeks of radical revolt by students: tens of thousands took part in protests, occupied universities across the country and organised walkouts in schools and FE colleges.[17] Instead of changing direction and meeting student demands, the state responded with some of the worst displays of police violence seen for two decades: horse charges, baton rams, kettling of children and teenagers, mass arrest, infiltration.[18] And this violent crackdown was just the beginning. Over the next few years, the state response morphed into a significantly increased police presence on campuses, the surveillance and arrest of student activists, and use of weapons like CS spray and tasers.[19] This sparked a national 'Cops Off Campus' campaign, of which Shanice was an active participant, seeing thousands of students take to the streets to protest police violence.[20] This was the first taste of state violence for many of the white, middle-class students in the movement. However, the working class and racialised kids who experienced regular police repression – many of whom were in schools and FE colleges – helped fuel the militancy and radicalism that would go on to character-ise the student movement. Already having an antagonistic relationship to state authority, these students were less bogged down in liberal hand-wringing over the protec-tion of property, favouring more radical expressions of resistance to the usual static demonstration or an A-to-B march.[21]

Having trialled their tactics of coercion, control and violence on students from 2010 onwards, police executed them with equal ferocity on the BLM youth uprisings of 2020. Netpol found that during the summer of revolt fol-lowing George Floyd's murder by police, Black protesters in the UK were disproportionately targeted with pepper spray, baton charges and horse charges. Black youth were regularly picked out by police, snatched from crowds and violently arrested.[22] Kettling re-entered the street theatre of violent social control, with BLM protesters being detained in kettles for up to eight hours with no social dis-tancing, no access to food and no access to toilets.[23] Many protesters reported that police refused medical attention to those who were injured,[24] including a 16-year-old Black boy who was stabbed in the face by far-right, anti-BLM protesters. He was searched by police and sent to find help elsewhere after he approached them for help.[25]

The increase in police violence against young people on the streets has occurred in tandem with an increase in police violence against young people in schools. Between 2010–11 and 2020–21, the number of police in London's schools has more than doubled, with 377 school-based police officers (SBPOs) now deployed in secondary schools across the capital.[26] In schools across the country, 683 SBPOs are deployed,[27] disproportionately distributed in schools with large working class and racialised student populations.[28] SBPOs are part of the 'safer schools' agenda, which is packaged as an attempt to make school life safe. But bringing the disciplinary function of police from the streets into the classroom has had the opposite effect: more children are now exposed to the horrors of police violence and criminalisation. In 2020, a Merseyside police officer, part of the 'safer schools' unit, assaulted a 10-year-old autistic child, dragging him along the floor by his clothes as he tried to crawl away in fear.[29] In December of the same year, a 15-year-old Black girl known as Child Q was strip-searched by police at school, in what can only be called a case of multi-agency child abuse. She was falsely accused of possessing cannabis, made to remove her underwear and sanitary towel while she was menstruating and was searched by two police officers alone in a room at her school. Neither the police nor the school informed her mother of what had happened, who only found out after her daughter returned home distressed and traumatised.[30] And it's vital to note, none of this would have been okay even if she *had* cannabis on her: we would much rather have cannabis in schools than the state-sanctioned sexual assault of children. From the streets to the school gates, austerity has expanded the number of children and young people targeted by the disciplining and coercive functions of the state.

In 2010, students ignited the flame of youth rebellion that had long been assumed to be dead. The following summer, Aviah was on a three-hour-long hold to Her Majesty's Prison Brixton, attempting to arrange a visit to a friend who had been nicked during the 2011 riots. With 1,400 people remanded during the uprisings,[31] it's little wonder the phones were jammed by those desperately trying to visit incarcerated loved ones. The 2011 riots were sparked in Tottenham by the police murder of an unarmed Black man: Mark Duggan.[32] The riots quickly spread across the capital and then across the country: Birmingham, Bristol, Manchester, Liverpool and other cities across England were lit up in rebellion. Some of those whose precarious route out of poverty had been destroyed by the end of the EMA and the decimation of further education, came out to the streets in solidarity with those for whom social mobility through education had always seemed like a pipe dream.[33]

While the mainstream media represented the riots as an apolitical looting fest, criminal justice targets remained central to the disturbances. For example, on the Pembury estate in Hackney, hundreds of participants built barricades and engaged in all-night hand-to-hand combat with the advancing line of riot police, as a means of protecting their estate.[34] Having since moved to another Hackney estate, a neighbour of Aviah's later recalled the gruesome intensity on Pembury that night, witnessing a police officer grab what he thought was the blunt slide of a machete only to see his fingers drop to the ground. Physical confrontation with the oppression of the state was clearly central to those participating in the riots. A

2019 Economic and Social Research Council (ESRC) report found that 'deprivation was the strongest predictor of whether a riot occurred in a London borough', and, crucially, that boroughs with more stop and search were more likely to experience rioting.[35]

In the three years leading up to the 2011 riots, large parts of London were subject to repeated use of Section 60 – suspending the 'reasonable suspicion' requirement for stop and search – and effectively giving police free rein to subject working class Black communities to sustained state harassment. Research based on interviews with those involved in the 2011 revolt found that poverty (86 per cent) and policing (85 per cent) were the most cited motivations for participation.[36] Interviewees also made repeated reference to the increase in tuition fees and scrapping of the EMA as motivating their participation.[37] By understanding the motivations of the 2011 uprisings beyond the trite, ideological musings on 'gangs' and looting by politicians and pundits, we can begin to reappraise this moment as political protest.[38] The 2011 uprisings shone a light on the combined effect of unemployment, violent policing, gentrification and the education cuts that disproportionately hit working class, racialised communities. The student rebellion of 2010, and the working class uprisings of 2011, were spurred on by the same conditions and motivations: hopelessness caused by declining life prospects and frustration caused by police repression.

A 2021 government report confirmed what we already knew about views of policing amongst Black people: confidence in policing is falling sharply, but this decline is particularly acute for young Black people. The confidence level for Black people aged 16–24 stood at 63 per cent, the lowest of all groups by race and age, rising to a mere 65 per cent for Black, full-time students.[39] Even those whose talents are recognised by the state remain wholly unprotected. Bestowing the status of 'young, gifted and Black' onto Grenfell Tower victim Khadija Saye did not prevent state violence from killing her. As well as a string of well-earned accolades, the up-and-coming artist had been awarded a scholarship to attend the sixth form at Rugby School, one of the country's best independent schools.[40] On the night Khadija and her mother, Mary Mendy, died in the 2017 Grenfell Tower fire, she was unable to call for help because police had seized her phone and refused to return it after a wrongful arrest.[41] In Khadija's story, we see the contours of modern life in Britain for Black youth: neoliberalism had torn through her west London community; corporate greed and criminal negligence turned her council housing block into a death trap; aggressive and racist policing made her vulnerable, not safe.[42] The lie of social mobility tells young people that hard work and education will save you, but even those ostensibly destined for status and stardom like Khadija find the odds stacked against them by systems deliberately hostile to working class Black life.

In this context, it is no surprise that young people, unaffiliated with traditional left-wing organisations, led the 2020 Black Lives Matter protests.[43] Yet despite the historically unique position of young people as militant political actors, who also experience the sharp end of state violence, there has been both a snobbery from the left about recent urban youth uprisings,[44] and a disconnect between students and poor, urban youth in grassroots anti-racist organising. A revolutionary abolitionist project cannot afford this disconnect; we must be unequivocal: the radicalism of the youth is invaluable to any movement that seeks systemic change. Abolition can be a vehicle for harnessing and directing the energy of young people towards the revolutionary goals of our time. Our work must bring students and marginalised youth together, connecting the dots between the politics of the streets, and the politics of the university. The power of youth radicalism, that has both a working class base and draws in socially mobile students whose conditions are also rapidly declining, can be seen in the recent Nigerian youth movement against police and state violence: #EndSARS.[45]

In October 2020, thousands of mostly young Nigerians came out onto the streets, cutting through ethnic and religious divides, to protest against the extra-judicial killings and unbridled brutality of the Special Anti-Robbery Squad, or SARS. The movement was sparked by intense police harassment of young Nigerians, who were finding new ways to make money from the Internet, with police assuming their windfall was down to criminal enterprise.[46] A lecturers' strike saw university students join the movement,[47] whilst long-standing police violence and harassment motivated the urban poor to show out.[48]

SARS was established as a national police unit during a time of war, military dictatorship, economic and political instability, and neoliberal restructuring. In this context, the government responded to the popular demand for safety and order, amidst rising rates of crime, with authoritarianism and violence.[49] SARS was given the power to determine guilt and carry out punishments, which could be administered on the streets,[50] including torture and the death penalty. Fears around crime were used to justify widespread surveillance at checkpoints and give SARS unrestricted powers to search vehicles, fuelling systemic corruption within the unit. SARS officers targeted young people with dreadlocks,[51] profiling them as criminals, and forcing them to pay massive bribes to secure release from detention, mirroring the anti-Black racial profiling, encountered the world over, that reconstructs symbols of Blackness as symbols of criminality.[52] Queer Nigerians were also a common target for SARS officers, who policed queer life with blackmail, extortion and violence.[53]

You will likely be unsurprised to learn that Nigerian policing has its roots firmly in colonial history. While policing on mainland Britain minimised the use of militaristic techniques, anti-colonial resistance in African colonies provided a pretext for developing violent strategies of social control. In Nigeria, SARS continues the legacy of violent, militaristic authority exerted over the region, primarily by commercial and financial colonial-era entities that were desperate to maintain and reproduce their power.[54] In order to broker legitimacy for police and military rule in colonial Nigeria, it was common to recruit officers from one region or tribe to police a different region or tribe. Colonisers exploited language and cultural barriers to decrease the likelihood of collectivised revolt.[55] This practice continues in Nigeria today, with police departments in each state coming from outside of the area they are policing:[56] tensions and divisions manufactured under colonial rule are perpetuated in the strategies of social control today.[57]

As the movement against SARS grew, the protesters turned their attention to blockading the Lekki toll gate in Lagos. Over several days, 234,000,000 naira (equivalent to around £400,000) was lost at the toll gate.[58] In a celebration of people power, protesters defied curfews and set up hair salons at the toll gate. But on 20 October as the sun began to set, military vehicles descended on the protesters. Lights at the toll gate were cut off, cameras were removed, and state agents opened fire.[59] Murder, a common tactic of colonial social control, spread across Nigeria as state forces unleashed increasing brutality on #EndSARS protesters. At least a dozen people were killed at the toll gate in Lagos, while dozens more were killed in attacks at other protests nationwide.[60] Radical, queer #EndSARS activist Ani Kayode Somtochukwu highlights that including as part of the movement's five demands a call to pay police officers a higher salary,[61] – which received strong support from middle-class sections of the movement – did not encourage officers' sympathies or restraint. They used tear gas, live bullets, water cannon, mass arrest and other military-style tactics to repress the #EndSARS movement. As the violence developed, the British government was forced to admit that it had provided equipment and training used by the SARS unit, demonstrating the enduring legacy of colonial power in the contours of British imperialism today.[62]

Despite the unrestrained violence meted out against them, #EndSARS protesters persisted, and by 11 October, the government were forced to disband the SARS unit.[63]

However, any cause for celebration quickly gave way to anger and suspicion, as SARS was replaced by a Special Weapons and Tactics Team, or SWAT.[64] Organisers such as Ani Kayode Somtochukwu expressed deep scepticism at the move, as SWAT were tasked with taking over the same duties of SARS: police power had not been abolished, but simply redeployed under another name. This mirrors strategies employed by the British state: the Independent Police Complaints Commission (IPCC), mired in scandal after family justice campaigns fought back against its long history of protecting police killers, was replaced by the Independent Office for Police Conduct in 2018.[65] But previously the IPPC had already replaced the Police Complaints Authority in 2004. And the Police Complaints Authority in turn had replaced the Police Complaints Board in 1985, following accusations of racism, and the Board's complete inability to hold police to account.[66]

Because the reformist and concessionary demand for increased police wages for officers did not stem the violence towards #EndSARS protesters, nor did it encourage any material compromise from the Nigerian state, Somtochukwu reasons the movement has become increasingly interested in abolition as a goal.[67] Despite the replacement of SARS with SWAT, the relationship between the police and the public continues to be tense, as justice still seems a distant goal,[68] and police violence continues to be a regular part of life for many Nigerians, particularly the urban poor.[69] The shallow attempt to make police violence more palatable by cosmetically rebranding it has exposed the vapidity of reformist demands: glaring and obvious, in all their uselessness, for all to see. This has created the conditions for the case for police abolition to grow stronger, and the space for abolition to become an organised political force in Nigeria. Here lies the potential for the increasingly politicised and militant youth base that has remained organised since 2020 to re-visualise their futures, now through the lens of abolition.

In the words of Nigerian feminist and activist Olu Timehin Adegbeye, 'Policing as it exists today is the result of the capitalist colonial project, so we must approach abolition knowing that it requires us to rethink not only policing but our entire social economic order.'[70] Abolition must be a revolutionary vision. As young Nigerians, bolstered by solidarity in the diaspora, call for an internationalist movement for police and prison abolition, we join them: there is no abolition without a united movement of the working class, built on solidarity across borders.

* * *

One of the most powerful and enduring legacies of the Black Panther Party was its central strategy of recognising and organising the revolutionary potential of 'the brothers on the block'[71] – the Black 'lumpenproletariat' – whilst simultaneously convincing college students to relinquish their Black elitist pretensions in favour of grassroots freedom fighting.[72] Although this strategy created tensions, the Black Panther Party's ability to organise young Black people by harnessing the radicalism of streets and the radicalism of the college in one organisation – guiding both towards an anti-imperialist, anti-capitalist future – made it one of the most influential and effective revolutionary organisations in both Western and Black history. This spirit of radicalism meant the Panthers were never afraid of, and in fact were strategically, politically and practically prepared for, street confrontations to defend the Black community from racist violence. This is why, with love and solidarity, we did not agree with our comrades when they called off the planned BLM demonstration in central London on 13 June 2020.

Far-right protesters, outraged at the toppling of slaver Edward Colston's statue in Bristol the previous week, were due to turn out to protest against planned BLM demonstrations. They were determined to 'defend' other colonial memorials, such as that of Winston Churchill, whilst initiating physical confrontations against BLM protesters. Typical of the BLM summer protests that year, young people unassociated with established organisations announced their intention to stand up to the far-right presence via social media. Black Lives Matter UK (BLMUK), who had not called the demonstration, took the unprecedented step of attempting to call it off by advising BLM protesters not to attend, in an understandable bid to prevent clashes and violence. Well-known public figures, such as rapper Akala and boxer Anthony Joshua, discouraged people from attending.[73] But our history tells us far-right racists are only ever emboldened when they believe they can run the streets, hunting for Black and Brown people, without being robustly confronted. From Cable Street to Lekki, Lewisham to Oakland, revolutionary and radical movements for systemic change have always involved confrontations with fascists and police.

This is not a reality we can shy away from, but one we must prepare our movements for.

The lack of organisational presence, alongside the inevitably reduced numbers that showed out as a result of the cancellation, created a more – not less – dangerous situation. Both BLM and fascist protesters dispersed in uncoordinated groups across central London. Whilst smaller groups of BLM protesters found themselves in police kettles, more mobile groups engaged in running battles and skirmishes with police and the far right, often down dangerously narrow side streets. Although 13 June was undoubtedly a victory, with the BLM contingent who turned up overwhelming the far-right presence and sending them packing with their tails between their legs, it was a victory secured by the working class roadman and roadgyal who turned out – with the more respectable and cautious supporters largely heeding BLMUK's call to stay at home.

Ex-cop Bryn Male, who had heeded racist Tommy Robinson's call to defend Churchill's statue,[74] wandered into a breakaway crowd of several hundred BLM protesters and was quickly set upon on the steps of the Royal Festival Hall.[75] Aviah watched with anxiety: worried about the futures of the young Black folk involved, should the retribution turn fatal. A group of Black personal trainers and martial arts experts led by Patrick Hutchinson, who similarly feared the incident with Bryn Male could quickly escalate to murder charges, removed him from the crowd. The image of Hutchinson, who is in his fifties, carrying a bloodied Male to safety was seized on by the media; keen to spin a story of the 'hero' saving Male from violent protesters. Yet Hutchinson later told reporters that he had attended to protect young Black people from the white supremacist violence he was forced to confront as a youth.[76] The presence of Black community elders with experience in community self-defence and physically confronting racists put paid to the idea that Black movements lack the discipline to confront the far right.

The 13th of June was a missed opportunity to bring the radicalism of our youth, and our rich history of anti-fascist resistance, into the broader base of the BLM movement. We all share in the responsibility to build strong, dynamic movement infrastructure so that pressure to make huge calls like this don't fall on just a few. The abolitionist call for radical, revolutionary change must at some point move from words to action – and our movements need to develop, or re-develop, the ethos and practice that makes the physical defence of our communities possible. Although the level of state violence each group experiences is certainly different, police repression, against both students and urban working class communities, demonstrates that the state is opting for an indiscriminate strategy of violent social control to manage crisis and instability: they will come for you whether you're on the street hustle or the study hustle. At a time when the state is escalating its violence, repression and authoritarianism against us, we must seize opportunities to organise the collective potential of youth radicalism, and create the space needed to escalate our strategies of resistance.

THESIS 10

Bordering and policing protects colonial, imperialist and capitalist wealth. Open borders is abolition and abolition is open borders!

'*I can't breathe*'
Jimmy Mubenga, October 2010, UK

'*I can't breathe*'
George Floyd, May 2020, US

FROM WINDRUSH 1948, TO WINDRUSH 2018

Growing up in the 1990s and 2000s, we were both fed the idea that Brits had turned their back on the old-fashioned racism our parents had experienced and were ready to embrace a truly multicultural society. Cutesy images of respectable, smartly dressed Caribbean migrants stepping off the HMT *Empire Windrush* could be found in local library displays, translated into Urdu or Hindi, with accompanying descriptions of how Britain had 'opened its doors' to migrants who built the NHS and transport systems. Since then our families have watched in real time as the act of crossing the border from one country to another has become an intensely controlled and criminalised act, with migrants from the 1950s, '60s and '70s realising they were never truly British after all. In 2018, the Windrush scandal exposed Britain's multicultural triumphalism as a lie: Caribbean migrants initially constructed as the 'good' type of hard-working migrant suddenly became the 'bad' type: 'illegal'. Many have been denied housing, benefits, NHS medical care and access to education.[1] Others were forced into homelessness or deported. The Home Office in the '70s failed to keep records of who was granted leave to remain, which the Home Office in the 2010s capital-ised on, with their right-wing 'hostile environment' policy pantomime. Contrary to what the state has claimed, the 'hostile environment' doesn't only target those without leave to remain: it has been used to rapidly expand the UK bordering regime, and more people under the status of insecure immigrant.

So where did this all begin? The low wages and pre-carious work that characterises working class life today is the result of the massive defeats workers sustained in the 1970s and '80s, and the criminalisation of immigration has always run alongside wider changes in the working class. The welfare state was established after the Second World War, as a response to growing class consciousness and worker militancy.[2] The ruling class were afraid that if they didn't make compromises, these movements could spill over into chaos or communism. This 'post-war con-sensus' involved widespread council house construction, the establishment of the NHS, publicly funded educa-tion, unemployment benefits and widespread availability of jobs to rebuild a country reeling from war. The trade union movement limited its activities to pay and con-ditions, de-emphasising workers' control, and settling instead for the nationalisation of key strategic industries such as coal, steel and the railways. Despite this, there was a shortage of workers and, crucially, British capitalism needed a 'reserve army' of cheap and disposable labour to help it manage the ebbs and flows of what had become a volatile, post-colonial economy. This is when the ruling elite turned towards the Commonwealth.

The 1948 British Nationality Act gave all Commonwealth subjects – former subjects of the British Empire – the right to work *and* settle in Britain. Colonialism had left the Commonwealth nations underdeveloped and poor, and many people saw the opportunity to move to Britain as a golden ticket to a prosperous life. But the relative poverty of the colonies – created and sustained by British colonialism – meant that workers migrating to Britain could be paid much less than British workers. Far from being a triumph of liberalism, the 1948 British Nationality Act was a way of boosting profits in the 'mother country' by maintaining a reserve army of cheap, colonial labour and driving down conditions in the British working class as whole. Meanwhile, the British state could keep the Commonwealth nations in the political and economic orbit of Britain, a now waning imperial power. The British state used race at the ideological level, nationality and contract law at the legislative level, and police terror at the street level, to protect what Nadine El-Enany calls the 'spoils of empire'.[3]

This period created a new racial order within mainland Britain, where bordering became a central tool to control the working class and the flow of capital and labour. Race – an ideological mechanism of dehumanisation – and borders – a physical mechanism of exclusion – combined to create a class of people whose capacity to work could be paid a pittance. The racialised migrant fleeing colonial poverty, that could at any point be replaced by another racialised migrant fleeing colonial poverty, existed in a constant state of vulnerability. This vulnerability, and in fact, disposability, meant that not only could their capacity to work be paid less, they could also be worked much harder than the native, white worker. And it's here the echoes of colonisation and enslavement could be heard in the racial and bordering regimes of mainland, capitalist Britain: racialised bodies could be made to work much harder, and racialised labour power valued for much less – the super-exploitation of modern times.

The ruling class was nervous about the political and social impact of formerly colonised people landing on Britain's shores, and initially tried to fill the gap with European workers, but soon found reliable ways to ensure the success of a new era of capitalism – one where race could be re-purposed from the colonies to differentiate and exploit the British workforce. Although post-war migrants came to Britain in the hope of accessing a secure living, it was crucial that the opportunities on offer were worse than their white British counterparts. When migrants arrived, they were met with racism in every aspect of social, political and economic life. Racism in employment meant Black people worked the lowest-paid, hardest jobs, ones that white British workers didn't want. Racism in housing meant they were often barred from buying and renting in all but a few areas – with racist, slum landlords and housing discrimination creating overcrowding and ghettoisation. Racism in education, and the categorisation of Black children as 'educationally sub-normal', prevented social mobility. Colour bars in pubs, bingo halls and across the white leisure industry forced Black people to create alternative leisure economies, with their own recreational institutions. Racial exclusion from society and the violent criminalisation of Black communities by police played a decisive role in disciplining the Black working class. The police created a conveyor belt between the border and prison systems, in the process reproducing the politically expedient idea of Black people as disorderly, immoral, threatening, criminal and undesirable. This cemented the status of Black people at the bottom of the social hierarchy, keeping our communities in check as a source of cheap and disposable labour. Here began what was to be an enduring and powerful friendship between the policing of the streets, and the policing of the border.

Fast forward to today and the new folk devil of 'foreign criminals' has been used to erode universal human rights and churn increasing numbers of people through immigration enforcement, with racialised people more likely to face deportation.[4] Operation Nexus, a joint project between the police and Home Office that disproportionately targets people of colour,[5] allows the state to deport people who have never been convicted of a crime, but who are still deemed criminal, often based on racist characterisations of 'gang' involvement.[6] The Met Police and Home Office run sting operations in London boroughs like Hackney and Wandsworth targeting migrant delivery drivers, with the Met chortling on Twitter after making immigration-related arrests and impounding workers' vehicles.[7] Yet it was only yesterday these same people were valorised as key workers and national heroes. Much like the Windrush generation would discover, migrants are only useful for as long as the latest national crisis runs. From the border to the borough, racist policing feeds migrant bodies into the voracious, violent gut of the capitalist anti-immigration regime.

THE RISE OF RACIALISED CAPITALISM

Although the state did a pretty good job of preventing British workers from becoming too radical or finding common cause with their migrant-descended colleagues, by the late 1950s and into the '60s, contradictions in capitalism that had once been held at bay were reaching crisis point. Workers' militancy was growing; Black Power had erupted onto the world stage, with the British ruling class worried Black revolution was making its way to the island; anti-colonial movements were linking with other struggles nationally and internationally; millions were organising against war in Vietnam in the US and around the world, and worker-student solidarity forced France to a standstill in May 1968. By the early 1970s, Britain had apparently become ungovernable! Revolution was knocking on the door once again. The UK government had no chance of regaining control over the masses unless they were able to separate workers from their power base: trade unions. After all, capitalism could be brought to its knees through the collective, organised power of working class labour in key strategic industries like coal and steel.

The working class of the 1970s developed dynamic strategies for winning workplace struggles, such as redistributing strikers using 'flying pickets', and organising large, mass picket lines that linked community and social justice struggles to the workplace. Laws criminalising the most effective trade union strategies came in fast, and violent police crackdowns on strikers came in faster – both being instrumental to breaking class power. In 1971 after mostly Asian, unionised workers in the North Acton Laricol Plastics factory were fired and told to accept a lower wage or go home, they went on strike. A few weeks into the dispute, police raided and arrested almost all of the 13-strong picket line. By the time the strikers were released from jail, 'the factory was in full production with non-union labour.'[8]

But, perhaps most crucially, during the 1980s, the government outsourced the labour of its most powerful industries to the Global South, where workers could be more intensely exploited. Successive laws had already begun to limit immigration. The Commonwealth Immigrants Act of 1962 restricted immigration from the colonies to those who had a work permit. The 1965 Labour government capped the number of work permits available and did away with permits for 'unskilled' workers; creaming the 'skilled' workers from the colonies while limiting overall 'coloured' immigration. These shifts culminated in the 1971 Immigration Act which removed the ability to settle, allowing *foreign labour* only – completing the transition from immigrant settler to migrant worker.[9] British national identity was crystallised at the state level as white, racial identity. As El-Enany highlights: 'Those exempted from control under the 1971 Act were primarily those born in Britain or with a parent born in Britain, thereby linking the right to enter Britain with whiteness.' This is because, El-Enany continues, in 1971, 98 per cent of those born in Britain were white.[10] These new borders birthed a new economic landscape: securing cheap labour in the Global South would only work if it could be ensured that poor workers in the Global South were unable to up sticks and move to Britain for better pay and conditions. It would be Thatcher who capitalised on this: reorganising the workforce, crushing the unions and outsourcing British industry to places it could pay pennies to non-unionised workers in poor, previously colonised countries.

Crucially, it's in this context that the ruling elite have grown intolerant of working-age migrants with steady jobs supplementing the wages of those in the Global South by sending money home to loved ones: this undermines the entire reasoning behind outsourcing labour and industry in the first place. You might wonder how much difference migrants sending a few pounds back home would make, but the World Bank estimates that remittances from the Global North to the Global South reached $440 billion in 2010, which is ten times more than the total amount of development aid flowing in the same direction.[11] The need to create a flow of cheap labour that is ever more disposable, precarious, and unable to settle for long enough to redistribute capital away from the Global North, dovetails with the need to satiate the rabid appetites of racist citizens looking for a scapegoat in uncertain times. Combined, these factors (at least partially) explain the hardening and militarisation of Britain's bordering regime over recent decades. This is why an abolitionist project in the UK that isn't also about building revolutionary, class power is doomed: the violence of borders is driven by the inherent violence of capitalist, class society. Workers' struggles and trade unions need to urgently drop their drooling fascination with flaccid party politics and take up the fight against state violence, which is a threat to us all.

The outsourcing of industry and labour to the Global South was intended to break workers' power and prevent interracial, internationalist workers' solidarity. But this is increasingly challenged by the growth of independent trade unions led by insecurely employed migrant workers. On 14 May 2022 on Ashwin St in Hackney, union-busting immigration raids were met with mass community resistance. Police had approached Deliveroo drivers under the guise of vehicle insurance checks, a blatant pretext for fishing for the driver's immigration status. An alliance that had begun to form in the weeks before swung into action: the union representing many of the riders, Independent Workers of Great Britain (IWGB), led the resistance with the support of Hackney CopWatch, Hackney Anti-Raids and close to five hundred community members. It was a success: several Deliveroo drivers avoided jail that afternoon, including one who had been de-arrested by the crowd.

Several solidarity protesters were badly beaten, and others were arrested by police,[12] confirming for any remaining doubters the violent lengths police will go to protect the interests of the state and capital, over the interests of ordinary people. In the midst of the IWGB's 'RooVolt' campaign – which has sparked a massive increase in unionised couriers and national strikes – the police have upped the ante against Deliveroo drivers. For example, whilst the IWGB has harnessed the radical potential of riders' hang-out spots to unionise and organise strikes, Hackney Council have designated these same locations – such as Ashwin Street – as 'anti-social behaviour hotspots',[13] partnering with police to criminalise them. And it's here we see the echoes of Patrick Colquhoun's policing theories discussed in Thesis 8: where the state, in cahoots with the bosses, redefines ordinary working class activity as 'crime'. Meanwhile, just days before the Ashwin Street resistance, Deliveroo announced that it had secured a sweetheart collective bargaining agreement with the conservative General Municipal and Boilermakers union (GMB). The GMB have no record of organising or unionising Deliveroo couriers, and Deliveroo had refused to engage with the IWGB.[14] This was a cynical backroom deal intended to undermine and quash the IWGB's success in organising the class power of migrant workers. With an electrifying energy and confidence, the Ashwin Street revolt confronted the behemoth that is interlocking systems of violence, criminalisation and punishment. In fighting back against the stop and search of the police, immigration checks of the borders and union busting of the bosses, the Hackney coalition of agitators drew a road map for abolition.

* * *

Ten years before George Floyd uttered his last words, Jimmy Mubenga was killed by private G4S security guards who restrained him on a deportation flight – witnesses heard him cry out 'I can't breathe', as he slowly died.[15] Despite his killing being ruled unlawful in 2013,[16] the guards responsible were found not guilty of manslaughter a year later.[17] Successive governments have shut down safe routes to the UK, causing untold horror and death, whilst criminalising the irregular and dangerous routes migrants are then forced to take.[18] Borders aren't just a way of hoarding wealth; they define, in quite literal terms, who will live and who will perish. Abolition must mean the free movement of people: open borders is abolition and abolition is open borders. Abolishing borders means redistributing wealth from the North back to the South, and building international networks of community.

THESIS 11

From the streets to the cell block, incarcerated people have organised to resist state violence.

This thesis is dedicated to Aviah's father Da'vid, whose long fight has seen him survive the care system, prison and the return of his only child from the brink of forced adoption.

In *Abolition. Feminism. Now.* Angela Davis, Gina Dent, Erica Meiners and Beth Richie trace the modern prison abolitionist movement to the Attica Prison uprising of 1971, and the Attica Brothers' 'passionate call for abolition during a 4-day rebellion that echoed across various movements and activist circles'.[1] The uprising was sparked by the murder of George Jackson, a Black revolutionary and political theorist who had been radicalised by his incarceration. Internationally, this period was punctuated by the mass withdrawal of consent to authority, sparking the imaginations of radicals – from the streets to the prisons – whose visions of a new world grew bolder and braver. Around this time, abolitionist ideas began to surface in Britain, as the criminalisation of anti-nuclear activists inspired an interest in prison organising. In 1970, the pressure group Radical Alternatives to Prison (RAP) was established.[2]

RAP argued that prisons, having proven to be a total failure, should be abolished. Those who perpetrate harm, they argued, should be dealt with in their community, with responses designed to prioritise negotiation and voluntary involvement.[3] In 1972, a newly formed prisoners union, Preservation of the Rights of Prisoners (PROP), organised a strike which saw as many as 10,000 prisoners withdraw their labour to demand union recognition and better pay and conditions.[4] RAP offered some support to the prisoners, but the strikes' reformist demands deterred them from throwing their weight behind a full coalition with PROP.[5] RAP's failure to recognise the radicalism of the prisoner's strike, and the abolitionist potential of their organising, is a prime example of prioritising political purity over political strategy. Coalitional organising between the groups could well have resulted in a powerful abolitionist movement, had PROP's willingness to take militant action been merged with RAP's abolitionist political theory.

Some of today's social justice movements take a similarly sectarian approach, holding back from going into coalition with those at the sharp edge of criminalisation, where their politics are perceived as not 'radical' enough. However, the militant action of those violently criminalised by police, prisons and borders is the foundation upon which abolition must be built: there is no revolution without recognising and centring oppressed people. With this in mind, we turn to two examples of revolt by incarcerated people in Britain: the Strangeways Prison uprising in 1990, and the Yarl's Wood 'hunger for freedom' strike in 2018. We highlight these powerful examples of resistance by incarcerated people whilst reflecting on the role of abolitionists and revolutionaries on the outside, when relating to and engaging with prisoner and detainee struggles. Neither of these revolts were explicitly abolitionist. Yet in both cases, incarcerated people took strategic direct action and risked extreme personal costs to assert their dignity and humanity – they led the way towards an abolitionist future.

Strangeways Prison was notorious for its brutal conditions. The prison was built for 970 people but at the time of the 1990 uprising was warehousing 1,647 souls.[6] The prison's regime was run by ex-army screws (slang for prison officers), with some proudly wearing far-right National Front badges, and donning steel toe cap boots as their weapon of choice against inmates.[7] Strangeways was known as a 'screws' nick' – that is, a prison run with the authoritarian commitment of the hardest prison officers[8] – and the regime had changed little since it was built in the Victorian era. Toilet facilities consisted of a bucket in the corner of a cell, each cell being occupied by up to three prisoners. Buckets would be left to fester for hours, until 'slopping out' times when prisoners were permitted to remove them.[9] These were the conditions in which prisoners were expected to eat their meals. Officially, prisoners spent 23 hours a day in their cells, but the 'screws' would frequently withdraw the hour of yard exercise.[10]

Prisons function to discipline unruly, mostly working class, people and prepare them for the hard graft of wage labour. The horrific conditions at Strangeways were the direct consequence of an authoritarian law-and-order agenda which would later spur on a new generation of British prison abolitionists. In 1990, at the dawn of neoliberalism, prisons were fast becoming warehouses where victims of successive financial crises – people capitalism no longer had a place for – were kept. Instead of jobs, housing and welfare, dispossessed working class people struggling to survive were increasingly met with cops and prisons. In 1990, the old Victorian prison estate had not yet been adapted for the new neoliberal strategy of warehousing 'surplus' populations;[11] prisons like Strangeways were at breaking point.

On Sunday, 1 April 1990, a group of prisoners taking part in a chapel service staged a protest. They had planned a 24-hour occupation of the chapel, hoping to win concessions that would improve their treatment and conditions. Instead, the protest exploded into a 25-day siege: the longest prison revolt in British history. The organic, spontaneous and unanticipated nature of the Strangeways mass rebellion reminds us that despair can give way to confident, militant action.

As groups of rebels wrestled to gain control of the prison from the screws, others looked for ways to communicate their protest to the outside world. Press releases were fashioned out of painted banners and messages written in chalk on a blackboard. Their powerful demand for democracy and justice displayed on a banner: '*Plebeius* [sic] *of the common people*'.[12]

The rebels were inspired by the Plebeian, or 'common peoples', assembly in Ancient Rome – and linked their struggle for self-governance with this historical example of democracy, that had been won through the resistance of oppressed people.[13] A phone call to the local press from inside the prison communicated their demands for increased physical contact arrangements, an end to

23-hour-a-day lock-up and longer exercise entitlements. The press having been alerted, within a few hours a crowd had assembled below the rooftop occupation, including relatives, ex-cons, journalists and solidarity activists. Back inside Strangeways, riot officers made desperate attempts to resume control of the prison, but over several days the rebels held them off with fierce resistance. Then, in a move which astonished many, the Prison Service leadership ordered the riot officers to retreat. The surprised but euphoric rebels took it as a victory, blaring out *We Got the Power* by the electronic dance group Snap, whilst dancing and chanting with fists to the sky.[14]

The decision by state authorities to stand down effectively secured the monumental 25-day siege of the prison. However, some of those leading the uprising have theorised that the retreat was an exercise in damage limitation: the Poll Tax riot had ripped through London the day before the Strangeways chapel protest began, and newspapers were collectively referring to the disturbances as a weekend of 'anti-authority violence'.[15] Alan Lord, a Black prisoner, was one of the uprising's instigators and was nominated to negotiate on the behalf of the others. He and others have since reflected that the 'negotiations' were not carried out in good faith and that the retreat was a prolongment ploy intended to distract the public from the mounting Poll Tax crisis.[16] If this was the government's strategy, it was made more difficult by a banner raised on the prison roof reading 'Smash the poll tax.'[17] With Home Office representatives repeatedly agreeing to the prisoners' demands and then retracting each deal, many of those on shorter sentences reasoned that the stakes were too high to invest in bad faith negotiations. Over the 25 days, most of the 1,100 prisoners who took part in the rebellion surrendered in dribs and drabs, and on day 23, Alan Lord was snatched by authorities during a negotiation meeting. A core group of rooftop rebels held out for another two days but eventually relented. Their 25-day siege came to an end with the remaining rebels lowered to the ground in a cherry picker, proudly raising their fists the whole way down.

While the rebels offered solidarity to the poll tax uprisings, the small showing of solidarity activists had not managed to convince the poll tax resisters to join forces with the Strangeways prisoners. A crucial lesson for abolitionists to heed is the importance of proactively organising solidarity and links between all groups resisting state violence – even if they appear to have little in common. Abolitionists must build active and mutual solidarity between those facing down state oppression. Over the course of the Strangeways 25-day siege, protests and disturbances took place in over a hundred prisons across the country. We wonder what the revolutionary potential might have been, had the hundreds of thousands of poll tax rebels made their way to the prisons to combine the rage on the streets with that in the cells.

Since the siege at Strangeways, successive governments have hardened their determination to criminalise working class survival. Those involved in the drug trade, sex work, or shoplifting find themselves locked away in prisons. Alongside building new prisons, the criminalisation of another form of working class survival strategy – immigration – has been aggressively enforced. Many of the tensions that bubbled to the surface at HMP Strangeways are today resurfacing in Britain's immigration detention centres. Migrant-led organising against immigration detention has always been militant, but in recent years has become increasingly visible. The most high-profile being the 2018 Yarl's Wood 'hunger for freedom' action by 120 women who staged a month-long hunger and labour strike in protest at the violent conditions of their incarceration. This was not the first protest led by detainees at Yarl's Wood, or indeed within Britain's wider detention estate. Earlier protests include a 2014 hunger strike organised by 60 men at Harmondsworth detention centre, a 2008 naked protest at Yarl's Wood by Ugandan women in protest at the violent deportation of a number of African detainees, and a 2015 three-day protest at Yarl's Wood, which was accompanied by a two-week action across five facilities that year. Between 2015 and 2019, 3,000 hunger strikes were inspired across Britain's detention estate.[18]

Much like the Strangeways rebellion, the 2018 hunger strikes were sparked by the inhumane nature of incarceration. Unlike most other nations, Britain detains migrants on an indefinite basis, with many languishing for months, even years, without a release date. Detainees are frequently refused access to medical care, which has led to a string of deaths spanning decades.[19] In 2014, ten members of staff at Yarl's Wood were sacked in relation to eight separate cases of sexual abuse against women detained at the centre.[20] These dismissals did little to shift the violent culture of Yarl's Wood, with a Channel 4 News exposé the following year uncovering racist and sexist abuse by guards, as well as details of a miscarriage brought on by the medical neglect of a pregnant detainee. It was in this context the 'hunger for freedom' action was launched, which was initially intended to last only three days. The women were spurred on by a letter released by Serco – a British company that provides security for carceral institutions – which implied that they had lied about not eating, shortly after a morale-boosting visit by Black Labour MP Diane Abbott. It was anger *and* hope that sparked the women's decision to escalate their action.

The strikers escalated to an indefinite hunger and labour strike, releasing a statement detailing their fight against 'offensive practices', including indefinite detention; poor access to medical services; the incarceration of victims of trafficking, torture and rape; prejudice against LGBT asylum seekers, including the withdrawal of hormones for transgender detainees; the super-exploitation of detainee jobs that were paid at £1 per hour,[21] and the violation of habeas corpus, the ancient protection against unlawful imprisonment.[22] These demands made a claim for basic human dignity. More than this, the month-long sustained action and intersectional demands spanning worker, gender, queer, trans and disability justice, showed the strikers' no-one-left behind radicalism is something to cherish and learn from.

Unlike the limited movement support for the Strangeways rebels, the Yarl's Wood strikers garnered broader support across the movement. SOAS Detainee Support,[23] Black Women's Rape Action Project and Detained Voices acted as critical channels of communication for the hunger strikers, ensuring they were able to publicise their action to the wider world beyond the detention centre walls. These groups also lent their knowledge and experience of previous actions and hunger strikes in guiding the women's strategy. Messages of solidarity went both ways, with the Yarl's Wood strikers releasing a statement in firm support of the Stansted 15 who were facing unprecedented terrorism charges for their 2017 blockade of a charter flight, which was due to deport 60 migrants (11 of whom continue to live in the UK as a result of the direct action).[24]

Those criminalised by immigration enforcement, stop and search, or encampment eviction often face down powers and strategies coming from distinct law enforcement agencies: police, immigration officers, high court bailiffs and many others. Writing in the 1980s, Sivanandan identified that anti-racist movements became fractured along racial lines, with Asian community resistance focusing on migrant justice and Black communities confronting police violence. Many were criminalised by both systems, but pressure to prioritise, and deliberate fracturing of communities by the state, led to a narrowing of focus.[25] The knowledge, skills and experience of how best to resist immigration and policing systems were developed in silos, fragmenting the movement along racial lines.

If we are to learn lessons from Sivanandan's warnings in the '80s, hitherto disconnected sections of the movement must work towards a united front. At the national level, this could mean a federation of groups, collectives and organisations resisting any and all forms of state violence. At the local level, practical alliances can be formed between those resisting stop and search, evictions and immigration raids, thereby swelling the numbers turning out for each other's struggles against the state. We are already seeing the beginnings of such local formations. In Hackney, an alliance has been established between migrant Deliveroo couriers in the Independent Workers of Great Britain, Hackney CopWatch and Hackney Anti-Raids to resist union-busting immigration raids by police and border agents. This style of joined-up action could do away with the asymmetrical power dynamics that characterises sections of the migrant justice movement – where people not directly affected by immigration detention lead the movement for migrant justice.

Returning now to Yarl's Wood, in response to the growing momentum of support for the women, the Home Office sent letters threatening accelerated deportations for anyone refusing to eat or drink. The use of deportation as a strike-breaking tool can neutralise dissent by simply disappearing the movement's most effective and ambitious organisers, in turn sending a message to potential recruits: join the struggle and we will hasten your exile.

But the 'hunger for freedom' strikers continued their action through the threat of punitive deportations, which were successfully prevented through activist, MP and legal interventions.[26] Correspondence with Tom Kemp from Detained Voices confirmed that after the strikes ended, seven of the action's leaders went on to receive leave to remain in the UK. This massive victory is a testament to the power of migrant-led organising. Migrants considering taking direct action will no doubt be plagued by the stories of those whose protests did not set them free or prevent their deportation. Yet we should hold in our memories the fact the Strangeways' rebellion achieved the

end of 'slopping out', improved family contact arrangements and a refurbishment of the ageing prison. When we
fight, we win.

The rebels at Strangeways and Yarl's Wood may not
have had explicitly abolitionist goals, but they risked
everything to take militant action in the hope of a dig-
nified life. As abolitionists, we must ask ourselves, what
risks are we willing to take to see abolition, to see revolution? Abolitionists across the country are taking radical
action; some are building coalitions with groups on the
front line of state violence, whether they be abolitionist
or not. But too many of us limit ourselves to academic
theory, purity politics or ally-ship models. As revolutionaries and abolitionists, we must close the gap between
the criminalised working class, racialised people taking
militant action against state violence, and those imagining
a world without prisons.

THESIS 12

The 'War on Terror' expanded policing powers into everyday institutions. Fighting Islamophobic racism is central to abolitionist struggle.

It is no accident that the language of the 'War on Terror' mirrors the language of the 'War on Drugs'. But why is the language of warfare so often the go-to lexicon of the state? A war puts boundaries around whose lives are to be protected and whose lives are to be disposed of. War defines victimhood, heroism and importantly, enemy status. During war, violence against the enemy is not only normalised and mundane but is necessary, even moral. And in the cases of both the 'War on Terror' and the 'War on Drugs', the primary weapons are not drones and guns – these come later – but racialisation and criminalisation: social processes that mark out the subjects of imperial and colonial power as the enemy within and without – to be contained and eliminated. The language of war, as it's used to communicate domestic politics, is not merely an attempt at metaphor or colourful discourse; in very material ways, it prepares one section of a population to tolerate, even celebrate, violence and prepares another section of that population to receive that violence. This thesis will look at how Prevent, part of the government's counter-terror strategy, brings home war, militarism and imperialism.

Prevent was launched in 2006, following the 2001 New York and 2005 London terror attacks. Prevent's stated aim is to identify those at risk of radicalisation, putting them through a corrective programme to deradical-ise and assimilate them within 'British values'. Launched by the Labour Party, and developed by the Conserva-tives, Prevent has been a core medium through which racialisation – the construction of both Britishness and otherness – has been formalised at the legislative level. Despite a more recent focus on right-wing radicalisation in order to placate accusations of racism, race as it's con-structed through religion and nationality, has always been the modality through which Prevent has operated. In 2020–21, 22 per cent of Prevent referrals were for Islamic extremism, yet Muslims make up only 5.7 per cent of the population.[1] The shift within Prevent towards right-wing extremism over recent years is nothing but a pantomime: when accused of being racist and Islamophobic, the gov-ernment is able to say 'oh no we're not!' This is an example of a reformist, not an abolitionist, reform; calls for Prevent to target right-wing extremists provides an equalising factor the state can point to in order to evade accusations of racism. This legitimises the function of Prevent whilst leaving the racist surveillance of Muslim communities perfectly intact.

But the statistics detailing the undeniable targeting of Muslims as terrorists is not the only metric of Prevent's racism and Islamophobia. The government's approach to right-wing extremists sees them as wayward individ-uals, sick 'lone wolves', completely disconnected from the colonial and imperial legacies and realities of Britain that creates them. By contrast, Prevent conceptualises Islamic extremists as being incubated within everyday life in the Muslim community – in its institutions, schools, families, even embedded in its religious beliefs and practices. This is what David Cameron meant when he said extremists are made in the 'swamp'.[2] He is pointing not just to individual people and their actions, but the *places* and *environments* they inhabit. Through this lens, the entire Muslim community becomes a factory of extremism – in on the terrorist plot one way or another. Prevent has never shied away from seeing Islamic spaces as terrorist spaces. The programme operates by focusing resources in Prevent Priority Areas (PPAs): areas targeted under the assumption they have populations at particular risk of extremism. 'The People's Review of Prevent' report, an incisive analysis of the racist rot at the heart of Prevent, estimated that 73 per cent of Muslims in England and Wales live in a PPA – which are also some of the most economically impoverished places in the country.[3]

On the day of the 2005 terror attacks, Tony Blair described the violence of Islamic extremists on London's streets as 'barbaric'. In the same statement, despite the fact that by this time tens of thousands of civilians had been killed in the Iraq War, he defined his coalition of imperialists as 'civilised'.[4] This language is telling: it plays on long-standing imperialist stereotypes of the 'Muslim world' being backwards and barbaric, while the 'Western world' (code for 'white' world) is enlightened and civilised. In a process of *othering*, the architects of Prevent define Islam outside of what David Cameron called 'fundamental British values': principles and behaviours that define British identity and divergence from which defines extremism. This not only provides a metric to measure enemy and criminal status against, but situates that enemy outside of the boundaries of national identity. This language – of a war against a foreign barbarism, that later becomes a domestic threat through notions of Muslim 'invasion' – has, from the very beginning, been the ideology at the heart of Prevent. This narrative goes hand-in-hand with that of a Western nation in crisis, where 'taking back control' from a racialised, criminalised enemy is offered as the solution to declining living standards within the nation. These narratives of national threat are then expressed in, and used to justify, the expansion of policing and bordering: the 2015 Prevent Duty, 2014 and 2016 Immigration Acts, 2022 Nationality and Borders Act, and 2022 PCSC Act. But crucially, the implementation of these new powers is designed to be hyper-visible, to draw citizens into their enforcement and permeate everyday life. As Arianne Shahvisi argues: 'Everyday bordering contributes to a sense of identity and security for those who are white and British, and may serve as a tangible, visible reassurance that resources are being reserved for these citizens, thereby securing their political support.'[5]

In 2013, weeks after British soldier Lee Rigby was murdered by men with connections to Islamic extremism, then Prime Minister David Cameron vowed to 'drain the swamp' that turns British citizens into Islamic extremists.[6] He pledged to do this by disrupting the 'conveyor belt' of radicalisation in schools and mosques. Animating the legacy of Thatcher, who in 1978 warned of Britain becoming 'rather swamped by people with a different culture',[7] the image of a 'swamp' is designed to create the feeling of a threat that's hidden and murky, growing nefariously within the boundaries of the nation, ready to emerge and attack at any point. As we discussed earlier, cultivating fear and anxiety is part of how the state manufactures consent for expanding the scope and reach of its coercive powers. To put a face to this anxiety, Cameron combines the idea of the swamp, with that of the 'conveyor belt' of radicalisation, where everyday Muslim life exists on a spectrum with extremism. It communicates the idea that, at any point, an ordinary Muslim can slide across the spectrum and drift into terrorism. This makes Muslim existence a threat, all Muslims a potential risk and so anything Islamic a justifiable target of surveillance and policing. In 2015, this idea became legislation as the Prevent Duty: the statutory duty for schools and other institutions to pay 'due regard to the need to prevent people from being drawn into terrorism', where the primary indicator of radicalisation is Muslimness.[8]

The murder of Lee Rigby was in the backdrop of the scandal that tore through the Muslim community a year later: the Trojan Horse. In late 2013, an anonymous letter arrived on a desk in Birmingham City Council. The letter alleged a systematic plot, run by ideological Islamist extremists, to take over schools across the country, starting in Alum Rock, a Muslim community in the heart of Birmingham. A series of reports and investigations – led from right at the top of government – found no plot, no Islamism, no extremism. But racialisation and criminalisation doesn't require reality. This scandal marked the Muslim community out as invaders, infiltrators taking over and Islamising schools, turning them into breeding grounds for extremism. Here were David Cameron's swamps; the next stage was to drain them. Not only were individual Muslim teachers at the heart of the scandal personally and professionally ruined, the Muslim community as a whole was systematically maligned. But at the structural level, this toxic atmosphere created the perfect conditions for the government to drive through its wider political agenda: they used this period to force through the academisation of schools, and beef up their counter-terrorism strategy. New powers of policing, surveillance and bordering were created and were normalised as part of everyday life. Teachers were turned into counter-terrorism police, doctors into border patrol, and Muslim community institutions were forced to become state informants. By 2015, a third of referrals to Prevent were made not by police, but by teachers.[9] Policing and surveillance have wormed their tendrils into the mundanity of civic life, meaning we must organise these spaces – the classroom, the hospital and the benefits office – as part of an abolitionist project. Workers and trade unions, particularly those who hold a strategic or powerful position within the public sector, like medical staff and teachers, can play a decisive role intervening in the expansion of surveillance powers.

Let's look a little deeper into the mechanics of criminalisation within Prevent – that is, how Prevent doesn't simply *find* criminals, but *creates* them. Prevent aims to do what it says on the tin: step in before a crime has taken place in order to prevent future ones occurring. But in order to operate in this pre-criminal space, you have to be able to predict who is likely to commit a crime, before they've actually done so. This is known as predictive policing, where analysing data – the who, what, when, where and hows of crime – is used to guess where pre-emptive policing strategies are more likely to be effective. In the case of Prevent, the data the government analyses in order to predict who might become a terrorist isn't a collection of facts or figures, but rests entirely on a racist understanding of ethno-religious identity. In other words, *race*. Signs of radicalisation featured in Prevent Duty training include what would for most people be considered completely normal child behaviour: being argumentative, changing friendship groups, keeping secrets, talking about political grievances, changing appearance. But for Muslims, these are signs of latent terrorism. Everyday engagement with Muslim religious, cultural and political life – choosing to wear a hijab, going to mosque more often, becoming more religious, caring about the treatment of Muslims by Western powers globally – becomes a sign of latent terrorism. By operating in a space of pre-criminality, Prevent constructs its own national identity for Muslims, one defined by suspicion, risk and threat. And guess what, readers? Using race to define pre-criminality isn't new. British rulers in colonial India passed a series of laws known as the Criminal Tribes Acts, designed to criminalise and control populations deemed a threat to colonial rule. These Acts proscribed entire ethnic groups as 'habitual criminals', subjecting them to draconian restrictions on their civil liberties, to hyper-surveillance and violent policing.

By definition, pre-criminality widens the definition of a criminal and therefore widens the reach of policing. This was the case for a 6-year-old girl in Newcastle Upon Tyne whose desire to wear a hijab was described by governors as 'threatening'; her mother's rightful frustration with the situation sparked concerns of radicalisation in the family, prompting the school to contact Prevent.[10] Then there's the 11-year-old boy referred to Prevent for wanting to give money to oppressed people, and the 4-year-old boy referred to Prevent for talking about a video game.[11] Another 4-year-old boy threatened with a Prevent referral for drawing a picture of his dad cutting a cucumber,[12] and a 27-year-old women referred to Prevent for converting to Islam.[13] The 14-year-old boy referred to Prevent for having an interest in Middle Eastern politics.[14] The 15-year-old boy referred to Prevent for not wanting to stay behind after school, because he wanted to attend Friday prayers.[15] We could go on. Behaviour that would be considered ordinary and innocent if the children were white, or Christian or otherwise quintessentially British, is perverted by the sickness of Islamophobia, becoming criminal behaviour because the 'suspects' are Muslim. But the hidden boon for the state in all of this, is normalising the idea of citizens as little cops, where policing begins before we ever get to a badge number. This is not only another mechanism for manufacturing consent to policing by making policing a civic action, but turns society into a giant panopticon, where everyday surveillance of each other forces us into policing the most intimate parts of ourselves – our bodies, our ideas and our identities.

* * *

Abolitionists in the UK cannot simply import movement demands from the US abolitionist movement, as our political and historical context is fundamentally different. One example of this is the call to defund the police. Over a decade of public service funding cuts has meant UK policing institutions are *already* defunded, with the Tories responsible for axing tens of thousands of policing jobs.[16] But far from being a reason for abolitionists to celebrate, this has laid the basis for policing work to be delegated to other public institutions. In many of the horrific cases of Muslim children being criminalised as terrorists-in-waiting, Prevent referrals came from teachers. Prevent has forced coercive state powers into institutions that should, at least theoretically, centre care and nurturing. This is the same dynamic in the NHS where medical professionals are legally obliged to check immigration status and snitch to the Home Office about unpaid patient costs, leading to patients refusing potentially life-saving care.[17] Instead of adopting slogans wholesale from the US movement, UK abolitionists need a more forensic approach to the idea of defunding the police, by identifying specific funding streams to campaign around. Why are police receiving multi-million pound contracts for domestic violence programmes, when the domestic violence sector has been gutted through austerity?[18] Why, during the biggest cost-of-living crisis for a generation, is Manchester's Mayor Andy Burnham robbing citizens through council tax hikes, in order to increase funding to the scandal-infested Greater Manchester Police, despite the fact that 77 per cent of residents voted against the increase during a consultation?[19] Police have been defunded under austerity, yet racist, sexist police violence has remained a constant. Our slogans must speak to our context; demanding the reduction of police power and resisting the creep of everyday policing.

Finally, not only has Prevent brought everyday life into the scope of policing, it has also expanded notions of *who* needs to be policed. Prevent has been developed to define any divergence from, or protest against, the state and 'British values' as extremism. With climate, migrant and pro-Palestine activists increasingly being referred into Prevent and censored in schools and on campuses, we can see how counter-terrorism is being used as a Trojan Horse to criminalise any form of dissent.[20] This authoritarian redefinition and expansion of extremism to mean virtually any divergence from hegemonic values, where the only acceptable political discourse is that of the establishment, set the tone for the 2022 PCSC Act, where the government has made disruptive or noisy protest and direct action a criminal offence. Policing, criminalisation and bordering is a relationship between the state and the rest of us; abolitionists need to be bold enough to defy the very basis upon which the state defines criminality. We need to push back against every instance of its encroaching power, by building cross-society coalitions with affected communities, trade unions, workers and activists to refuse participation in coercive programmes like Prevent. We need to withdraw the consent they work so hard to manufacture, abolish Prevent, resist the securitisation of everyday life and restructure our institutions so they prioritise care not social control.

THESIS 13

Capitalist crisis, neoliberalism and gentrification drive racist 'gangs' policing in Black communities. Abolition is a struggle against the whole system!

Blackness, crime and violence: dominant racist narratives that filter down from the media and political establishment often treat these things as interchangeable. There are lots of ways it happens, one being through Black cultural production. Music has always been used to communicate the realities, joys, struggles and spirit of Black life. The blues speaks to what life was like for Black Americans, venturing out into the world to redefine and discover themselves after slavery. Reggae speaks to social upheaval and spiritual renewal within Black life in the Caribbean and diaspora. Grime is the voice of a younger generation, mapping the contours of urban life and survival in a post-industrial world. But powerful institutions rarely see Black music for its complex and deep beauty. In the courts, participation in music videos is used as evidence of gang membership; tying people to crimes there is no evidence they participated in.[1] Known as 'joint enterprise', these laws are used by the state to construct narratives of 'gang' crime – creating collective culpability out of offences that only had one perpetrator.[2] In a harrowing case in Manchester, ten young Black boys – grieving the death of a friend – were sent to prison on life-changing conspiracy charges, after a majority white jury decided text messages, drill music videos and a blue Arsenal t-shirt confirmed they were part of a 'gang'.[3]

Resurrecting the ghost of The Mangrove restaurant, where prominent Black community leader and campaigner Frank Crichlow saw his restaurant raided by police twelve times between 1969 and 1970, in 2016 the Met Police demanded a club in Croydon stop playing bashment music in order to prevent 'crime and disorder'.[4] Black artists up and down Britain, such as Fumez the Engineer and Pa Salieu,[5] had shows cancelled in 2021 with police and other authorities citing security concerns. Combined with the disproportionate use of joint enterprise against Black people, it is clear the criminal justice system sees existing in a Black space, participating in Black culture and being around other Black people as a potential act of crime. The London Assembly Tory leader Susan Hall summed up the establishment position clearly when she said in 2021 the 'black community has a crime problem.'[6]

The association of Blackness with criminality isn't new. It stems from the exploitation of Black people; first as slaves and colonial subjects, and now as surplus and cheap labour power. Under these systems, state violence has been a vital tool in both generating and protecting wealth and class privilege. Stereotypes that link Blackness with criminality do important work for the political class, enabling them to justify violent social control, while outsourcing responsibility for social problems onto Black communities. But what is unique about 'gang' narratives is the idea, as Jasbinder S. Nijjar highlights, that 'Black people now fulfil some supposed compulsion for (violent) crime *col-*

lectively, as well as individually.'[7] The interplay between collective notions of criminality in the Black community, joint enterprise and the wholesale criminalisation of working class Black culture is fast-tracking Black people – especially Black youth, into the prison system. Black people are 13 per cent of the prison population, skyrocketing to 32 per cent of the under-18s prison population, despite only making up around 3.5 per cent of the general population.[8]

Contrary to trends of declining prison populations across Europe, the Ministry of Justice (MoJ) predicts the prison population in England and Wales will increase by nearly 24 per cent between 2021 and 2026.[9] This increase is not due to any prediction in the rise of crime but, according to the MoJ, 'is largely a result of the recruitment of an extra 23,400 police officers.'[10] With the MoJ building new adult prisons across the country, and the PCSC Act set to expand youth imprisonment through 'Secure Schools',[11] the coffers of private companies like G4S, Sodexo and Serco will continue to fatten as they are handed an increasing number of contracts to run detainment services.[12] Private companies also benefit from the hyper-exploitation of prison labour, with prisoners being paid an average of £9.60 a week,[13] often doing gruelling hours, where work is compulsory, and with no recourse to workers' rights. And it is here that the political economy of 'gangs' becomes clear, as collective punishment is used to feed bodies into the voracious maw of an ever-expanding private prison industry accruing ever-expanding profits. And once again, as with all aspects of criminalisation in the twenty-first century, we hear the 'echoes of empire'.

Similar to 'gangs' narratives and joint enterprise today, the colonial Criminal Tribes Act marked out specific ethnic groups as inherently criminal – which created sub-classes of workers who could be super-exploited, to make huge profits for pennies: 'the identification and investigation of suspect castes and tribes by police, and their subsequent registration and punishment through hard labor, proved convenient for developing an extensive pool of penal labor [in the British colonies].'[14]

Narratives of collective Black criminality allow the state to blame the moral character of Blackness, instead of the political and economic character of wider society, for social problems ranging from unemployment and educational attainment, to youth violence and disproportionate policing. Under neoliberalism, this has laid the ideological basis for the withdrawal of state investment in Black communities. In order to address youth violence, we are told we don't need youth services, mental health support, domestic violence services, family support services, good and secure employment, and high-quality education. Instead, we get criminalisation, policing and prisons. Prisons are already violent places with people often coming out more destitute, more traumatised and more hopeless than when they went in. Private prisons in particular concentrate and intensify this violence, with 47 per cent more assaults taking place in private prisons.[15] This shatters any pretence that the growing number of prisons and prisoners is about anyone's safety: prisons create more violence, not less. And more violence means cycles of repeat offending that feed the state's expansion of the prison system, causing countless harm along the way.

When economic and political crisis rocked Britain in the early '70s, the government pivoted to a 'law-and-order' discourse that involved criminalising migrant descended communities who had, by that time, become unemployed and therefore surplus to labour demands. As Stuart Hall argues in *Policing the Crisis*, criminalisation, race and policing are key tools that the state mobilises during times of instability and upheaval. When policing is understood in this way – as a tool to create an image of stability during times of chaos – we can begin to contextualise one of the most blatant forms of police racism in the last decade: the Gangs Matrix. The Gangs Matrix is an intelligence database compiled by the Metropolitan Police that ranks people it deems to be at risk of gang violence. Unsurprisingly, the trope of collective Black criminality structures how the Gangs Matrix is used: 78 per cent of those on the Gangs Matrix are Black, despite the fact Black people make up only 27 per cent of youth violence convictions.[16] While the police claim the criteria for getting on the database is participation in violent crime, it's clear the actual criteria is skin colour. In 2016, watershed research showed the issue was spread right across the country: 89 per cent of people on Greater Manchester Police's gangs database were Black, yet only 23 per cent of those convicted of youth violence were Black.[17] Thirty-five per cent of people on the Met's Gangs Matrix have never committed a serious offence,[18] they are added to the Gangs Matrix through their association – in online, social and public spaces – with friends and peers. Once again, in the eyes of the police, simply being Black, in a Black space, around other Black people, makes you a criminal.

Do you recall we said the state uses criminalisation and race to police crises? The Gangs Matrix emerged in the throes of upheaval: four years after the 2008 financial crash, two years after the start of austerity (and the concomitant wave of resistance it created) and one year after the 2011 riots. All the while, neoliberalism – the deregulation of financial markets and shrinking of public assets in order to enrich the private sphere – was drumming along in the background. So what change or upheaval does the Gangs Matrix help the state to manage? You might be surprised we found some answers when looking at housing. Central to neoliberal strategy, from Thatcher to Blair, is turning social housing into commodities – where housing is no longer about human need, and instead becomes a lucrative opportunity for capital speculation. Tony Blair's 'Urban Renaissance' strategy kickstarted gentrification, where working class council estates were knocked down, and working class people cleansed out of urban areas, all to make space for middle-class buyers and the climbing house prices they brought with them. Initially articulated through the language of class – 'sink estates', 'social exclusion', 'deprivation' – the political establishment seized the moment to accelerate their neoliberal housing agenda by coding declining council estates with race through the use of 'gang' narratives.

Days after the 2011 riots shook the country, Prime Minister David Cameron declared 'a concerted, all-out war on gangs and gang culture'. As discussed earlier, 'gang' is a racially loaded word; regularly used to point to a collective Black criminality. And where was Cameron's war on gangs to be fought? The '*streets and estates* across our country', he claimed. He vowed to make fighting gangs a 'new national priority'.[19] In a 2019 Institute of Race Relations (IRR) report,[20] Jessica Perera maps out the policies that unfolded over the years following the riots: these became the essential artillery used to fight the war on gangs in council estates. Anti-gang policing strategies like Boris Johnson's Operation Shield specifically targeted housing estates in working class Black areas. The Anti-Social Behaviour, Crime and Policing Act of 2014 ushered in new powers that enabled local authorities to police anti-social behaviour, made it easier for landlords to evict tenants and introduced new powers to disperse people on the streets. These new powers were intended to not only clear space for gentrifiers to buy in working class areas, but made the streets more palatable to their tastes when they arrived. Just like with counter-terror strategy, anti-gang strategy brought civil society institutions and ordinary people into the dirty work of policing, diffusing police power into the hearts and minds of public servants and institutions.

In 2016, David Cameron committed to rooting out the 'gangs' and 'ghettos' in working class estates by razing them to the ground, and letting loose the regeneration and development sharks. Once again, highly racialised language reared its ugly head, intended to build a picture of social decay in the Black community.[21] In a *Sunday Times* piece, Cameron clearly laid out his plans to eviscerate council estates, concluding: 'I believe that together we can tear down anything that stands in our way.'[22] And indeed, tear down is what they did. Building on earlier austerity policies – such as the 60 per cent cut in affordable housing funds, and the 2013 bedroom tax which cleared working class people from council homes[23] – the Tories drove through an aggressive housing agenda that bowed to the interests of increasingly aggressive property developers. By 2017, there were 40 per cent fewer council-rented dwellings in London than there had been in 1994.[24]

So what of the Gangs Matrix? Amnesty International's 2018 report *Trapped in the Matrix* showed that information sharing across multiple agencies, including housing associations and local authorities, created housing and tenancy instability.[25] In some cases, police were threatening the families of those on the Gangs Matrix with eviction, including in cases where police had no evidence the individual was actually in a gang. In 2018, the Home Office said it would begin rolling out a scheme where convicted gang members' families would be evicted from council homes, cementing in no uncertain terms the fact that policing, social cleansing and gentrification go hand-in-hand.[26]

But strong communities can defend themselves against the dual attacks of policing and gentrification. Broadwater Farm Estate in Tottenham is an estate of 3,000 people, many of whom have Caribbean or African heritage, and is an inspiring example. In the 1980s, Broadwater Farm was policed with 'one officer for every 20 people'.[27] Systematic racist policing was the backdrop to the uprising that erupted on the Farm in 1985, when police killed Caribbean mother Cynthia Jarrett. For decades, campaigners and organisations from Broadwater Farm have led the struggle against deaths in custody and police violence. And it's this same community that sprang into action in 2017 when the council threatened to demolish the estate and turn it into private housing as part of the Haringey Development Vehicle (HDV). Local campaigners built a grassroots case against social cleansing and for social housing, ultimately defeating the HDV in 2018 and booting out the pro-gentrification councillors, replacing them with anti-HDV representatives. The groups involved in the anti-HDV campaign were made up of stalwart anti-racists, with strong histories of fighting police violence, such as Tottenham Rights, Haringey Solidarity Group and many others.[28]

Gentrification drives racist policing in working class communities and this is why housing campaigns, eviction resistance and renters' unions must be embedded in struggles to resist police violence. We have to make these links! The state obscures the connections between our realities and struggles, often leaving our resistance disjointed and singular. Revolutionary abolitionists can play a key role in making visible the wider social relations at play, linking working class and anti-racist struggles and making the case for a society where everyone has access to secure, quality housing. Three years after the defeat of the HDV, Haringey Council successfully applied for the compulsory purchase of two buildings on Broadwater Farm, which are due to be demolished.[29] Although it remains to be seen if it will be honoured, at the time of writing, tenants in those buildings will have the right of return and the right of first refusal: this is the legacy of the decades of struggle against racist policing and gentrification. Broadwater Farm is an inspiration to us all.

By now, you may have noticed the similarities between the Gangs Matrix and Prevent. Both schemes define pre-criminality through race, where proximity to a particular racial or ethnic identity means proximity to a specific type of crime. This allows new technologies of surveillance and policing to be trialled in communities deemed undesirable. Both schemes weaponise race and deploy it in the public imagination in order to drive through political and economic agendas. Both schemes turn racialised groups into a criminal class, allowing their rights and freedoms to become disposable and conditional. In the struggles of the 1960s, '70s and '80s, Black and Asian communities used their shared experience of colonialism and racism on the mainland as a basis for unity in struggle. Groups like the Organisation for Women of Asian and African Descent (OWAAD) and the British Black Panthers were made up of Black and South Asian activists. Yet today, the politics of antagonism and irreconcilable difference dominates the political relationship between our communities.

The PCSC Act will create a Gangs Matrix version of the Prevent Duty, where teachers in schools will once again be turned into cops, this time to police the Black community.[30] We already know about the devastating role teachers can play in criminalising Black children, as seen in the horrendous case of state-sanctioned child sexual abuse experienced by Child Q. The presence of police in schools has already increased the contact working class and racialised children have with state violence. Resisting new powers of policing in schools is not just a matter of politics, but one of child safety.

The state is using the technologies of racialisation and criminalisation it trialled in the Muslim community to expand police powers in the Black community. Political Blackness was an organising tool that brought together the communities resisting colonialism at home and abroad, under one banner. And the politics of neoliberalism – individualism, competition, grift – drove these communities apart again. As racialised communities today find ourselves under siege from interlocking systems of violence, abolition can be the collective language through which we re-articulate our shared struggles. Abolition can be the antidote to the individualistic style of identity politics that has left communities – who have a fundamentally shared history and reality – in competition with one another for the trophy of greatest grievance and prize of biggest crumb. As the state builds its powers of policing and surveillance, and expands them from one community to the next, our side should rebuild its power with solidarity and coalitionism: without these, there can be no prospect of an abolitionist future.

PART 4
Abolitionist Futures

THESIS 14

Gypsy, Roma and Traveller communities have led fierce resistance to state violence. Abolition must unite different struggles.

When the movement to kill the PCSC Act kicked off in March 2021, it's safe to say neither of us knew a great deal about Gypsy, Roma and Traveller (GRT) communities. We came to the movement as Black women, with backgrounds in feminist and anti-racist organising, but no contact with GRT organising. No doubt Priti Patel thought she was exercising efficiency by targeting protesters, migrants, travellers and Black folk in one fell swoop, with a single piece of legislation. As a result, what unfolded was a movement based on solidarity between oppressed groups that, before the Kill the Bill (KTB) movement, rarely had anything to do with each other.

A few days after the violent police crackdown of the Sarah Everard vigil, Sisters Uncut held an online public meeting to launch the Kill the Bill movement. Three thousand people attended to hear from abolitionists and activists in No More Exclusions, Sex Worker's Advocacy and Resistance Movement (SWARM), Black Lives Matter UK (BLMUK), Public Interest Law Centre, Disability Justice, and the GRT collective Traveller Pride and Dikhlo Collective. Lolo, of Traveller Pride and Dikhlo Collective, gave voice to her community's bitter disappointment with the mainstream British left's perpetual sidelining of GRT struggle. It was a call-out (or rather a call-in) that we felt chastened by, but were determined to address. Lolo was also upfront about the existence of anti-Black racism in GRT communities, and was keen to find ways to build a coalition that could provide political education and a shared sense of understanding between two racialised groups targeted by the bill.

The Kill the Bill coalition was formed of too many groups to mention, but included: feminist, anti-racist, Black, youth, GRT, migrants rights, education, disability justice, trade union, squatter, abolitionist, queer, sex worker and police monitoring groups. This coalition announced a national day of action against the bill on 1 May 2021: ten thousand people gathered in protest. In London, the march twisted through the city centre's streets, stopping off at the Home Office for speeches, before coming to its final destination at Vauxhall Pleasure Gardens for a political education festival. GRT Socialists, a GRT campaign group, spoke on the history of gypsy and traveller oppression in the UK. They pointed to the need for mass, solidarity action to resist the inevitable evictions that would come as a result of draconian new trespass laws.[1] BLMUK provided a know-your-rights skill share on stop and search, contextualised by an explanation of how policing operations are used as a tool to oppress Black communities.

Listening to GRT Socialists and BLMUK lay the groundwork for mass resistance in defence of their respective communities, we were struck by the commonalities between Black and GRT positioning within British capitalism. Romani Gypsies, it was explained, came to England five hundred years ago from India, whilst Irish travellers, or Pavees, hailed from a Celtic nomadic tradition. There was a time when nomadism was the norm and settled communities did not always react with hostility at the arrival of Gypsies or travellers, who were often a valuable source of trade for more immobile communities.[2]

Over several hundred years, common land underwent the process of enclosure, where peasant workers were evicted from land where they, and generations of their ancestors, had toiled for centuries. Landlords realised they could make more money by creating artificial scarcity through gate-keeping access to survival resources, and only giving jobs to the most productive peasants.[3] Remaining land was turned over for sheep rearing.[4] Privatising land meant that peasants could only survive by competing with each other, as they were no longer free to fish, hunt, or forage. To seal the deal, the ruling class then set about criminalising 'vagrancy', a deliberately loose term which referred to forms of survival that existed outside of paying rent or accepting waged work in the landlord's burgeoning and booming industries.[5] In 1530, Henry VIII passed the 'Egyptian Act',[6] branding Gypsies as 'outlandish' and criminalising them for 'wandering' and 'fortune telling'. In 1554, his daughter Mary I followed in her father's footsteps by passing further anti-Gypsy legislation which targeted them for 'idle' and 'ungodly' lifestyles, and punished them if they refused legal employment. Gypsies posed a threat to the development of early capitalism, as their free and wandering existence tempted peasants away from the industrious competition and productivity that landlords wanted for them. Vagrancy legislation has violently criminalised nomadic lifestyles ever since. Fundamentally, use of free land, mobility, and survival outside of waged labour continues to be seen as incompatible with modern capitalism.[7]

As BLMUK spoke about the racism underpinning stop and search in Britain, it occurred to us that the same vagrancy legislation used to control GRT communities had also been weaponised against Black people. When deep financial crisis rocked Britain in the 1970s, the ruling elite strategised to shift attention away from the economic crisis (for which they could find no enduring solution), towards a law-and-order panic: in the early 1970s, senior politicians had declared Britain to be 'ungovernable'.[8] In order to justify more repressive state powers, the courts, the media and politicians manufactured a Black crime 'problem', which they argued could only 'solved' with force.[9] Black communities were the first to be sacrificed to the dole queue, and were disproportionately hit by deep public-sector cuts, which resulted in run-down and neglected Black neighbourhoods. It's in this context that the state repurposed the 1824 Vagrancy Act to initiate a campaign of police terror in Black communities. Known as 'sus' laws, the Vagrancy Act 1824 gave police the power to stop and search anyone, at any time, without suspicion they had been involved in a crime. Sus laws were used to harass Black people in places like Tottenham, Brixton and Handsworth, sparking Black revolts in the '70s, and into the '80s.

As the KTB coalition developed, so too did our understanding of the different communities represented within it. Through discussions with comrades in GRT Socialists, Drive2Survive and Dikhlo Collective, the parallels, across a range of issues, between Black and GRT experiences of state violence became clear. Aviah, after having been taken into foster care by racist social workers, was moved by the astronomically high numbers of GRT children taken into care and adopted into non-GRT families: these policies perpetuate similarly violent assimilation against Black children. The racism against GRT families is beyond doubt. An analysis of data produced by the Department for Education,[10] shows that Gypsy and Roma children are one-and-a-half times more likely to have an initial referral to children's services – which is a gateway into the care system – than children from all other ethnic groups. Travellers of Irish heritage are 2.74 times more likely. At the other end of that spectrum, by 2017–18, Gypsy/Roma children were 2.11 times more likely to live in care than children from all other ethnic groups. Children of Irish traveller heritage were 2.55 times more likely to live in care.[11] The same data shows that Black children were more likely to be looked-after (7 per cent) and less likely to be adopted (2 per cent) compared with their share of the under-18 year old population (5 per cent).[12] Strikingly, the data shows that between 2015 and 2020, the number of Black looked-after children who were adopted went down by 47 per cent. And completing the horrific picture, we learned from our comrades that GRT children face a similar pupil referral unit to prison pipeline, as we knew Black children did.[13]

Oppression towards GRT and Black communities has intensified under neoliberalism, in different yet connected ways, as successive governments have sold off large amounts of public land. Through schemes such as the 'right to buy' – programmes that sold off council estates, and gentrified working class communities – previously publicly owned land is now largely in the hands of profiteering multinational property developers.[14] David Harvey refers to this process of gentrification as 'accumulation by dispossession',[15] whereby the ruling elite make working class people destitute by depriving them of publicly owned land and goods – a process evocative of the early capitalist enclosures. This has led to extortionately high property prices, as local authorities increasingly decide that public land occupied by working class people can be put to more profitable use in the private sector. As discussed in an earlier thesis, Black communities have been violently policed throughout this process of racialised social cleansing. So too have GRT communities, who have faced a relentless intensification of racism. Landowners anxious not to see the value of their land and property drop have turned to violent dispersal methods, either through the police or through vigilantism.[16]

GRT and working class Black communities are under siege by the state: both are criminalised as 'vagrant' classes under neoliberalism. The landslide victory won by the Tory Party in the 2019 general election secured a democratic mandate to advance what has become the most radically authoritarian power grab in a generation. The PCSC Act takes the state one step closer to reintroducing the suspicionless searches of the Vagrancy Act through the new Serious Violence Prevention Orders (SVROs). SVROs will give police more powers to stop people without needing to suspect a crime has taken place. After being defeated in the House of Lords, the government is also bringing back Serious Disruption Prevention Orders through a new public order bill,[17] which will also give police more powers to conduct suspicionless stop and searches. Further, the proposed 'Prevent-style' duty on gangs expands the culture of surveillance that already criminalises Muslim childhood into the lives of Black children. For most nomadic people in GRT communities, the PCSC Act will lead to evictions for unauthorised encampments, whilst refusing to address the real issue of woefully inadequate, and declining numbers of, legal sites – even as the number of Traveller caravans rises.[18] Racism in the application of property and land planning laws means that even when Gypsies and travellers purchase land, councils often refuse to give them permission to reside on it. The PCSC Act makes the previously civil, non-arrestable offence of trespass a criminal matter. By accompanying this with harsh sentencing guidance, GRT life has now become entirely criminalised. Those found guilty will face seizure of their mobile homes, a £2,500 fine and up to three months in prison.[19] This pincer operation, designed to eradicate GRT life, criminalises travellers whilst manoeuvring to make legal nomadism a near impossibility.

By targeting two of Britain's most racially and politically marginalised groups, the Tories were banking on expanding repressive police powers with minimal dissent. The KTB movement, and its reconfiguration through the radical abolitionist CopWatch network, has robbed the government of its hope for a smooth-sailing, uninterrupted process. CopWatch is building a national solidarity network across urban and rural areas, preparing to physically resist the new powers in the PCSC Act. City-based CopWatch groups are organising in Black and working class communities to scale up resistance to policing on the streets and in schools. More and more groups that cover rural areas, such as Cambridge CopWatch, are springing into action by establishing GRT solidarity networks to resist evictions, whilst lobbying local councils to enhance legal site provision. CopWatch organisers have linked up with the activists who established the solidarity camp to resist the eviction of travellers from Dale Farm in 2011. This action ran for months, with a show of brave resistance from travellers, solidarity activists and community members, who collectively fought back against police use of tasers, batons and dogs. Ultimately, the scale of the racist police operation and extreme use of violence were overwhelming, and the state managed to secure the eviction of Dale Farm. Those involved in resisting the eviction have shared their learning with members of the CopWatch network to ensure the success of future GRT defence campaigns, one example being improvements in coordination to ensure carefully rotated solidarity camps never fall below minimum numbers of people needed.[20]

The summer of 2020 saw the biggest anti-racist demonstrations Britain had ever known. Hundreds of thousands turned out onto the streets in small rural villages and towns for BLM demonstrations; organised largely by white residents in solidarity with Black communities. We believe the conditions for a broad-based anti-racist movement, across both urban and rural areas, are likely to be more favourable than they've been for a long time. Groups resisting the criminalisation of trespass span both urban and rural settings. For example, Resist Anti-Trespass faces down criminalisation by squatting urban properties. But there's also action up north. Marking the ninetieth anniversary of the Kinder Scout mass trespass against the denial of public access to nature, the April 2022 Kinder in Colour action saw hikers of colour lead an interracial delegation of ramblers, conservationists and environmental campaigners through the Peak District's forbidden territories. One of the action's partners, Right to Roam, coordinates regular rural trespass in resistance to anti-trespass laws. As resistance to state violence in urban and rural areas grows, abolitionists must seize the moment to build a combative and fearless national network of resisters – with solidarity between Black and GRT communities at its core.

THESIS 15

Crime is a social construct, but harm is real. Revolution is an essential ingredient to building transformative approaches to harm from the community level up.

Crime is a social construct, but harm is real. What does this mean? Put simply, it means what is and isn't treated as criminal is determined by social processes. These processes are made up of a complex intermingling between economic, political, cultural and historical contexts. Despite the myth that policing and prisons exist primarily to keep us safe, there is no linear line between what is harmful and what is criminalised, and between what is criminalised and what is policed. In 1995, Brian Douglas' skull was fractured by a baton strike to the head; he died after police refused to take him to hospital for twelve hours. In 1998, police left Christopher Alder to die on the floor of a police station, while they made monkey noises over his dead body. In 2008, Sean Rigg entered a police van alive and came out dead, after police restraint put him in cardiac arrest. In 2015, Jermaine Baker was shot by a police officer as he slept in his car. In 2017, Rashan Charles choked to death in a shop, after a police pursuit ended in him being thrown to the floor and restrained in a headlock.[1] In none of these cases had a law been officially broken, despite the fact that in each case, untold harm was caused. Criminality is defined by those with wealth and power, which means criminal justice systems are built to protect ruling-class interests. From Hillsborough in 1989 to Grenfell in 2017, the capitalist state has protected the rich and powerful from accountability and justice.

One of the ways behaviour becomes criminal is through the act of policing itself. As more of our lives come under the watchful eye of the state and the scope of policing increases, so too does the list of things deemed criminal. More and more behaviour is becoming criminalised as new legislation, like the PCSC Act, extends the reach of police powers; as joint working between police and other organisations, like local authorities and private businesses, increases; citizens become drawn into the work of everyday policing through programmes like Prevent, and public and specialist support services have their funding decimated by austerity. This reality has meant police are now often the first agency responding to social problems, after these problems have been left to fester and boil over, through state neglect and disinvestment, into serious harm or violence. But we know care- and health-based solutions that prioritise prevention and harm reduction have been proven to work. For example, knife deaths among young people have been dramatically reduced in Scotland by shifting from a police-centred approach to a public health approach. Those identified as being at risk are offered support with 'housing, relocation, employment and training', as meaningful routes away from violence, with many people taking them up. From an abolitionist perspective, the Scottish approach is far from perfect: the programme doesn't offer a systemic analysis of the way capitalist society breeds violence, and although police are kept at 'arms length', it still leans on them as a partner organisation.[2] But it validates the abolitionist instinct that there are real solutions to social problems, away from criminalisation and punishment.

The fact that police are often the first responders to disputes in the community, youth violence, homelessness, substance use, or acute mental ill-health is directly related to the fact no alternative infrastructure exists that can facilitate a different response. With police responding to everything, the deeper roots of social problems become mystified behind the smokescreen of criminalisation. This approach reframes social problems as individual failures – and punishment, meted out by the criminal justice system, is presented as the only solution. This is where abolitionists in the anti-austerity and labour movements can play a fundamental role in fighting police power: struggles to refund vital public and specialist services should go hand-in-hand with calls to shift power away from police. For example, we should not only be fighting for investment in person-centred mental health services, but also investment in new ideas: specialist mental health first responders, with no powers of force or coercion, who are trained to respond to crisis situations with mental health first aid and care, not force or violence. These services would be democratically run and non-hierarchical, run in partnership with local communities and workers, not police, the state, or capital, where they can be guided by the needs and values of people, not power.

But surely there will always be violence? How would we manage it without police? What will we do with the rapists and murderers? These are all-important questions abolitionists should work hard to develop satisfying answers to. But let's be clear: police have never themselves answered the question of how to solve violence. They have never done anything much with rapists, with only 1.6 per cent of them facing charges.[3] And the police themselves don't protect us from violence: 1,815 people have died following police contact since 1990.[4] Politicians avoid asking the question of how to tackle the root causes of social problems because they don't want to hear real, transformative answers. Destitution, poverty and inequality are core drivers of crime both nationally and internationally.[5] Even some senior police officers know this. Retired Chief Constable of Merseyside Police, Andy Cooke, said in 2021: 'Why do people get involved in crime and serious crime? It's because the opportunities to make money elsewhere aren't there for them.'[6] Destitution creates powerlessness and hopelessness, low self-esteem and isolation: the breeding ground of harm and violence. Abolition must be revolutionary because poverty and inequality are endemic to life under capitalism, and therefore so is harm and violence. Capitalism structures human relations on the basis of power, greed, individualism, competition and ruthlessness. As we've shown throughout this book, violence is essential, not incidental, to how society is organised and this violence leaks throughout society; punching down along lines of race, class, gender, sexuality and ability.

But committing to a wholly revolutionised future does not mean a passive acceptance of the way things are now. Transformative justice – an abolitionist framework for responding to interpersonal harm outside of the criminal justice system (CJS) – commits us to responding to systemic and interpersonal violence as part of the same project. Transformative justice recognises the state as a primary organiser of violence in society and looks instead to localised communities for collective responses to harm. Groups like Cradle Community are building on the work of US groups such as Critical Resistance and INCITE! to develop transformative justice responses to violence in Britain. Alternatives to the CJS are vital in a context where police are an additional threat of harm. Dalian Atkinson, Mouayed Bashir and Kingsley Burrell were all killed by police after experiencing mental health crises. In Dalian's and Mouayed's cases, family members called police to seek help. In Kingsley's case, he called the police himself.[7] For all three, men who needed support ended up dead following police contact.

Communities of colour often refuse to involve police in personal matters for fear of violence and criminalisation. And who can blame us: the Met Police are four times more likely to use force against Black people,[8] and Inquest have found that 'the proportion of BAME deaths in custody where restraint is a feature is over two times greater than it is in other deaths in custody' – with the same true for the number of BAME deaths involving force.[9] The criminalisation and demonisation of sex work, substance use, insecure immigration status, homelessness, mental ill-health and GRT life, as well as rampant ableism, transphobia, sexism and racism within police forces, makes traditional routes of justice inaccessible to the oppressed

and working classes. In this context, radical and transformative alternatives to criminal justice are a necessity in
the here and now.

But transformative justice approaches to harm presup-
pose the existence of strong communities; communities
with the resources, skills, will and cohesion to hold what
is often difficult and draining work. Neoliberalism has
left our communities fragmented, gentrification means
communities hold conflicting class interests, austerity has
gutted our public resources, and workplaces are increasingly precarious. How can abolitionists help rebuild out
of the neoliberal ashes left in our communities? Abolitionist organising must be coalitional, and abolitionists
embedded in radical struggles for systemic change nationally and internationally. Ours is a fight against powerful
systems of violence and terror. Although that violence
manifests in specific and localised ways, it is organised by a global nexus of capitalist power working across
borders and nations. Even at the local level, state violence
isn't limited to the bodies of the most marginal, but is an
ever-expanding practice of coercion and control against
people and the environment. In recognising the inter-
connectedness of systems of state violence, abolition can
be the basis of a new solidarity: one that acknowledges
specific experiences of violence in particular communities, whilst building a unified, internationalist resistance.

Abolition doesn't understand the concept of solidarity as an airy-fairy call for different oppressed groups to
'just get along'. Solidarity is a vital strategic response to
the prevalence and ubiquity of state violence. We live in
a world of vast wealth and resources, and yet of endemic

poverty and inequality. In order to maintain hegemony and control, particularly at times of crisis when the cracks begin to show, the state constructs 'enemies within' to outsource responsibility away from itself and capitalism. It divides ordinary people horizontally, along lines of identity and culture, as opposed to vertically, along lines of class. So for them the problem is not the historic experience of racism and the legacies of slavery and colonialism: it's Black 'gangsters' on our streets. It's not disinvestment from and neglect of working class communities: it's Syrian migrants in our hospitals. It's not military and imperial domination of vast swathes of the world: it's Muslim extremists in our schools. Constructed 'enemies within' like these provide a constant justification for the use and expansion of state violence in order to maintain control; they tie people's lived experience of the world to divisive narratives that weaken the collective consciousness of ordinary people. Solidarity, given this, is a way of building power in the direction of marginalised people. It weakens the tools the state relies on to maintain power, by building connections between the exploited and oppressed people the system would rather keep in contest.

Abolitionist organising must connect the local to the national, and the national to the international. Our work must be community-based, building shared values and radical political consensus through local resistance to state violence and police power. We must build against the idea of static, permanent concentrations of coercive force and power in institutions like the police, and fight for new ways of democratising power and decision-making in working class life; in our campaigns, in our communities and in our workplaces. We must build resistance at the street level and generalise out into the whole world.

The idea of transformative justice goes hand-in-hand with *social* justice: the notion that we can prevent a whole load of harm by building a fair and just world. But we go one step further and believe the idea of social justice requires *revolutionary* justice: total social justice demands a fundamental, revolutionary, reorganising of class relations, state, wealth and power. And this leads us to a final, critical point: policing isn't primarily a response to interpersonal harm at the community level. At every moment in history when there has been an insurgent social movement, uprising, or mass class mobilisation – since 1829 all the way up to the BLM protests of 2020 and the Kill the Bill protests of 2021 – the police have met people with repression, brutality and violence. During the 2021 Bristol uprisings against the PCSC bill, protesters sustained injuries from police officers; including kicks, punches, baton and shield strikes, pepper spray and police dogs.[10] Meanwhile, Bristol police chief Mark Runacres apologised after police were caught fabricating their injuries.[11] Police exist primarily to protect the state, maintain the status quo, defend the interests of the powerful and control ordinary people. This has been their function since day one in the colonies. In this context, there cannot be what some radical reformists and left realists call 'minimal policing'.

Minimal policing, as it's been recently articulated in the UK, is the idea that sometimes, in particularly acute situations where there is a real threat of violence, police are needed. However, their role would be to first and foremost make a situation safe, instead of acting in a way that criminalises any individual. In situations where they may need to detain someone, the response thereafter should be a 'social, rather than [a] criminal justice, response'.[12] Advocates for minimal policing argue we can dramatically reduce police power by transferring the autonomy and decision-making they currently hold to external bodies with no coercive powers. These independent bodies will then decide how to respond in emergency and non-emergency situations, not the police. Now, that's all well and good, but the question still remains: *in whose interests* will these institutions operate? In a world where power and wealth is wildly, unequally distributed and concentrated among a ruling elite, it certainly won't be in the interests of ordinary people. The idea of minimal policing assumes the issue is the police as an institution per se. In truth, the issue is that we live in a society organised in such a way that it *creates the conditions where a coercive police force becomes a necessity*. The idea of 'minimal policing' is precluded by the fact that capitalist, imperialist nations require *maximal* policing in order to maintain the day-to-day functioning of the system and balance of power in their favour. Policing is because capitalism is.

THESIS 16
Revolution needs you ...

[George Floyd] suffocated with a cop kneeling on his neck for ... 10 minutes. If one person woulda thrown a brick at that cop, if one person woulda thrown a coca-cola can, he might have got off his neck and might be alive today. We have been so programmed into believing that violence doesn't accomplish anything, that it only begets other violence, that we fail to take steps to defend ourselves, because we believe that we will lose.

Dhoruba Bin Wahad, Black Panther 21[1]

In the summer of 1977, twenty thousand people turned up to the picket line at Grunwick Film Processing Laboratory to defend six Asian women strikers from a violent police operation that was determined to see scabs (strike breakers) get into work. The strike leader, Jayaben Desai, travelled the length and breadth of the country speaking at trade union branch meetings and in community halls to mobilise mass support. Her hard work paid off: the pickets swelled with anti-racists, feminists and a trade union movement dominated by white men, each turning out to back migrant women in their fight for union recognition. The notoriously racist Dockers' Union, which had marched in favour of Enoch Powell's 'rivers of blood' call for immigration controls a decade earlier, were found at the Grunwick gates, teaching the migrant strikers how to

beat back the police line. The state branded this solidarity a 'rent-a-mob', yet deployed their own massive salaried
mob of cops to batter the crowds, and clear the way with
mass arrests. In defending the picket line, a bottle was
thrown, hitting a cop upside the head and hospitalis-
ing him. This twenty-thousand strong crowd mobilised
to withdraw consent from union-busting police violence
towards migrant women workers, launching an open
challenge to racial capitalism in Britain.

Despite such monumental strength, to quote Derek
McGuinness, a trade unionist who picketed Grunwick in
solidarity, 'defeat was snatched from the jaws of victory.'[2]
The Trades Union Congress and the strikers' union capitulated to the police violence and government pressure,
withdrawing their support from the Grunwick strike in
a double-crossing backroom deal. A two-year dispute,
which was on the brink of victory, was defeated. The
revolutionary threat posed by Grunwick had to be neu-
tralised: racial capitalism could not function without the
super-exploitation of both women and migrant labour,
alongside the bribery of superior status for white workers.
The twenty thousand workers who turned up in solidarity
with the Grunwick strikers were on the cusp of overcom-
ing the deep divisions set in place by racial capitalism.
In the years that followed, the state saved capitalism
from revolutionary threats by exploiting the movement's
hitherto poor record on internationalism and anti-racism. By the late 1980s, the unions were crushed, industries
were outsourced and militarised borders were established
to maintain the super-exploitation of an industrialising
Global South workforce. Meanwhile, Black communi-

ties in Britain were thrown on the landfill scrapheap as a 'surplus population' through state-sponsored neglect and violent policing. The state connects the dots on policing, immigration enforcement and union busting. Our aim must be to outmanoeuvre state attempts to rule through division and violent policing, with mass resistance rooted in solidarity.

Policing is violence. But alongside the batons, cuffs and beatings they used at Grunwick, police also rely on a culture of compliance to carry out violence without challenge. The defeat of revolutionary movements in the 1960s, '70s and '80s resigned many to feeling that resistance to police violence is futile. In the months after Sarah Everard's murder, details emerged that her killer, PC Wayne Couzens, had kidnapped her in full view of witnesses. He used his warrant card, handcuffs and the additional Covid-19 powers bequeathed to him by Home Office Minister Priti Patel to arrest her. Understandably, the onlookers did not intervene. It wouldn't occur to most people to do so in a culture where deference to carceral institutions is normalised. In 2017, 20-year-old Rashan Charles suffocated to death in a shop in Hackney, when a police officer restrained him in a headlock, with the active and enthusiastic help of a member of the public.[3] As Dhoruba Bin Wahad said, if only someone had thrown a brick; this is why British abolitionists have taken up physically intervening in carcerality as a key abolitionist strategy. Public compliance is police power. Withdrawing our consent is people power.

With trust in police at an all-time low,[4] in autumn 2021, Sisters Uncut – in coalition with BLMUK, Manchester

KTB, Netpol, the London Campaign Against Police and State Violence (LCAPSV), the Northern Police Monitoring Project (NPMP), Anti-Raids Network and Bristol CopWatch – put on a series of police intervention trainings. The training took the despair and anger people were feeling, and channelled it towards a strategy of challenging the legitimacy of police powers: over five thousand people signed up. Regional workshops took place across the country: from North, East, South and West London, to Bristol, Manchester, Sheffield, Leeds, and Wales. Off the back of this, tens of CopWatch groups sprung up,[5] and the national CopWatch Network was formed. Many police monitoring groups established in the 1980s focused on informing people of their legal rights when interacting with police, as well as casework and campaigns to support those whose rights had been violated. Building on this radical history, CopWatch focuses on intervention in, as opposed to observation of, all police activity: transforming a radical response to policing, into an abolitionist one, where all police activity is illegitimate.

Intervention builds the confidence needed to harness class power. We don't need to wait for, or appeal to, politicians for reforms: we can short circuit carceral systems ourselves. Intervention can generate the quick wins needed to sustain and grow our movement, such as the beautiful eviction resistance that Shanice took part in at Seven Sisters' Latin American village in May 2022, organised by local groups including N15 CopWatch. Local residents turned out en masse to block police from entering the building: after several hours of stand-off, the cops left empty handed. Having local CopWatch groups that coordinate at the national level has enabled CopWatch to organise mass actions; whilst being responsive to, and disrupting, local carceral systems without getting trapped in the silos of hyper-localism. But we need a diversity of tactics. We need people challenging legislation at the national level, and its implementation at the local authority level. We need workers in care services to fight for harm-reduction approaches, as opposed to punitive and carceral ones. We need to develop collective accountability models for our activist groups, and bring these to our neighbourhoods. We need to build mutual aid infrastructure outside of the confines of the state machinery. We need strategic direct action, mass movement building and strikes, to harness the potential of working class power. CopWatch does some of this work but nowhere near it all. We need you to start building towards this vision too.

Mass resistance to state violence is growing. But today we face a state on steroids, pumped with powers that block us from reaching our revolutionary potential. Radical struggles must have strategies for confronting and dismantling state enforcement in order to have any realistic hope of success. For intervention to further revolutionary goals, it cannot limit itself to reactively springing into action when cops swarm our streets; strategic use of intervention means proactively building working class power by turning out to protect rent strikers or traveller sites from eviction, and providing a barrier between cops and workers struggles. In 2021, we saw the triumphant victory on Kenmure Street, Glasgow when intervention by a thousand local people saw two people released from an immigration enforcement van. In 2022, an explosion of mass resistance took place on Ashwin Street, Hackney, when five hundred community members successfully prevented union-busting immigration raids which targeted several Deliveroo riders. In both instances, mass resistance happened organically, spontaneously. Local coalitional organising, that tapped into national networks and resources, laid the groundwork for this spontaneity.

Years of community organising by Glasgow No Evictions provided the infrastructure to hold the organic explosion of resistance on Kenmure Street. In Hackney, the Independent Workers of Great Britain (IWGB) union, who led the resistance on Ashwin Street, were supported by Hackney CopWatch (HCW) and Hackney Anti-Raids (HAR), after recently forming a local coalition. In the weeks before the raid, HCW and HAR ran joint intervention training on the Ridley Road market – adjacent to Ashwin Street. Spontaneous rebellion is reinforced by community infrastructure, outreach and political education, which in turn builds confidence to rebel. Withdrawing our consent through mass, organised and spontaneous resistance will bring us one step closer to an abolitionist revolution. Patient community organising can prepare us for these spontaneous rehearsals in revolution, where mass withdrawal of consent becomes possible.

But a revolutionary and abolitionist vision cannot limit itself to dismantling carceral systems. As important as this is, it is not the end goal of our liberation. It is true that state enforcement is currently the barrier to us fighting back, and is thwarting our ability to survive and thrive under racial capitalism. They evict us from our homes; they destroy our encampments; they brutalise us on our picket lines, and they use deportation to break workers' power. When we have the audacity to survive outside of this broken system, through selling sex or drugs, they criminalise our communities. In protecting the interests of the ruling class, police, prisons and borders act as a violent buffer between the most marginalised in the working class, and the things we need for a life of dignity and self-determination. Abolition must work towards the wider goal of seizing the land, natural resources and wealth stolen from us by capitalists: abolition must work in service of proletarian revolution.

At the height of global revolutionary fervour in 1968, French students withdrew their consent by proactively defending themselves against police brutality: eventually sparking a general strike that involved 11 million workers. Seeing students resist the state on the streets gave workers the confidence to exercise their own lever of power to withdraw their labour, and bring the country to a standstill. Simultaneously withdrawing labour in the workplace and withdrawing consent from policing would drain the lifeblood of oppression, by making capitalist exploitation and state violence impossible. In the words of Marxist revolutionary Rosa Luxemburg:

Political and economic strikes, mass strikes and partial strikes, demonstrative strikes and fighting strikes, general strikes of individual branches of industry and general strikes in individual towns, peaceful wage struggles and street massacres, barricade fighting – all these run through one another, run side by side, cross one another, flow in and over one another – it is a cease-lessly moving, changing sea of phenomena.[6]

Today, systems of exploitation and control have been turbocharged across the globe, in a bid to subdue the revolutionary potential of ordinary people. This can only be beaten with deep, sustained internationalist solidarity. We must build internationalist infrastructure, share skills and strategies to resist, and support each other's work to resist capitalist exploitation and state enforcement. A serious project to end police violence and the siege of marginalised communities cannot be anything but revolutionary: a total transformation of the international world order, the unequivocal abolition of the conditions that give rise to policing and a rebuilding in the interests of ordinary folk – as equals, as collaborators, as comrades. Abolition. Revolution. Now.

Black and audacious
Black and we're famous
Black and we're hated
Black isn't basic
Black is the love that's objected by racists
Black's what my face is
Black meant plaques
But a life full of dangers
Black meant no housing … evictions
No access to education
Black meant mass incarceration, why not
   desegregation?
a war on drugs –
Black meant dividing a nation?
'White' thinks Black's life is for the taking
Black thinks black's life is for the taking?
… one thing I could tell you about is institutional
   exploitation
Told the truth so Exclusions attacking my social status
13, 14, 15 used to pose on blocks?
Grown now … demonstrations outside of Government
   occupations
But I can't change that the courts are racist
Can we state that the judge was brainless
Not focused on law mostly falsified statements
By constables who forgot to formalise so of course they
   were strangers
By the neglect, of course I'm in danger
Want me to serve but of course I can't cater
Memories blank but my needs were so major,
Enquire our status

Life in a A class
Live from a strays path
Rights? Tryna take ours …

Kadeem Marshall-Oxley
No More Exclusions

PART 5

Symposium: Abolition in the UK

Abolition is a theory and practice with roots in many communities, traditions and organisations: from community organisers, direct action activists and academics, to incarcerated folk, trade unionists, and policy advocates. In this final section, we gather together comrades who have played a significant role in the development of abolitionist politics in the UK. In conversation with the authors, they discussed where next for the movement. We recognise this conversation is incomplete, and doesn't touch many of the topics or communities that abolition needs to touch. Whilst we initially hoped the conversation would have an internationalist scope, time constraints led us to focus squarely on the UK context. However, readers should use this as a springboard for building their own connections with abolitionist organisers across the globe, and as a small contribution to the many hundreds of conversations already happening, we hope it offers helpful reflections for our movement. Joining Aviah and Shanice in conversation are:

Zara Manoehoetoe – *Northern Police Monitoring Project, Manchester CopWatch*

Lydia Caradonna – *Decrim Now, United Voices of the World Sex Workers Branch*

Zahra Bei – *No More Exclusions*

Adam Elliott-Cooper – *Black Lives Matter UK, The Monitoring Group*

Temi Mwale; *The 4Front Project*

Shanice
So the first question: what does abolition mean to you and the groups that you're organising with?

Zara Manoehoetoe
For me, more than anything, it means potential. Potential for new, potential for different, potential for safety, potential for rediscovering or discovering what's right for us. It's about community-led solutions to issues that existed long before I graced this planet. It's about re-imagining what society can look like. Abolition doesn't just look at one area, but a whole system of different, individual and collective harms. Within an organising context, I think it's funny because a lot of people focus solely on policing. Whereas for me, it's not just about police on the street but how policing sits within society, within the structures that we all have to navigate. It's policing in schools, it's policing through statutory services, it's the prison system, it's the whole criminal justice system. There's also a lot of work to do to dismantle the constructs and attitudes we hold in society, which feed into this wider policing – and ultimately become policy and legislated harm.

Temi Mwale
The 4Front Project exists to serve young people who have experienced trauma, violence and racial injustice,

by fighting for their rights and supporting them to heal. 4Front emerged out of necessity – responding to the violence that children and young people face in our communities. My friend was shot and killed a month before his 18th birthday. There was no support for me, as a young person grieving. There was no support available for his family – let alone his friends. His murder was labelled as 'gang-related', so within 24 hours I saw the ways police narratives shape the stories of our lives – and deaths – and the empathy and compassion we receive. Policing is framed as being about reducing violence – but it doesn't. At the beginning, 4Front wasn't an explicitly abolitionist organisation: this emerged from recognising the failures of policing and imprisonment. These systems don't reduce violence – nor do they support the healing that's required once the violence takes place. We asked ourselves, who is going to do that work? Who is going to offer that support? That aftercare is vital. Supporting people to process their grief, to hold that emotion, is what reduces retaliation and cycles of violence. The police don't have a role to play in that.

But the more we worked with young people impacted by violence in communities, the more clear it became: you can't separate violence in the community from the violence of the state – that's how our work developed. For us, abolition means re-imagining what justice looks like, what safety feels like. What the state tells us 'justice' looks like directly harms our communities: putting young people on conveyor belts into prison, where they experience more trauma, violence and harm. They justify the harm inflicted by the police and prisons as being about responding to violence. But we're saying there must be a way to address violence and harm without inflicting more violence and harm. And that's what abolition looks like for us.

Zahra Bei

So, to me the first thing is refusal. There has to be a politics of refusal, without compromise. Because what we're faced with is an utter dehumanisation project, right across the board. That starts, and it's always going to start, with the most marginalised and excluded historically. So yeah, refusing to be complicit, refusing to be neutral, refusing to stand and watch, refusing to continue to be gap-ified, deficit-ised and pathologised – all these things that reproduce master narratives. That's what it means to me right now, but it means a lot more than that too.

Adam Elliott-Cooper

It means so many different things right. I guess that's part of the power of abolitionism. So for an organisation like The Monitoring Group (TMG), that does advocacy work, it's really about a politics which meets people at the sharpest end of police violence and prison violence and border violence. But it doesn't stop there. It doesn't say these are the problems with policing – but only when they beat someone up. It's about wanting to build a different kind of world in which these institutions don't exist, rather than a world where they function 'properly'. It's about taking people on that journey: a lot of the people who call up TMG because they've experienced these things, aren't there politically. They think the police have done something wrong, when in fact the police have done exactly what they're supposed to do, what they were created to do. We need to think about how abolition can be everywhere and anywhere. How even in a school or a college – which the government is trying to turn into spaces run by security, policing and prison logics – we try to carve out spaces for radical learning, spaces of creativity, where people can imagine alternative systems of safety, care and harm reduction. I see abolition as a process, rather than simply a moment.

Lydia Caradonna

On a very basic bitch level for sex workers, abolition means that our work is no longer going to be criminalised. But taking it one step further, we are getting rid of all the systems that mean we have to do this work in the first place. I'm hoping in an abolitionist future, my job won't exist to be criminalised. I will have access to food. I will not have to beg the benefits system for money. We'll get rid of the violence done to us by poverty.

On a personal level, abolition means accountability: being accountable to the people around me, my friends and my neighbours. When someone does you wrong, and you go to the cops, all you're doing is outsourcing accountability to someone out there. We're not accountable to our neighbours, or our friends. We have to appeal to the state for harm and violence to be recognised, and then hope that we're going to be handed some kind of solution – and we're never actually given a solution. A big part of this is rejecting a culture of overwork under capitalism that means the idea of sorting things out as a community is unthinkable. No one has time to be doing big account-ability sessions in their community, because no one has time to be in their community. So I think we have to start building networks with our neighbours in order to really be able to envision a solution in which we are all account-able to each other.

Aviah

I want to ask a question about gendered violence. After Sarah Everard, the state has been giving police more powers to deal with gendered violence, even though in that moment the role police play in maintaining gendered violence became clear. What examples of organised resistance to misogynistic violence can you share from your work?

Lydia Caradonna

Sex workers are very limited in what we can do to stand up directly to the police, because that just puts us in more danger. And actually, the best abolitionist work coming out of the sex worker movement has been less about challenging the police directly, and more about creating infrastructures that offer an alternative to police as a solution to violence. This is the same for drug users. We can't run to the police when things go wrong, so natu-rally we've been creating communities of care, places we can turn to for safety and accountability. Like brothels for example. Criminalisation and policing make us more vulnerable to violence: because a brothel is criminalised, we're often targeted by armed robbers – they know we're not going to report it, so we become victims.

We have alternative methods of safety to prevent violence in the first place. Lots of sex workers will offer a buddy service to other workers, who they might not even know. They will say 'check in with me after this client; we will come around if we don't hear from you.' We have informal whisper networks where we pass on information about clients. We'll even turn it into formalised blacklists, so people know who to avoid. We do a lot of work on educating each other on our rights. The first time my brothel was raided, the reason that I was okay is because other sex workers had taken the time to explain 'they could raid you for all of these reasons, and here's how you avoid being arrested in that circumstance.'

We also have the sex worker breakfast, which is mainly a London thing but is currently being rolled out all over the UK. It's an informal, harm-reduction space for sex workers to come, get fed, do needle exchange, and get information about how to access blacklists. It's because we have these community resources that we're able to keep each other safe. We have informal networks of mutual aid: if I am on a brothel shift and I get raped, I'm not going to go to a station and do a police report. That's not going to happen because my brothel would get shut down. So as a community, we've had to come up with ways to help each other when bad things happen.

Zara Manoehoetoe
I want to touch on my experience at work, as I'm reflecting on the day-to-day way children are weaponised and used against mothers by the state. It is horrific for everybody involved. They know what a mother, or a parent, or

a carer, will go through to be able to provide for a child, and yet will use that child to attack them. That community safeguarding that Lydia just touched on is something that I've really seen in terms of mothers rallying together and making sure that a child is then cared for and that there's somebody to step into so the state can't remove the child into care. Communities can react fast and often what then develops is something beautiful.

Shanice
Adam, I know you talk about the role of women in anti-racist, abolitionist organising in your book …

Adam Elliott-Cooper
A lot of the people who contact TMG are women, who may not necessarily be calling up because they've had an experience themselves, but very often because someone in their family has. There are two things that may be interesting about that. Part of it is this proactive and quite radical form of care, with people making connections to community organisations or advocacy groups to try to challenge what someone in their community has experienced from the state. It's this radical reconceptualisation of care that we need to build an abolitionist movement. But also there's the fact that almost every campaign against a Black death in custody is led by a woman. The different ways these women are portrayed in the press (like Carole Duggan who was described as a 'Ja-fake-an' by the tabloids) demonstrates how sexist, as well as very racist and classist, narratives are really fundamental to trying to repress

resistance against policing. But it also shows us how care is supposed to be the normal role of a woman: I'm caring for my deceased nephew or son or brother. Yet as soon as it is confronting the state, that care becomes criminalised, that care becomes deviance. That care becomes the wrong type of care. You should be caring for your nephew or your son or your brother or your husband, if you're a woman, but not if it is challenging the power of the state.

Shanice
Zahra, you've been doing lots of work on abolition in schools. Can you talk to us about the role criminalisation is playing there?

Zahra Bei
Okay, so this is a very important question. I'll talk about it from the perspective of a teacher, but also as a parent and auntie, as well. We know about all the pressures that teachers complain about: workload, being overworked and underpaid, Ofsted, the tyranny of measuring and league tables – all of that. Then at the same time we get cuts to funding. Not just cuts to what is available for schools to use, but also cuts to what was available for teachers to have a fuller life. So for example, a scheme that was available when I first started was help with mortgages, so teachers could get on the housing ladder. And other key workers could get on the housing ladder. Now, of course, no one can get on the fucking housing ladder, and teachers are pissed off and angry. And some of that anger, unfortunately, gets passed downwards in the hierarchy to children.

Another thing that I've really resented, and I've said it before publicly, is that for me teachers have always been plantation supervisors. But now it's really obvious. Our role isn't to be intellectuals, to be critical, to be thinking about what it is that we are asked to do in any shape or form. Our job is simply to service without any kind of criticality. Children are now given the bare minimum. They want us to show up, take the register, make sure you code and categorise, make sure you've monitored attendance, make sure you've recorded who has free school meals; we need to make sure we get that Pupil Premium money in.

Safeguarding is being operationalised to criminalise. So instead of supporting young people, kids are like, 'there are things going on in my home that I'm worried about. But I don't want to tell teachers because they might tell social services, and they might take me away.' You've got children who are possibly at risk, possibly in need of support of some kind, or maybe just want someone to talk to, but they can't go to the teacher. So for me, one of the things that's really contributed to the criminalisation of students, and particularly black and working class students, is the fact that the role of the teacher, who the teacher is and what their function is, has completely changed and eroded to one of plantation supervisor, snitch, inequality overseer. You're not there to have human connections or be a comrade to these kids. And that is what I am fundamentally angry about; that's why I've withdrawn my consent as a teacher, and as an abolitionist. They do not have my consent to turn me into a snitch, prison guard, cop, whatever it is – that's not what I trained for.

Shanice
Given the shocking state of education, what does abolition in education look like?

Zahra Bei
So what does abolition in education look like? The way we've organised so far focuses on five things. Number one: teacher education. Secondly, the curriculum. Thirdly, a lot of the work that we do revolves around parent and carer advocacy, building their power, getting them to organise and know their rights, peer support groups, places they can go to to talk – all of that. Law and policy change is the fourth thing. We started with that, but I think that was in the naive days when I thought law and policy could take us to liberation. It fucking won't. However, we're not going to let law and policy off the hook because they govern our lives. So we still have to be in that game without selling out our hopes and dreams and pinning them on that wagon, because that's a wagon that's taking us nowhere close to liberation. And the final thing is youth voice, but also youth development, because our young people – Black, excluded, disabled young people – have had their future lives, their present lives, their imagined selves destroyed. So there is a project of reconstruction, and I don't want to over romanticise it, but it's true. We've got to really rebuild who they believe themselves to be, their skills. For the education denied, we need to provide spaces where that education can happen again.

Zara Manoehoetoe
What really pisses me off about compulsory education in this country is that people are like: be grateful for it.

But it removes power from the child, parent and family. Schools are breeding grounds for oppression: schools can authorise meetings with the police, with social services, with early help – without informing parents. The policies might not say that, but that's what happens daily. We have, under the guise of safeguarding, infiltration into children's lives, which then becomes infiltration into their parents lives, their family's lives, what's going on in the estate – data and intelligence gathering.

Aviah
What is the role of trade unions in the abolitionist movement – and of abolitionists within trade unions?

Lydia Caradonna
A lot of criminalisation that happens isn't at the hands of cops. It's by ordinary working people who are being asked to act in proxy, which means that trade unions are a key site of resistance for the abolitionist movement. Speaking from my position as a prozzie, quite often the people used against us are hotel staff, frequently trained to spot a prostitute and dob us in. And it's the same with estate agents and landlords: clauses in contracts stop you using the premises for prostitution, and there are checks to make sure you're not a hooker before you rent. University staff even. One of the best ways we can resist this is by trade unions understand it's their business to stand with criminalised communities and say 'no, fuck you. I'm not I'm not doing your prevent strategy. I'm not spotting sex workers and telling the police.' I've only ever seen one per-

tinent example of this in the last few years. Deliveroo had training and policy where you were not allowed to deliver food to a prostitute, and drivers had to profile people: if someone looked like a prostitute, you weren't supposed to deliver food! How is that even enforceable? What does a prostitute look like? But striking Deliveroo drivers who were working with IWGB, stood with us and made it one of the demands of the strike. And you know what? They won. And now I guess I'm allowed to order on Deliveroo again. So that's nice.

And then of course the other side of the coin is having rights in a criminalised workplace. If your job is criminalised, like sex work, or if you are criminalised at your job because you have shaky migration status and you're not hired legally, you have absolutely no rights to assert – you have no bargaining power at all. This puts the union movement on the back foot, because we have all of these criminalised workers who can't take their bosses to employment tribunals, who can't fight back at work. This is part of the reason why we started Decrim Now, to decriminalise the sex industry, at the same time as we started a trade union branch for sex workers. We understand that ending the criminalisation of our workplaces is not going to fix everything. But it is going to help us assert our rights as workers, and be able to strike. You can't strike against an illegal boss, you can't pitch a picket line outside a brothel – we'd all get arrested. You can't say 'I'm entitled to this' because you're entitled to nothing if you're criminalised. Abolition helps the union movement, and the union movement has so much power it can help abolitionists with.

Zahra Bei

This is a thorny subject for me because I believe in the labour movement, but not in its current iteration. At the same time, I've been paying subscriptions for over twenty years, even through the times of unemployment, to my own union, which is now the National Education Union (NEU) – and they keep boasting that they're the largest union in Europe. Okay, so behave like it! I'm seeing reports going decades back, anti-racism in education motions that have been passed before, saying isn't it terrible? Isn't it awful? Look at the over-representation of excluded Black children. Why are these motions being passed year after year? The union will put out reviews and reports, and then suddenly they still need another piece of research, and then they need another review. Then they need a review that's going to review the research and then they need a working group. Who do they think they're taking the piss out of? What happened last year with the moratorium on exclusions was really important. What happened this year with no police in schools was a fucking miracle. They did some filibustering; they used some nasty, dirty tactics to make sure that they would come out with a motion that was basically a lot of hot air right and nothing else, that made the union's leadership look good but wouldn't be shaking any trees let alone get to the roots of the problems Black children, young people and educators face daily. And we were like, no, fuck that. But I know they can just ignore these motions anyway. So that then leads us to the question of, should we stay? Should we pay subs? Should we be funding our own oppression? Is it time to start setting up abolitionist unions led by the most affected? Yes, it is. Yes, yes, yes.

Aviah
Young Black people are not the face of the abolitionist movement, nor are they in leadership positions. How can we ensure young people at the sharp edge of police violence are central to abolitionist organising?

Zara Manoehoetoe
There are multiple reasons why young people aren't more involved with resistance, organising and the movement in general. Part of that has to do with the schooling system. Part of that is to do with fear from parents, and this belief that young people need to toe the line, do well at school, get a job and comply, comply, comply. But I also think part of it has to do with the over-policing and infiltration of communities, the fact that key leaders have been removed from communities, elders have been batted down and people have left England because they've had enough: there's been a breakdown of intergenerational mentorship. Youth Work is also no longer the way that it was because of funding. Youth Work used to be community-led, it used to be radical. It was mums, dads, aunts, uncles, big sisters, you name it – off the estate. The space to just be a child and make mistakes has been taken away. Everything has gone into these funding models where every single youth organisation becomes a competitor. My dream is to have a community centre that caters from birth to death, that is independent of any kind of state funding, any kind of state

involvement, that is run by the community for the community and counteracts the harm that people are facing.

Adam Elliott-Cooper

I only worked as a youth worker full time for a couple of years. But in those two years, I remember seeing a lot of the kinds of funding opportunities that came our way, as a small organisation in Hackney, being really centred around crime reduction. So as abolitionists, we're saying, 'right, we want more youth projects because youth projects are a way we can reduce harm in our society, not the police.' Then the funders and the government say 'right, okay. We're going to let you apply for a pot of money. And you're going to tell us how many active gang members you work with in your youth project. And at the end of the twelve months when the money's finished, you're going to write a report about how many of them are no longer active gang members.' So they take that kind of abolitionist rhetoric which says 'defund the police and fund these youth projects', and turn it into the most crass, reductionist, almost factory conception of youth work.

Temi Mwale

It's complicated and challenging work. How do we support young people by responding to their immediate needs – addressing the systemic barriers that they're facing, whilst providing them with the educational opportunities to make sense of the oppression that they experience? It's about helping them to not just know that their voices are powerful, but to experience just how powerful their voices are. And that comes by giving them opportunities to speak, uplifting their voices and amplifying their stories. Just because they've experienced police violence doesn't automatically mean they're going to be abolitionist. It's a journey for everyone. We're going to prioritise supporting you to challenge systemic barriers that you're facing, we're also going to give you the space to heal from these things, and then we're going to give you the space to get politically active. And not everybody will want to do that. And that's fine. But there has to be a way to incubate that.

But it's also about safety: recognising that young people on the sharp end of police violence are scared of targeting and harassment. So it's not always appropriate for them to be standing on a stage at a protest. These are real fears. So it's about being able to create opportunities for people at all ends of that spectrum to engage with this work. And really, I think it's about that process of being with young people and holding space for them to imagine. And that's why I said it's a journey because they're not going to wake up and say, 'Oh, actually, let's build a world that doesn't have police and prisons.' It's about saying, 'well, what would make you feel safe? What would it take to keep your friends safe? What would have made you feel held or supported? What did your family need at that time?'

Shanice

We wanted to think about the technologies of everyday policing. From your experience, what are the ways the state brings the work of police, borders and prisons into everyday public life? Connected to that: how are struggles for migrants and struggles against police and prisons connected?

Lydia Caradonna

When it comes to border politics, sex work occupies a really interesting space in which we're not just impacted by the legislation, we're used as an excuse for the legislation that affects everyone else. The best example of this is the huge mythology we have around sex trafficking, that was used to bring in the Modern Slavery Act in 2015. What we know about trafficking is that the people who are the most vulnerable are people in countries recovering from colonisation, who are trying to migrate, but who have no safe, cheap, or legal route. So they end up becoming indebted to people smugglers, in order to be in this country and have more opportunities in their lives. Lots of people end up in things like debt bondage because of that. And then they become victims of domestic violence, once they're over here. But that's not what is ever being talked about when politicians argue about laws targeting trafficking. What is being talked about is this bullshit image of white girls on holiday in France being kidnapped by Albanian gangs, and having to be rescued by Liam Neeson in the *Taken* movies. Because of hostile environment policies, we're criminalising people coming over here, we're reducing the number of legal routes to migrate, causing more people to fall prey to human smugglers, creating more trafficking.

One of the really stark things about it is the way that it's called the Modern Slavery Act. When people call themselves abolitionist, and they say that they're abolishing the new slavery – co-opting the language of people like us who are actually doing abolitionist work – it sets it up as this thing that no one can argue against. Imagine having to stand up and say, 'I'm against anti-trafficking legislation.' Imagine saying that. You can't, because they've co-opted this language. They've co-opted rare cases of victimhood, taken people's trauma, stripped it of its name, stripped of its meaning, and they use it to perpetuate laws that fuck us all over. And they're using ordinary citizens to police it. I've been part of a modern slavery raid, and I'm beginning to come to the conclusion that most of the time it's happened, it's because of neighbours going 'Oh, lots of men coming into that property.' 'Oh, the women there seem foreign.' 'This must be trafficking. So it's my moral duty to get the police involved and rescue people.' But no one gets rescued from a brothel raid. I have never heard of a single fucking case in my entire life where a sex worker has been trafficked into a brothel, the police have come in, and they've gone 'thank God, I'm rescued.' No. What happens is you get sent to immigration detention, you get deported back to the very place you were trying to get away from in the first place. There is absolutely no help for people. There is no rescue happening in the rescue industry.

Zahra Bei

I want to mention the case of Osime Brown, and how there's an absolutely fucking dead straight line you can chart between school exclusion; the way he was not diagnosed as autistic until after school exclusion at 17; being put in care and taken away from his mum, even though he had a very loving, supportive home; how he was criminalised for an act he didn't even commit, that had nothing to do with him and put in prison for years; then finally threatened with deportation on release. So when we talk about the school-to-prison pipeline, I think we need to start adding school-to-prison-to-deportation. And also not miss all the other services. We haven't mentioned the social services element that was complicit. We haven't mentioned the educational psychologists that didn't do their job. We need to name all these other nexuses, all these other points of criminalisation, of state failure, state violence.

Shanice
Finally, what do you think are the main priorities of the abolitionist movement moving forward and how do we build from where we are now?

Zahra Bei
I'm going to quote Linda Tuhiwai Smith when she says, 'the challenge is always to demystify.' So for me, our challenge is to continue to demystify what abolition is, what it isn't, all the ways that abolition is already happening in schools, in communities, in families, in neighbourhoods, and people don't call it abolition, but it is abolitionist. And finally, I think there's something in reparations we need to talk about. There is no justice without a reparative framework. So what are we saying as a movement about the generations of young people that have been made educationally subnormal? What are we saying about the generations of people who have been incarcerated – what are we saying about that? Well, I think we need to talk about reparations sometime soon.

Adam Elliott-Cooper

There's two things that popped to mind. One of them is that the abolitionist movement has to be really careful not to be co-opted by social democrats. Because it's easy to say, 'we want less funding for police, prisons and borders, and more funding for social services and youth services.' It's very easy, therefore, for the end goal of that to be like, 'oh, well, what you want is what the welfare state looked like in the 1960s.' Actually, the 1960s wasn't really that great for a lot of people. So I think being able to navigate that very carefully, and saying of course we want to survive and thrive in the short and medium term. But we need to survive and thrive pending revolution. Another thing is trying to, as difficult as this can often be, to think internationally. And I think that the opportunities arise for that when we think about things like Prevent and the global, as well as the domestic, war on terror. The global, as well as the domestic, war on drugs. Trying to push that when it's very easy to remain focused on local community policing issues, or the prison that's being built, or the detention centre in this specific location is, again, something that is really crucial if we're going to be able to move towards our vision.

Lydia Caradonna

I have three main priorities. So the first one is we have to build soft power in our communities by doing the less glamorous work. We have to create the infrastructure we need to make abolishing the police seem a very possible reality. And that's the unglamorous work of creating collective childcare, cooking for your neighbours, organising community food sources, things like that. Because no one is going to trust their community with their safety, if they can't even trust their community to help them out of a tight spot. The second thing is, I think we need to be doing more political education to get people comfortable with the idea of harm reduction. Lots of people reject harm reduction because they believe if there's enough criminalisation, harm won't happen. We have to collectively work out how to reduce harm, and how to cope with it when it happens. The final thing is that there is a lot of trauma that people hold, because of carceral attitudes we have, that needs to be undone. Lots of people fear being accountable to their peers, and admitting when they've done wrong and confessing to crimes, because the punishment has always been violence. And it means the idea of a society where if you do something wrong and you admit it and talk about it, is scary to people. We need to look within our own movement spaces, and figure out how we create accountability that's healthy – so it is a site of growth, rather than a site of punishment.

Zara Manoehoetoe
I think in part that's dictated as the movement grows and develops, to think that we can plan out the future would be naive, and probably quite arrogant. This is about community, it's about drawing on the strengths and lessons learned. It's about understanding harm, and the fact that harm develops and changes, increases and decreases, that fluctuation will dictate immediate priorities, as well as longer-term goals. And it's about remaining steadfast: there is no one person that is in charge, and there is no

one person who is the expert, and there is no specific one answer, other than we want to be safe. And we want the generations that come after us to be safe. That is what we do this for. And I think CopWatch is a beautiful example because that was born out of multiple movements, and multiple acts of resistance and campaigns.

Notes

THESIS 1

1. Aamna Mohdin, Glenn Swann and Caroline Bannock, 'How George Floyd's death sparked a wave of UK anti-racism protests', *Guardian*, 29 July 2022. www.theguardian.com/uk-news/2020/jul/29/george-floyd-death-fuelled-anti-racism-protests-britain
2. Rahman Khaleda, 'Black Lives Matter co-founder requests meeting with Biden, Harris: "We want something for our vote"', *Newsweek*, 9 November 2020. www.newsweek.com/black-lives-matter-co-founder-requests-meeting-biden-harris-1545913
3. Jeff Mordock, 'Biden signs three bills to expand counseling, benefits for law enforcement', *Washington Times*, 18 November 2021. www.washingtontimes.com/news/2021/nov/18/biden-signs-three-bills-expand-counseling-benefits/
4. William Roberts, 'After 2020's BLM protests, real police reform proves a struggle', *Al Jazeera*, 13 April 2021. www.aljazeera.com/news/2021/4/13/after-2020s-blm-protests-police-reform-still-a-struggle-in-us; Zusha Elinson, Dan Frosch and Joshua Jamerson,.'Cities reverse defunding the police amid rising crime', *Wall Street Journal*, 26 May 2021. www.wsj.com/articles/cities-reverse-defunding-the-police-amid-rising-crime-11622066307
5. Andy Gregory, 'Black Lives Matter: Keir Starmer takes knee in solidarity with "all those opposing anti-Black racism"', *Independent*, 9 June 2020. www.independent.co.uk/news/uk/politics/black-lives-matter-keir-starmer-labour-take-knee-george-floyd-funeral-a9557166.html; Chris York, 'Keir Starmer criticised for saying calls to defund police

are "nonsense'", *Huffpost UK*, 29 June 2020. www.huffingtonpost.co.uk/entry/kier-starmer-black-lives-matter_uk_5efa0069c5b6ca970912eda2

6. 'Labour puts crime top of May election agenda to hurt PM', *Observer*, 13 February 2022. www.theguardian.com/politics/2022/feb/13/labour-keir-starmer-may-election-agenda-crime-law-and-order-; Jon Stone, 2022. 'Climate activists say Keir Starmer has "betrayed" them', *Independent*, 13 April 2022. www.independent.co.uk/climate-change/news/keir-starmer-climate-protest-ban-injunction-b2056999.html

7. John Grayson, 'Wecome to Britain: "Go home or face arrest"', *Open Democracy*, 6 September 2013. www.opendemocracy.net/en/shine-a-light/welcome-to-britain-go-home-or-face-arrest/

8. Ambalavaner Sivanandan, *A Different Hunger: Writings On Black Resistance*. London: Pluto, 1991.

9. Ibid., p. 20.

10. Ibid., p. 117.

11. Sarah Lamble, 'Bridging The gap between reformists and abolitionists: Can non-reformist reforms guide the work of prison inspectorates?', *Institute For Criminal Policy Research*. 22 March 2022. www.icpr.org.uk/news-events/2022/bridging-gap-between-reformists-and-abolitionists-can-non-reformist-reforms-guide

12. House of Commons Scottish Affairs Committee, 'Problem drug use in Scotland', London: House of Commons Scottish Affairs Committee, 2019.

13. Mure Dickie, 'How UK drug policy is being challenged by Glasgow safe consumption van', *Financial Times*. 9 October 2020. www.ft.com/content/68fd5d13-0725-497d-9acd-c6ff77f00a8d; Matha Busby, 'Operator of Glasgow safe drug-use van charged at service', *Guardian*, 24 October 2020. www.theguardian.com/society/2020/oct/24/operator-of-glasgow-safe-drug-use-van-peter-krykant-arrested-and-charged

14. John Strang, 'Randomised trial of take-home Naloxone to prevent heroin overdose deaths post-prison release', KCL.ac.uk, 2022. www.kcl.ac.uk/research/n-alive#:~:text=For%20UK%20prisoners%2C%20the%20risk,four%20weeks%20of%20leaving%20prison

15. Samuel Bowles and Arjun Jayadev, 'Guard labor: An essay in honor of Pranab Bardhan', *Economics Department Working Paper Series* 63, 2004.

THESIS 2

1. Aviah Sarah Day, 'Dream of a new world', *Dope Magazine* 17, 13 March 2022.
2. '"Squatting is a part of the housing movement"': Practical squatting histories 1969 – 2019', 2019. *Maydayrooms.Org.* https://maydayrooms.org/wp-content/uploads/MAYDAY-BOOK-DESIGNS-FINAL-UNPAGINATED-MARCH-2019.pdf; Lucy Brownson, 'Feminist housing activism in the 1970s–1980s, #1: Making space for feminist infrastructures | Glasgow Women's Library', *Glasgow Women's Library*, 17 August 2021. https://womenslibrary.org.uk/2021/08/17/feminist-housing-activism-in-the-1970s-1980s-1-making-space-for-feminist-infrastructures/
3. Rahila Gupta, *Homebreakers To Jailbreakers: Southall Black Sisters*, London: Zed Press, 2003.
4. 'Sisters Uncut: Feministo', *Sisters Uncut*, 2022. www.sistersuncut.org/feministo/
5. Matt Myers, *Student Revolt: Voices of the Austerity Generation*, London: Pluto, 2017.
6. Ibid. Also Adam Elliott-Cooper, *Black Resistance To British Policing*, Manchester: Manchester University Press, 2021.
7. Kevin Rawlinson, 'UK Uncut protesters blockade Vodafone stores across country', *Guardian*, 14 June 2014. www.theguardian.com/uk-news/2014/jun/14/uk-uncut-vodafone; Roxanne Escobales and Tracy McVeigh,

'Starbucks hit by UK Uncut protests as tax row boils over', *Guardian*, 8 December 2012. www.theguardian.com/business/2012/dec/08/starbucks-uk-stores-protests-tax

8. UK Uncut, *The Missing Billions*, Video, 2012. https://think-left.org/2012/06/19/the-missing-billions-ukuncut-new-video/

9. Ellie Mae O'Hagan, 'In 2014 feminists spoke up. This year we're taking to the street', *Guardian*, 29 January 2015. www.theguardian.com/commentisfree/2015/jan/29/2014-feminists-sisters-uncut-domestic-violence-direct-action-feminism; Lizzie Dearden, 'Trafalgar Square fountains dyed blood red as Sisters Uncut demonstrators protest against women's refuge cuts', *Independent*, 28 November 2015. www.independent.co.uk/news/uk/home-news/trafalgar-square-fountains-dyed-blood-red-as-sisters-uncut-demonstrators-protest-against-women-s-rcfuge-cuts-a6752861.html. See also Gaptooth ft. Sisters Uncut, *They Cut We Bleed*, Video, 2022. www.youtube.com/watch?v=oykTtUldOLE, and Gargi Bhattacharyya et al., *Empire's Endgame*, London: Pluto, 2021.

10. Anaïs Brémond, 'Feminist activists occupy women's prison after 10-hour standoff with police', *Vice.Com*, 1 June 2017. www.vice.com/en/article/gyppy9/sisters-uncut-holloway-prison-occupation

11. Sarah Kwei, 'Why I protested with Sisters Uncut at the Suffragette premiere', *Independent*, 8 October 2015. www.independent.co.uk/voices/why-i-protested-with-sisters-uncut-at-the-premiere-of-suffragette-a6685686.html

12. Annette Hastings, Peter Matthews and Yang Wang, 'Unequal and gendered: Assessing the impacts of austerity cuts on public service users', *Social Policy And Society*, 2021, pp. 1–21. doi:10.1017/s1474746421000543

13. Office for National Statistics, 'Homicide In England And Wales: Year ending March 2018', London: Office for National Statistics, 2019 (average taken over ten years).

14. Armine Ishkanian, and Anita Peña Saavedra, 'The politics and practices of intersectional prefiguration in social move-

ments: The case of Sisters Uncut', *The Sociological Review* 67(5), 2019, pp. 985–1001. doi:10.1177/0038026118822974. See also 'Sisters Uncut: Meetings', *Sisters Uncut*, 2022. www.sistersuncut.org/meetings/

15. Julie Tomlin, 'South Yorkshire women strike back', *Big Issue North*, February 2017. www.bigissuenorth.com/news/2017/02/south-yorkshire-women-strike-back/

16. 'Sisters Uncut: This is how we know we can win', *Sisters Uncut*, 2016. www.sistersuncut.org/2016/08/02/this-is-how-we-know-we-can-win/

17. Helen Thomas, 'Burning the Daily Mail with Sisters Uncut', *New Statesman*, August 2015. www.newstatesman.com/politics/2015/08/burning-daily-mail-sisters-uncut

18. Siobhan McGuirk, 'Video report: Shut down Yarl's Wood!', *Red Pepper*, 20 August 2015. https://www.redpepper.org.uk/video-report-shut-down-yarls-wood/

19. 'Why Sisters Uncut support Black Lives Matter UK #Shutdown', *Sisters Uncut*, 2016. www.sistersuncut.org/2016/08/05/why-sisters-uncut-support-black-lives-matter-uk/

20. P. Patel, 'The tricky blue line: Policing Black women', in R. Gupta (ed.) *Homebreakers To Jailbreakers: Southall Black Sisters*, London: Zed Press, 2003. See also Women's Aid, *Statement on the Domestic Violence Crime and Victims Act 2004*, London: Women's Aid, 2004, and P. Patel, 'The multi-agency approach to domestic violence: A panacea or obstacle to women's struggles for freedom from violence', in N. Harwin, G. Hague and E. Malos (eds), *The Multi-Agency Approach to Domestic Violence: New opportunities, old challenges?* London: Whiting and Birch, 1999, pp. 62–85.

21. M. Hester, 'Who does what to whom? Gender and domestic violence perpetrators in English police records', *European Journal of Criminology*, 10, 2013, pp. 623–37, O. Brooks and D. Kyle, 'Dual reports of domestic abuse made to the police in Scotland: A summary of findings from a pilot research study', *Scottish Centre for Crime & Justice Research*, 2015.

22. V. Frye, M. Haviland and V. Rajah, 'Dual arrest and other unintended consequences of mandatory arrest in New York City', *Journal of Family Violence*, 22(6), pp. 397–405. https://doi.org/10.1007/s10896-007-9094-y

23. Catrin Nye, Natalie Bloomer and Samir Jeraj, 'Victims of serious crime face arrest over immigration status', *BBC News*, 14 May 2018. www.bbc.co.uk/news/uk-44074572

24. Amelia Hill, 'Vulnerable women "still locked up in Yarl's Wood immigration centre"', *Guardian*, 1 November 2017. www.theguardian.com/uk-news/2017/nov/01/vulnerable-women-still-locked-up-in-yarls-wood-immigration-centre

25. Women Against Rape, 'Rape & sexual abuse in Yarl's Wood Immigration Removal Centre,' Women Against Rape, 14 June 2017, p. 3. https://womenagainstrape.net/rape-sexual-abuse-in-yarls-wood-irc/

26. Lorraine Radford and Aisha Gill, 'Losing the plot? Researching community safety partnership work against domestic violence', *The Howard Journal Of Criminal Justice*, 45(4), 2006, pp. 369–87. doi:10.1111/j.1468-2311.2006.00429.x. And J. Sudbury, 'Rethinking antiviolence strategies: Lessons from the Black Women's Movement in Britain', in INCITE! Women of Color Against Violence (eds) *Color of Violence: The INCITE! Anthology*. Durham, NC: Duke University Press, 2016.

27. Andrea J. Ritchie, 'Law enforcement violence against women of color', in INCITE! Women of Color Against Violence (eds) *Color of Violence: The INCITE! Anthology*. Cambridge, MA: Duke University Press, 2006.

28. A. Gill and B. Banga, 'The reality and impact of the Domestic Violence, Crime and Victims Act 2004 on BMER women', *SAFE*, 2008, pp. 11–13. See also Sudbury, 'Rethinking antiviolence strategies: Lessons from the Black Women's Movement in Britain'.

29. Lawrence W. Sherman and Richard A. Berk, 'The specific deterrent effects of arrest for domestic assault', *American Sociological Review* 49(2), 1984. p. 261. doi:10.2307/2095575.

Also Lawrence W. Sherman, 'Policing domestic violence 1967–2017', *Criminology & Public Policy* 17(2), 2018, pp. 453–65. doi:10.1111/1745-9133.12365, and Frye, Haviland and Rajah, 'Dual arrest and other unintended consequences of mandatory arrest in New York City'.

30. Patel, 'The tricky blue line: Policing Black women'.
31. Ishkania and Saavedra, 'The politics and practices of intersectional prefiguration in social movements: The case of Sisters Uncut'.
32. 'Sisters Uncut: How can she leave if she has nowhere to go? Housing and domestic violence', *Sisters Uncut*, 2015. www.sistersuncut.org/2015/09/15/how-can-she-leave-if-she-has-nowhere-to-go-housing-and-domestic-violence/
33. Day, 'Dream of a new world'.
34. Eve Hartley, 'Sisters Uncut celebrates "win" over Hackney Social Housing with Town Hall stunt', *Huffpost UK*, 19 September 2016. www.huffingtonpost.co.uk/entry/sisters-uncut-hackney-fight-for-social-housing_uk_57dedc33e4b0d584f7f172b0
35. Damien Gayle, 'Sarah Reed told family of alleged sexual assault in hospital', *Guardian*, 4 February 2016. www.theguardian.com/society/2016/feb/04/sarah-reed-wrote-to-family-she-had-been-sexually-assaulted-in-hospital
36. Damien Gayle, 'Woman assaulted by PC who lost his job found dead in Holloway cell', *Guardian*, 3 February 2016. www.theguardian.com/society/2016/feb/03/sarah-reed-assaulted-by-pc-dead-holloway-prison
37. 'Sarah Reed', *4Front Project*, 2021. www.4frontproject.org/sarah-reed
38. Gayle, 'Woman assaulted by PC who lost his job found dead in Holloway cell'.
39. Inquest, 'Jury concludes unnecessary delays and failures in care contributed to death of Sarah Reed at Holloway Prison', *Inquest*, 20 July 2017. www.inquest.org.uk/sarah-reed-inquest-conclusions

40. Ritchie, 'Law enforcement violence against women of color'. Also Frye, Haviland and Rajah, 'Dual arrest and other unintended consequences of mandatory arrest in New York City'.

41. Leah Lakshmi Piepzna-Samarasinha and Ejeris Dixon, *Beyond Survival*, Oakland, CA: AK Press, 2020.

42. 'Reclaim Holloway: The opportunity of a generation to re-imagine women's services and spaces in the UK', *Reclaim Holloway*, 2022. https://reclaimholloway.mystrikingly.com/

43. 'Alternatives To Holloway', *Reclaim Justice Network*, 2016. https://downsizingcriminaljustice.wordpress.com/2016/03/16/alternatives-to-holloway/. Also 'History Of UK abolition', *Abolitionist Futures*, 2022. https://abolitionist futures.com/resource-collector-practice/vq3y xjxknds3g8hd7jsq54ck6kmkby, and Mick Ryan and Tony Ward, 'Prison abolition in the UK: They dare not speak its name?', *Social Justice: A Journal Of Crime, Conflict & World Order* 41(3), 2014, pp. 107–19.

44. 'Holloway Prison: Community perspectives', *Community Plan For Holloway*, 2017. www.crimeandjustice.org.uk/sites/crimeandjustice.org.uk/files/plan-for-holloway-community-views-oct-2017.pdf

45. Reclaim Holloway, 'The opportunity of a generation to re-imagine women's services and spaces in the UK'.

46. 'This is a political occupation', *Vice*, Video, 2017. https://video.vice.com/en_uk/video/sisters-uncut-this-is-a-political-occupation/59a0407ddbbe67f12357ceb8.e67f1 2357ceb8

47. Angela Y. Davis et al., *Abolition, Feminism, Now*, London: Penguin, 2022. Also 'Press release: Feminists occupy Holloway Prison to demand more domestic violence services', *Sisters Uncut*, 27 May 2017. www.sistersuncut.org/2017/05/27/press-release-feminists-occupy-holloway-prison-to-demand-more-domestic-violence-services/

48. SamGelder, 'Holloway Prison: 1,000 homes to be built by Peabody after £42m loan from Sadiq Khan', *Islington*

Gazette, 8 March 2019. www.islingtongazette.co.uk/news/
holloway-prison-1-000-homes-built-peabody-42m-loan-
sadiq-3812814

49. 'Holloway Prison site to be 50% "genuinely affordable"',
council rules', *BBC News*, 5 January 2018. https://www.bbc.
co.uk/news/uk-england-42571302

50. Will Ing, 'Council defers decision on AHMM'S contro-
versial Holloway Prison plans', *The Architects' Journal*, 11
February 2022. www.architectsjournal.co.uk/news/ahmm-
holloway-prison-plans-deferred

51. 'No police in our women's building', *Sisters Uncut*, 2020.
www.sistersuncut.org/2020/11/30/no-police-in-our-
womens-building/

52. Alison Phipps, *Me, Not You: The Trouble With Mainstream
Feminism*, Manchester: Manchester University Press, 2020.

53. Jess Carter-Morley, 'Blackout on the red carpet: 'Best
dressed' a non-issue at Baftas', *Guardian*, 18 February
2018. www.theguardian.com/fashion/2018/feb/18/baftas-
red-carpet-blackout-times-up

54. Prime Minister's Office, 'Prime Minister's plans to transform the way we tackle domestic violence and abuse',
17 February 2022. www.gov.uk/government/news/prime-
ministers-plans-to-transform-the-way-we-tackle-domes-
tic-violence-and-abuse

55. 'Time's up Theresa: Why Sisters Uncut stormed the BAFTAs
red carpet', *Gal-Dem*, 19 February 2018. https://gal-dem.
com/times-up-theresa-sisters-uncut-storm-baftas/

56. 'Press release: Domestic violence protesters crash BAFTA
red carpet to call 'time's up' on Theresa May', *Sisters Uncut*,
18 February 2018, www.sistersuncut.org/2018/02/18/
press-release-domestic-violence-protesters-crash-bafta-
red-carpet-to-call-times-up-on-theresa-may-call-times-
up-on-theresa-may/

57. 'Majority of women in prison have been victims of domestic
abuse', *Prison Reform Trust*, 2017. www.prisonreformtrust.
org.uk/PressPolicy/News/vw/1/ItemID/494

58. Gwilym Mumford, 'Domestic violence activists Sisters Uncut invade BAFTAs red carpet', *Guardian*, 18 February 2018. www.theguardian.com/film/2018/feb/18/sisters-uncut-baftas-red-carpet-protest-theresa-may. See also Graeme Demianyk, 'Domestic violence activists "Sisters Uncut" storm the red carpet at BAFTAs 2018', *Huffpost UK*, 18 February 2018. www.huffingtonpost.co.uk/entry/baftas-2018-protest_uk_5a89d5b4e4b004fc31936715, and Pascale Day, 'Domestic violence activists Sisters Uncut take over BAFTAs red carpet', *Metro*, 18 February 2018. https://metro.co.uk/2018/02/18/domestic-violence-activists-sisters-uncut-take-baftas-red-carpet-7323216/

59. Kyra Hanson, 'Sisters Uncut has hijacked London's Tube adverts to protest cuts to domestic violence services', *Time Out London*, 21 November 2016. https://www.timeout.com/london/blog/sisters-uncut-has-hijacked-londons-tube-adverts-to-protest-cuts-to-domestic-violence-services-112116

THESIS 3

1. Stuart Hall, 'Race, the floating signifier', Lecture, Goldsmiths College, London, 2002.

2. Betsy Barkas, 'Framing the death of Mark Duggan', *Institute Of Race Relations*, 17 April 2014. https://irr.org.uk/article/framing-the-death-of-mark-duggan/

3. Paul Lewis and Sandra Laville, 'Mark Duggan death: IPCC says it inadvertently misled media', *Guardian*, 12 August 2011. www.theguardian.com/uk/2011/aug/12/mark-duggan-ipcc-misled-media

4. Barkas, 'Framing the death of Mark Duggan'.

5. David Pilditch, 'Gangsta salute for "fallen soldier" Mark Duggan who sparked riot', *Express*, 10 September 2011. www.express.co.uk/news/uk/270299/Gangsta-salute-for-fallen-soldier-Mark-Duggan-who-sparked-riot

6. 'The killing of Mark Duggan', *Forensic Architecture*, June 2020. https://content.forensic-architecture.org/wp-content/uploads/2020/06/2020.06-Report-The-Killing-of-Mark-Duggan.pdf

7. Ibid.

8. 'Jean Charles De Menezes' cousin wants truth over "smear" stories', *BBC News*, 9 November 2020. www.bbc.co.uk/news/uk-england-london-54839505

9. 'Sarah Everard was a wholly blameless victim, court hears', *BBC News*, 30 September 2021. www.bbc.co.uk/news/uk-england-london-58745581

10. Paul Gilroy, *There Ain't No Black In The Union Jack*, 2nd ed., London: Routledge, 2002, p. 84.

11. Jen Mills, 'Black boys "nine times more likely to be murdered than white boys"', *Metro*, 29 November 2020. https://metro.co.uk/2020/11/29/black-boys-nine-times-more-likely-to-be-murdered-than-white-boys-13672200/

12. Diane Taylor, 'Black boy in stop and search "30 times" accuses Met Police of racist profiling', *Guardian*, 15 November 2021. www.theguardian.com/uk-news/2021/nov/15/black-boy-in-stop-and-search-30-times-accuses-met-police-of-racist-profiling

13. Jamie Grierson, 'Met carried out 22,000 searches on young black men during lockdown', *Guardian*, 8 July 2020. www.theguardian.com/law/2020/jul/08/one-in-10-of-londons-young-black-males-stopped-by-police-in-may

14. Michael Howie, 'No-one is being targeted with stop and search because of the colour of their skin, says Dame Cressida Dick', *Evening Standard*, 29 November 2020. www.standard.co.uk/news/crime/cressida-dick-met-police-black-stop-and-search-b102451.html

15. 'Drugs and diversity: Ethnic minority groups learning from the evidence', UK Drug Policy Commission, 2010. www.ukdpc.org.uk/wp-content/uploads/Policy%20report%20-%20Drugs%20and%20diversity_%20ethnic%20minority%20groups%20(policy%20briefing).pdf

16. Pippa Crerar, 'Notting Hill Carnival bosses reject plan to make people pay for tickets', *Evening Standard*, 24 December 2015. www.standard.co.uk/news/london/notting-hill-carnival-bosses-reject-plan-to-make-people-pay-for-tickets-for-the-first-time-a3144216.html
17. Justin Parkinson, 'Parliament drug use claims to be raised with police this week', *BBC News*, 5 December 2021. www.bbc.co.uk/news/uk-politics-59539589
18. 'Police powers and procedures: Stop and search and arrests, England And Wales, year ending 31 March 2021 second edition', London: Home Office, 2022.
19. Parkinson, 'Parliament drug use claims to be raised with police this week'.
20. Lammy Review, 'An independent review into the treatment of, and outcomes for, Black, Asian and minority ethnic individuals in the criminal justice system', 2017, p. 5. https://assets.publishing.service.gov.uk/government/uploads/system/uploads/attachment_data/file/643001/lammy-review-final-report.pdf
21. Ibid., p. 33.
22. Cedric Robinson, *Black Marxism, The Making Of The Black Radical Tradition*, 3rd ed., Chapel Hill, NC: North Carolina University Press, 2021, pp. 26–27.
23. Stuart Hall et al., *Policing The Crisis*, London: Palgrave Macmillan, 2013, pp. 13–21.
24. 'Obituary: Sir Edward Heath', *Independent*, 18 July 2005. www.independent.co.uk/news/obituaries/sir-edward-heath-299884.html
25. Hall et al., *Policing the Crisis*, p. 13.
26. Grahame Allen and Megan Harding, 'Knife crime in England And Wales', London: House of Commons Library, 2021. https://researchbriefings.files.parliament.uk/documents/SN04304/SN04304.pdf
27. Emma James and Alex Winter, 'London gripped by bloodiest teen murder epidemic EVER as boy, 16, knifed', *Sun*, 31 December 2021. www.thesun.co.uk/news/

16849346/london-crime-epidemic-most-teens-killed/. See also Joe Duggan, 'Britain's knife crime at highest level in a DECADE as blade offences soar in UK', *Sun*, 16 January 2020. www.thesun.co.uk/news/10751008/britains-knife-crime-at-highest-level/, and Isabella Nikolic, 'London's murder toll hits shameful high as boy is stabbed to death', *Mail Online*, 31 December 2021. www.dailymail.co.uk/news/article-10358203/Londons-teenage-murder-toll-hits-shameful-record-high-boy-16-stabbed-death-Hillingdon.html

28. Allen and Harding, 'Knife crime in England and Wales'.
29. Home Office, 'Practitioners' guidance (accessible version)', London: Home Office, 2022.
30. Elliott-Cooper, *Black Resistance to British Policing*, p. 158.
31. Allen and Harding, 'Knife crime in England and Wales'.
32. Matt Dathan, 'Knife-related murders and sex attacks soar in a year', *The Times*, 25 February 2021. www.thetimes.co.uk/article/knife-crime-murders-and-sex-attacks-using-knives-soared-in-a-year-in-worsening-crime-epidemic-doq5owfwl, and James Mutch, 'Sexual assault reports involving knives and sharp instruments in Greater Manchester double', *Bolton News*, 9 February 2021. www.theboltonnews.co.uk/news/19076319.sexual-assault-reports-involving-knives-sharp-instruments-greater-manchester-double/
33. Stanley Cohen, *Folk Devils And Moral Panics*. London: Routledge, 2011, p. 1.
34. Hugh Muir and Yemisi Adegoke, 'Were the riots about race?', *Guardian*, 8 December 2011. www.theguardian.com/uk/2011/dec/08/were-the-riots-about-race
35. 'England riots: "The whites have become black" says David Starkey', Video, *BBC Newsnight*, 13 August 2011. www.bbc.co.uk/news/av/uk-14513517
36. Robbie Shilliam, *Race And The Undeserving Poor*, Newcastle Upon Tyne: Agenda Publishing, 2018.
37. Ibid.

THESIS 4

1. Sami Quadri, 'Met Chief Dame Cressida Dick tells officers "Enough is enough" as she seeks to root out "nasty" behaviour', *Evening Standard*, 7 February 2022. www.standard.co.uk/news/london/cressida-dick-met-police-letter-iopc-report-racism-sexism-prejudice-b980994.html
2. Charles Reith, *A Short History Of British Policing*, Oxford: Oxford University Press, 1948.
3. Home Office, 'FOI release: Definition of policing by consent', London: Home Office, 2012.
4. Audrey Farrell, *Crime, Class and Corruption: The Politics of the Police*, London: Bookmarks, 1992, pp. 50–51.
5. Cressida Dick, 'Rebuilding trust', Metropolitan Police, 2021. www.met.police.uk/police-forces/metropolitan-police/areas/about-us/about-the-met/rebuilding-trust/
6. Cressida Dick, 'Cressida Dick: The Met is not perfect, but let us regain your trust', *Evening Standard*, 4 October 2021. https://www.standard.co.uk/comment/cressida-dick-metropolitan-police-not-perfect-trust-sarah-everard-murder-b958656.html
7. John Besley, 'Sadiq Khan aims to rebuild trust in the Met with new police and crime plan', *Independent*, 24 March 2022. www.independent.co.uk/nws/uk/sadiq-khan-police-met-cressida-dick-london-b2042837.html
8. Metropolitan Police, 'Rebuilding trust – immediate priorities', 2021. www.met.police.uk/SysSiteAssets/media/downloads/met/about-us/rebuilding-trust--our-priorities.pdf
9. Ibid., p. 2.
10. The Strategic Review of Policing in England and Wales, 'A new mode of protection: Redesigning policing and public safety for the 21st century', London: The Police Foundation, 2022, p. 5. www.google.com/search?q=cressida+dick+rebuilding+trust+immediate+priorities&oq=cressida+dick+rebuilding+trust+immediate+priorities&aqs=chrome..69i57.10717j0j7&sourceid=chrome&ie=UTF-8

11. 'Policing by consent', *Abolitionist Futures*, 2021. https://abolitionistfutures.com/latest-news/policing-by-consent/

12. 'Our response to issues raised by the crimes of Wayne Couzens', Metropolitan Police, 2021. www.met.police.uk/notices/met/our-response-to-issues-raised-by-the-crimes-of-wayne-couzens/

13. Metropolitan Police, 'Rebuilding trust', p. 8.

14. 'Enhanced response to tackling violence against women and girls in London', Metropolitan Police, 2022. https://news.met.police.uk/news/enhanced-response-to-tackling-violence-against-women-and-girls-in-london-445454

15. Tobi Thomas, 'Charities warn over "frightening" plan to put plainclothes police in nightclubs', *Guardian*, 16 March 2021. www.theguardian.com/uk-news/2021/mar/16/charities-warn-plainclothes-police-nightclubs

16. Ellena Cruse, 'Fury as women "told not to go out alone" after Sarah Everard disappearance', *Mylondon*, 10 March 2021. www.mylondon.news/news/south-london-news/anger-after-police-tell-women-20047944

17. Shaheen Rahman, 'Sarah Everard vigil cancelled', *UK Human Rights Blog*, 13 March 2022. https://ukhumanrightsblog.com/2021/03/13/sarah-everard-vigil-cancelled/

18. Vikram Dodd and Jamie Grierson, 'Priti Patel wanted police to stop people gathering at Sarah Everard vigil', *Guardian*, 19 March 2021. www.theguardian.com/uk-news/2021/mar/19/priti-patel-wanted-police-stop-people-gathering-sarah-everard-vigil

19. Jamie Grierson and Vikram Dodd, 'Protest exemption set to be removed from England lockdown rules', *Guardian*, 3 November 2020. www.theguardian.com/world/2020/nov/03/protest-exemption-set-to-be-removed-from-england-lockdown-rules

20. Molly Blackall, 'Sarah Everard: Reclaim These Streets cancels its South London vigil', *Guardian*, 13 March 2021. www.theguardian.com/uk-news/2021/mar/13/sarah-everard-vigil-in-south-london-cancelled-organisers-say

21. John Berger, 'The nature of mass demonstrations', *International Socialism*, 34, 1968, pp. 11–12.

22. 'Stop and search dashboard', Metropolitan Police, 2022. www.met.police.uk/sd/stats-and-data/met/stop-and-search-dashboard/

23. Jamie Grierson, 'Black people five times more likely to have force used on them by police', *Guardian*, 17 December 2020. www.theguardian.com/uk-news/2020/dec/17/black-people-five-times-more-likely-to-be-subjected-to-police-force

24. Joint Committee on Human Rights, 'The government response to Covid-19: Fixed Penalty Notices', 27 April 2022. https://publications.parliament.uk/pa/jt5801/jtselect/jtrights/1364/136402.htm. And 'BAME people more likely to be arrested under Coronavirus laws, figures suggest', *ITV*, 6 March 2020. www.itv.com/news/london/2020-06-03/bame-people-more-likely-to-be-arrested-under-coronavirus-laws-figures-suggest

25. Unmesh Desai, 'Policing with consent', Greater London Assembly, 2020, p. 4. www.london.gov.uk/sites/default/files/policing_with_consent.pdf

26. 'Polling London: Londoners' priorities ahead of the local elections', The Mile End Institute, 2022, pp. 18–19. www.qmul.ac.uk/mei/media/mei/tgc-media/filesx2f publications/161_22-MILEEND_Polling-report_V5_final-WEB.pdf

27. 'Almost half of women have less trust in police following Sarah Everard murder', *End Violence Against Women*, 2021. www.endviolenceagainstwomen.org.uk/almost-half-of-women-have-less-trust-in-police-following-sarah-everard-murder/

28. The Mile End Institute, 'Polling London', pp. 18–19.

29. Desai, 'Policing with consent', p. 6.

30. 'Over 11,000 police hired with more women than ever before', London: Home Office, 2021.

31. 'Confidence in the local police', London: Office for National Statistics, 2021.

32. 'Leafy suburbs': Ben Hill, 'Shocking figures show Britain's knife epidemic move from cities to suburbs', *Sun*, 16 July 2020. www.thesun.co.uk/news/12138857/britain-knife-crime-epidemic-stabbing-moved-from-cities-suburbs/. 'Shires': David Collins and Iram Ramzan, '"County lines" drug gangs spread knife crime epidemic to shires', *The Times*, 6 May 2018. www.thetimes.co.uk/article/county-lines-drug-gangs-spread-knife-crime-epidemic-to-shires-3zg2v9tlj

33. Sarah Marsh, 'Middle-class "consume more drugs and alcohol" than poorest', *Guardian*, 16 September 2018. www.theguardian.com/society/2018/sep/16/middle-class-consume-more-drugs-and-alcohol-than-poorer-people

34. Lizzie Dearden, 'Children as young as seven being used by "county lines" drug gangs', *Independent*, 4 July 2019. www.independent.co.uk/news/uk/crime/county-lines-drug-dealing-gangs-children-uk-exploitation-a8988916.html

35. Kit Malthouse, House of Commons Debate, 27 May 2015, UIN 8765. https://questions-statements.parliament.uk/written-questions/detail/2021-05-27/8765

36. Mike Doherty, 'Drive 2 Survive rally to protest anti-Traveller law "makes history"', *Travellers Times*, July 2021. www.travellerstimes.org.uk/news/2021/07/drive-2-survive-rally-protest-anti-traveller-law-makes-history

37. 'Green and pleasant? Policing rural England', *Criminal Justice Matters* 63(1), 2006, pp. 34–35. doi:10.1080/09627250608553118

38. Micha Frazer-Carroll, 'Copaganda: Why film and TV portrayals of the police are under fire', *Independent*, 9 July 2020. www.independent.co.uk/arts-entertainment/tv/features/police-brutality-tv-copaganda-brooklyn-nine-nine-paw-patrol-cops-george-floyd-a9610956.html

39. Sara Chitseko, 'Copaganda: A powerful and dangerous police PR tool', *4Front*, 24 July 2020. www.4frontproject.org/post/copaganda-a-powerful-and-dangerous-police-pr-tool

40. Aaron Bastani, 'Do the police actually solve crime?', *Novara Media*, 29 April 2021. https://novaramedia.com/2021/04/29/do-the-police-actually-solve-crime/

41. Caelainn Barr and Alexandra Topping,'Fewer than one in 60 rape cases lead to charge in England and Wales', *Guardian*, 23 May 2021. www.theguardian.com/society/2021/may/23/fewer-than-one-in-60-cases-lead-to-charge-in-england-and-wales

42. Charles Hymas, 'Police solving lowest proportion of crimes ever, even as number of sex offences soars', *Telegraph*, 27 January 2022. www.telegraph.co.uk/news/2022/01/27/police-solving-lowest-proportion-crimes-amid-record-numbers/

43. Farrell, *Crime, Class and Corruption*, pp. 24–28.

44. Ibid., pp. 28–32.

45. Hall et al., *Policing the Crisis*, pp. 40–45.

46. Adam Forrest and Lizzie Dearden, 'Boris Johnson says stop-and-search policy "kind and loving" way to get weapons off streets', *Independent*, 27 July 2021. www.independent.co.uk/news/uk/politics/boris-johnson-stop-search-police-b1891317.html

47. Criminal Justice And Public Order Act. 1994. www.legislation.gov.uk/ukpga/1994/33/section/60/1995-04-10

48. UK Government, 'Beating crime plan', 2021, p. 6. https://assets.publishing.service.gov.uk/government/uploads/system/uploads/attachment_data/file/1015382/Crime-plan-v10.pdf

49. Nannette Youssef and Emmanuelle Andrews, 'Listen to us: It's time to scrap the Policing Bill', *The Runnymede Trust*, 2021. www.runnymedetrust.org/blog/listen-to-us-its-time-to-scrap-the-policing-bill

50. 'Liberty's briefing on the Police Crime Sentencing And Courts Bill for second reading in the House of Commons', *Liberty*, March 2021, p. 17. www.libertyhumanrights.org.uk/wp-content/uploads/2021/03/

Libertys-Briefing-on-the-Police-Crime-Sentencing-and-Courts-Bill-HoC-2nd-reading-March-2021-1.pdf

51. Rhydian McCandless, Andy Feist, James Allan and Nick Morgan, 'Do initiatives involving substantial increases in stop and search reduce crime? Assessing the impact of Operation BLUNT 2', London: Home Office, 2022. https://assets.publishing.service.gov.uk/government/uploads/system/uploads/attachment_data/file/508661/stop-search-operation-blunt-2.pdf

52. Sisters Uncut, 'It's time we policed the police', *Huck Magazine*, 2021. www.huckmag.com/perspectives/sisters-uncut-its-time-we-policed-the-police/

53. Sisters Uncut, Twitter post. 25 April 2022, 1.30 p.m. https://twitter.com/SistersUncut/status/1518568218251730948?s=20&t=A7WeJsXm7HawFh44c6p8Iw

54. Lisa Smith, 'I'm a Romany Gypsy – the government's Police Bill will criminalise my culture', *Independent*, 24 April 2021. www.independent.co.uk/voices/police-bill-gypsy-traveller-b1836882.html

55. 'Stopwatch's position on Serious Violence Reduction Orders'. *Stopwatch*, 22 June 2021. www.stop-watch.org/news-opinion/stopwatchs-position-on-serious-violence-reduction-orders/

56. Damien Gayle, 'Feminist protesters set off 1,000 rape alarms outside London police station', *Guardian*, 12 March 2022. www.theguardian.com/world/2022/mar/12/feminist-pro-testers-set-off-1000-alarms-outside-london-police-station

57. David Woode, 'IOPC uncovers "disgraceful" Met Police behaviour including officers having sex while on duty', *Inews.Co.Uk.*, 1 February 2022. https://inews.co.uk/news/metropolitan-police-watchdog-iopc-disgraceful-behaviour-officers-sex-on-duty-1434979

58. Sisters Uncut, Twitter post, 29 September 2021, 1.31 p.m. https://twitter.com/SistersUncut/status/1443191808167710725?s=20&t=m4NuHQsHugWX2QmoRKArBA

59. Sisters Uncut, 'Why we're launching national intervention training after Sarah Everard's kidnap by cop', *Gal-Dem*, 30 September 2021. https://gal-dem.com/wayne-couzens-arrested-sarah-intervention/

60. Nosheen Iqbal and Alexandra Topping, 'The shameful strip search of Child Q', Podcast, *Guardian*, 25 March 2022. www.theguardian.com/news/audio/2022/mar/25/shameful-strip-search-of-child-q-today-in-focus-podcast

61. Patrick Butler, 'England's poorest areas left far behind with lack of social infrastructure', *Guardian*, 28 June 2021. www.theguardian.com/society/2021/jun/28/england-poorest-areas-left-far-behind-lack-social-infrastructure

62. 'Press release: New prison strategy to rehabilitate offenders and cut crime', London: Ministry of Justice, 2021.

63. 'Press release: Thousands of new prison places to rehabilitate offenders and cut crime', London: Ministry of Justice, 2022.

64. 'UK's greenest and most innovative prison unveiled', London: Ministry of Justice, 2021. See also 'The new prisons programme: June 2021 public consultation on plans for a new prison in Chorley', London: Ministry of Justice, 2021; 'The new prisons programme: Public consultation', London: Ministry of Justice, 2020, p. 8, and 'The new prisons programme: New prisons in Wethersfield, Braintree District public consultation', London: Ministry of Justice, 2021.

65. 'Press release: New prisons go green', London: Ministry of Justice, 2021, and The Parole Board, 'Guidance on prisoners who are transgender', 2022. https://assets.publishing.service.gov.uk/government/uploads/system/uploads/attachment_data/file/987027/Guidance_on_Prisoners_who_are_Transgender.pdf.

66. Ministry of Justice, 'Public consultation on plans for a new prison in Chorley', p. 18.

67. Ministry of Justice, 'The new prisons programme: Public consultation', p. 19.

68. Ministry of Justice, 'Press release: Thousands of new prison places to rehabilitate offenders and cut crime'.

69. 'Prison population projections 2021 to 2026, England and Wales', London: Ministry of Justice, 2021.

70. Council of Europe, 'Europe's imprisonment rate continues to fall: Council of Europe's annual penal statistics', 2021. www.coe.int/en/web/portal/-/europe-s-imprisonment-rate-continues-to-fall-council-of-europe-s-annual-penal-statistics

71. 'Revised Prevent Duty guidance: for England and Wales', London: Home Office, 2021, and 'Police, Crime, Sentencing And Courts Act 2022: Serious Violence Duty factsheet', London: Home Office, 2022.

72. 'Purposeful collaboration to combat retail crime', *Mitie Intelligence Services*, 2022. https://mitie-intelligence.com/case-studies/purposeful-collaboration-to-combat-retail-crime/

THESIS 5

1. Chris Harman, *A People's History Of The World*, London: Verso, 2008, p. 323.

2. Farrell, *Crime, Class and Corruption*.

3. Connor Woodman, 'How British police and intelligence are a product of the imperial boomerang effect', *Verso Blog*, 10 June 2020. www.versobooks.com/blogs/4390-how-british-police-and-intelligence-are-a-product-of-the-imperial-boomerang-effect

4. Bryan Knight, '"They were afraid of us": The legacy of Britain's Black Panthers', *Al Jazeera*, 7 December 2020. www.aljazeera.com/features/2020/12/7/they-were-afraid-of-us-the-legacy-of-britains-black. Also Seumas Milne, 'During the miners' strike, Thatcher's secret state was the real enemy within', *Guardian*, 3 October 2014. www.theguardian.com/commentisfree/2014/oct/03/miners-strike-thatcher-real-enemy-within-extremism, and Rob Evans and Paul Lewis,

'Undercover officer spied on green activists', *Guardian*, 9 January 2011. www.theguardian.com/uk/2011/jan/09/undercover-office-green-activists

5. Rob Evans, 'Black undercover officer who spied on Stephen Lawrence campaign named', *Guardian*, 16 July 2019. www.theguardian.com/uk-news/2019/jul/16/black-undercover-officer-who-spied-on-stephen-lawrence-campaign-named. See also Rob Evans and Steven Morris, 'British BLM group closes down after police infiltration attempt', *Guardian*, 15 February 2022. www.theguardian.com/uk-news/2022/feb/15/swansea-black-lives-matter-british-blm-group-closes-down-after-police-infiltration-attempt

6. Alexandra Topping, 'Police must call out sexism in force, says chief taking on violence against women', *Guardian*, 7 March 2022. www.theguardian.com/uk-news/2022/mar/07/policing-attracts-men-who-want-to-coerce-vulnerable-people-says-female-police-chief

7. Jaymi McCann, 'Why Wayne Couzens was known as "The Rapist", the origins of the nickname explained', *inews*, 3 October 2021. https://inews.co.uk/news/uk/wayne-couzens-the-rapist-nickname-why-known-as-sarah-everard-killer-explained-1227129

8. Benn Quinn, 'Met officers charged over alleged messages in Wayne Couzens Whatsapp group', *Guardian*, 17 February 2022. www.theguardian.com/uk-news/2022/feb/17/met-police-officers-charged-over-whatsapp-messages

9. Tammy Hughes, 'Shocking details emerge about Wayne Couzens' preference for prostitutes', *Evening Standard*, 3 October 2021. www.standard.co.uk/news/uk/shocking-details-emerge-about-wayne-couzens-preference-for-prostitutes-b958529.html

10. Owen Jones, *The Establishment: And How They Get Away With It*. London: Penguin, 2014.

11. Koshka Duff, 'The Met just apologised after strip-searching me. I don't believe a word of it', *Novara Media*, 24 January 2022. https://novaramedia.com/2022/01/24/

the-met-just-apologised-for-strip-searching-me-i-dont-believe-a-word-of-it/

12. 'About us', *Forever Family Ltd.*, 2022. www.foreverfamilyfund.co.uk/about

13. Sinai Fleary, 'Community groups and activists tackle attempted child abductions', *Voice Online*, 6 February 2021. www.voice-online.co.uk/news/2021/06/02/community-groups-and-activists-tackle-attempted-child-abductions/.

14. Sarah Lamble, 'Practicing everyday abolition', in Koshka Duff (ed.) *Abolishing The Police*, London: Dog Section Press, 2021, p. 148.

THESIS 6

1. Pat Carlen, 'Carceral clawback', *Punishment & Society* 4(1), 2002, pp. 115–21. doi:10.1177/14624740222228509. Also Mimi E. Kim, 'The carceral creep: Gender-based violence, race, and the expansion of the punitive state, 1973–1983', *Social Problems* 67(2), 2019, pp. 251–69. doi:10.1093/socpro/spz013

2. Silvia Federici, 'Preoccupying: Silvia Federici', *The Occupied Times*, 26 October 2014. https://theoccupiedtimes.org/?p=13482

3. Selma James and Mariarosa Dalla Costa, *The Power of Women and the Subversion of the Community*, Bristol: Falling Wall Press, 1972. See also Selma James, *Sex, Race and Class*, Bristol: Falling Wall Press, 1972.

4. Angela Davis, 'Joanne Little – The dialectics of rape (Reprint of 1975 article)', in Joy James (ed.) *The Angela Y Davis Reader*, Oxford: Blackwell, 1998.

5. Beverley Bryan, Stella Dadzie and Suzanne Scafe, *The Heart Of The Race: Black Women's Lives In Britain*, London: Virago, 1993.

6. Angela Davis, *Women, Race & Class*, 1st ed., London: Penguin Classics, 2019.

7. Michael A. Robinson, 'Black bodies on the ground: Policing disparities in the African American community— An analysis of newsprint from January 1, 2015, through December 31, 2015'. *Journal Of Black Studies* 48(6), 2017, pp. 551–71. doi:10.1177/0021934717702134

8. Maydayrooms.org, '"Squatting is a part of the housing movement"'.

9. Sarah Joseph, 'Book review: *Debating Marxist-Feminism Women And The Politics Of Class* by Johanna Brenner', *Economic & Political Weekly* 42(35), 2007.

10. James, *Sex, Race and Class*, and Bryan, Dadzie and Scafe, *The Heart Of The Race*.

11. Kelly Henderson and Yoric Irving-Clarke, *Housing And Domestic Abuse: Policy Into Practice*, London: Routledge, 2020, and Christine Wall, 'Sisterhood and squatting in the 1970s: Feminism, housing and urban change in Hackney', *History Workshop Journal* 83(1) 2017, pp. 79–97. doi:10.1093/hwj/dbx024.

12. Muneeza Inam, 'Taking or giving refuge? The Asian women's refuge movement', in R. Gupta (ed.) *Homebreakers To Jailbreakers: Southall Black Sisters*, London: Zed Press, 2003. And also Amina Mama, *The Hidden Struggle: Statutory and Voluntary Sector Responses to Violence Against Black Women in the Home*, London: London Race and Housing Research, 1989.

13. Inam, 'Taking or giving refuge?'.

14. Ibid.

15. May Bulman, 'Nearly 200 domestic abuse victims turned away from refuges each day, charity finds', *Independent*, 25 November 2017. www.independent.co.uk/news/uk/home-news/domestic-abuse-refuges-victims-uk-turned-away-stats-a8074661.html

16. R. Emerson Dobash and Russell P. Dobash, *Women, Violence and Social Change*, London: Routledge, 1992.

17. Elizabeth Bernstein, 'Carceral politics as gender justice? The "traffic in women" and neoliberal circuits of crime,

sex, and rights', *Theory And Society* 41(3), 2012, pp. 233–59. doi:10.1007/s11186-012-9165-9

18. Melanie. F. Shepard and Ellen. L. Pence, *Coordinating Community Responses to Domestic Violence": Lessons from Duluth and Beyond*, Thousand Oaks, CA: SAGE Publications, 1999.

19. Cheryl Hanna, *The Paradox of Hope: The Crime and Punishment of Domestic Violence*, Williamsburg, VA: The William and Mary Law Review, 1998.

20. College of Policing, 2015, 'Criminal sanctions to prevent domestic violence', quoted in Penelope Gibbes, 'Domestic violence prosecutions clumsy and costly', Centre for Crime and Justice Studies, 2018. www.crimeandjustice.org.uk/resources/domestic-violence-prosecutions-clumsy-and-costly

21. Sylvia Federici, *Going to Beijing: How the United Nations Colonized the Feminist Movement*, Toronto: Between the Lines Press, 1997.

22. Nancy Fraser, *The Fortunes of Feminism: From Women's Liberation, to Identity Politics, to Anti-Capitalism*, London: Verso, 2013.

23. Federici, *Going To Beijing*.

24. Jules Falquet, 'Hommes en armes et femmes "de service": tendances néolibérales dans l'évolution de la division sexuelle internationale du travail', *Cahiers de Genre* 40, 2006, 15–37, cited in Silvia Federici, *Witches, Witch-Hunting, and Women*. Oakland CA: PM Press, 2018.

25. Nancy Fraser, 'How feminism became capitalism's handmaiden – and how to reclaim it'. *Guardian*, 14 October 2013. www.theguardian.com/commentisfree/2013/oct/14/feminism-capitalist-handmaiden-neoliberal

26. Juno Mac and Molly Smith, *Revolting Prostitutes: The Fight for Sex Workers' Rights*, London: Verso, 2018.

27. Dorothy Roberts, *Torn Apart: How the Child Welfare System Destroys Black Families – and How Abolition Can Build a Safer World*, New York: Basic Books, 2002.

28. Kirstin Bumiller, *In an Abusive State – How Neoliberalism Appropriated the Feminist Movement Against Sexual Violence*, Durham, NC: Duke University Press, 2008. See also Roberts, *Torn Apart*.

29. Charlie Owen and June Statham, 2009. 'Disproportionality in child welfare: The prevalence of Black and minority ethnic children within the "looked after" and "children in need" populations and on child protection registers in England', London: Institute of Education, 2009. https://dera.ioe.ac.uk/11152/1/DCSF-RR124.pdf

30. Hester, 'Who does what to whom?', and 'Domestic Abuse Bill', *End Violence Against Women*, 2021. www.endviolenceagainstwomen.org.uk/campaign/domestic-abuse-bill/

31. Meda Chesney-Lind and Joycelyn Pollock, 'Women's prisons: Equality with a vengeance', in A. Merlo and J. Pollock (eds) *Women, Law, and Social Control*, Lexington, MA: Lexington Books, 1995, pp. 155–75.

32. Polly Neate and Glen Poole, 'Should domestic violence services be gender neutral?', *Guardian*, 5 August 2014. www.theguardian.com/commentisfree/2014/aug/05/domestic-violence-services-gender-neutral

33. Moya Lothian-Mclean, '"If they sound like a man, hang up" – How transphobia became rife in the gender-based violence sector', *Gal-Dem*, 2022. https://gal-dem.com/transphobia-in-sexual-violence-services/. See also Phipps, *Me, Not You: The Trouble with Mainstream Feminism*.

34. Beth Ritchie, *Arrested Justice: Black Women, Violence, and America's Prison Nation*, New York: New York Univiersity Press, 2012. See also Davis et al., *Abolition, Feminism, Now*.

35. 'Women prisoners "coerced into sex with staff"', *BBC News*, 25 February 2014. www.bbc.co.uk/news/uk-26324570. See also 'Yarl's Wood: Six sex assault allegations investigated', *BBC News*, 15 July 2016. www.bbc.co.uk/news/uk-england-beds-bucks-herts-36804714

36. Ritchie, 'Law enforcement violence against women of color'.

37. Alexandra Topping, 'Sarah Everard murder sparked UK reckoning with male violence, say charities', *Guardian*, 3 March 2022. www.theguardian.com/uk-news/2022/mar/03/sarah-everard-sparked-uk-reckoning-with-male-violence-say-charities

38. 'Workers launch the first ever UK trade union group for workers in the Violence Against Women And Girls (VAWG) and Gender-Based Violence (GBV) sector', *UVW*, November 2019. www.uvwunion.org.uk/en/news/2019/11/workers-launch-trade-union-group-for-gbv-vawg-sectors/

39. Holly Chant, 'Hundreds protest plans to move Hackney domestic abuse charity into "unsuitable premises"', *Hackney Gazette*, 13 July 2020. www.hackneygazette.co.uk/news/hundreds-protest-plans-to-move-hackney-domestic-violence-charity-3666144

THESIS 7

1. Simon Childs, 'Guess how much cops spent kicking 4 people out of a Russian oligarch's mansion', *Vice. Com*, 13 May 2022. www.vice.com/en/article/wxdvqz/russian-mansion-occupied-police-cost

2. Stanley H. Palmer, *Police and Protest in England and Ireland, 1780–1850*, Cambridge: Cambridge University Press, 1988.

3. George F.E. Rudé, 'The Gordon Riots: A study of the rioters and their victims', *Transactions Of The Royal Historical Society* 6, 1956, pp. 93–114. doi:10.2307/3678842. See also Charles Tilly and George Rude, 'The crowd in history: A study of popular disturbances in France and England 1730–1848', *American Sociological Review* 30(4), 1965, pp. 604. doi:10.2307/2091357, and Peter Linebaugh, *The London Hanged*, London: Verso, 2003.

4. Jerry White, 'The history of riots in London shows that persistent inequality and injustice is always likely to breed periodic violent uprisings. | British politics and policy at

LSE', *LSE Blog*, 25 October 2011. https://blogs.lse.ac.uk/politicsandpolicy/london-riot-history/

5. Palmer, *Police and Protest in England and Ireland, 1780–1850*.
6. Ibid. Also, Linebaugh, *The London Hanged*.
7. Linebaugh, *The London Hanged*.
8. Joseph Kay, 'Intakes: Communities, commodities and class in the August 2011 riots', *Libcom.Org*, 17 November 2011. https://libcom.org/article/intakes-communities-commodities-and-class-august-2011-riots
9. Andy Gregory, 'Bristol Kill the Bill protester found guilty of arson on night police station attacked', *Independent*, 7 February 2022. www.independent.co.uk/news/uk/home-news/bristol-kill-the-bill-conviction-b2009573.html. See also Vala Z. Francis, 'A Kill the Bill protester's court case is all the evidence you need for police abolition', *Novara Media*, 14 February 2022. https://novaramedia.com/2022/02/14/a-kill-the-bill-protesters-court-case-is-all-the-evidence-you-need-for-police-abolition/
10. Linebaugh, *The London Hanged*.
11. 'Prisons data', Ministry Of Justice, 2022. https://data.justice.gov.uk/prisons
12. Diane Taylor, 'Jailing of most mothers for non-violent crimes should stop, says report', *Guardian*, 25 October 2021. www.theguardian.com/society/2021/oct/25/jailing-of-most-mothers-for-non-violent-crimes-should-stop-says-report
13. Linebaugh, *The London Hanged*.
14. Stella Akua-Mensah, 'Abolition must include psychiatry', *Disability Visibility Project*, 2020. https://disabilityvisibilityproject.com/2020/07/22/abolition-must-include-psychiatry/. Also, Liat Ben-Moshe, *Decarcerating Disability: Deinstitutionalization and Prison Abolition*, Minneapolis MA: University of Minnesota Press, 2020.
15. Linebaugh, *The London Hanged*.
16. Midnight Notes Collective, 'The delivery of Newgate 6 June 1780', *Libcom.Org.*, 1985. https://libcom.org/article/delivery-newgate-6-june-1780

17. Ibid. Also, Linebaugh, *The London Hanged*.

18. Midnight Notes Collective, 'The delivery of Newgate 6 June 1780'. Also, Linebaugh, *The London Hanged*.

19. Jenny Bourne, 'Mental health and black custody police deaths', Institute Of Race Relations, 2021. https://irr.org.uk/article/mental-health-police-deaths/

20. Elish Angiolini, 'Report of the independent review of deaths and serious incidents in police custody', London, 2017, p. 33. https://assets.publishing.service.gov.uk/government/uploads/system/uploads/attachment_data/file/655401/Report_of_Angiolini_Review_ISBN_Accessible.pdf

21. Campaign for Psychiatric Abolition, 'There is no abolition without anti-psychiatry: The fight for psychiatric abolition', *Dope Magazine*, 2022, p. 17.

22. Frantz Fanon, *The Wretched Of The Earth* (translated by Constance Farrington). London: Penguin, 1967. See also Jonathan M. Metzl, *The Protest Psychosis*, Boston, MA: Beacon Press, 2014.

23. Palmer, *Police and Protest in England and Ireland, 1780–1850*. Also, Linebaugh, *The London Hanged*.

24. Randall Williams, 'A state of permanent exception: The birth of modern policing in colonial capitalism', *Interventions* 5(3), 2003, pp. 322–44. doi:10.1080/1369801032000135602

25. Palmer, *Police and Protest in England and Ireland, 1780–1850*.

26. Carole Boyce Davies, *Left of Karl Marx: The Political Life of Black Communist Claudia Jones*, Durham, NC: Duke University Press, 2008.

27. Claudia Jones, 'A people's art is the genesis of their freedom' in Carole Boyce Davies (ed) *Claudia Jones: Beyond Containment*. Banbury: Ayebia Clarke Publishing, 2011.

28. Marika Sherwood, Donald Hinds and Colin Prescod, *Claudia Jones: A Life In Exile*, London: Lawrence & Wishart, 1999.

29. Andrew Marr, *The Making of Modern Britain*, London: Macmillian, 2009.

30. Sarah Glynn, 'East End immigrants and the battle for housing: a comparative study of political mobilisation in the Jewish and Bengali communities', *Journal Of Historical Geography* 31(3), 2005, pp. 528–45. doi:10.1016/j. jhg.2004.07.019

31. David Rosenberg, *Rebel Footprints: A Guide to Uncovering London's Radical History*, London: Pluto, 2015.

32. Danny Dorling and Sally Tomlinson, *Rule Britannia: Brexit and the End of Empire*, London: Biteback, 2019.

33. Zaina Alibhai, 'Unemployment at lowest level since 1974 as UK wages fall sharply', *Independent*, 17 May 2022. www.independent.co.uk/news/uk/home-news/uk-unemployment-wages-ons-b2080717.html

34. Richard Partington, 'UK households face biggest fall in living standards since 1950s, say experts', *Guardian*, 26 February 2022. www.theguardian.com/business/2022/feb/26/uk-households-face-biggest-fall-in-living-standards-since-1950s-say-experts

THESIS 8

1. Anita Mureithi, 'Why isn't Sabina Nessa getting the attention Sarah Everard did?', *Open Democracy*, 2021. www.opendemocracy.net/en/opendemocracyuk/why-isnt-sabina-nessa-getting-the-attention-sarah-everard-did/

2. Aviah Sarah Day, 'We must stop comparing Sabina Nessa's murder with Sarah Everard's', *Novara Media*, 23 September 2021. https://novaramedia.com/2021/09/23/we-must-stop-comparing-sabina-nessas-murder-with-sarah-everards/

3. Azfar Shafi and Ilyas Nagdee, *Race to the Bottom: Reclaiming Antiracism*, London: Pluto, 2022.

4. Robinson, *Black Marxism: The Making of the Black Radical Tradition*.

5. Neil Faulkner, *A Radical History of the World*, London: Pluto, 2013. See also Mark Neocleous, *A Critical Theory of Police Power: The Fabrication of the Social Order*, London: Verso, 2000, and Jason Hickel, *The Divide: A Brief Guide to*

Global Inequality and Its Solutions, London: William Heinemann, 2017.

6. Silvia Federici, *Caliban and the Witch*, London: Penguin, 2004.

7. Hickel, *The Divide*.

8. Neocleous, *A Critical Theory of Police Power*.

9. Liam Geraghty, 'The "archaic" Vagrancy Act is officially being scrapped after 200 years', *The Big Issue*, 22 February 2022. www.bigissue.com/news/the-vagrancy-act-will-be-scrapped-government-confirms/

10. Keith Laybourn, *A History Of British Trade Unionism, c. 1770–1990*, Stroud: Alan Sutton, 1997.

11. Emma Dabiri, *What White People Can Do Next: From Allyship to Coalition*, London: Penguin, 2021.

12. Peter Linebaugh and Marcus Rediker, *The Many-Headed Hydra: The Hidden History of the Revolutionary Atlantic*, London: Verso, 2000. See also Theodore W. Allen, *The Invention of the White Race*, London: Verso, 1994.

13. Jacqueline Battalora, *Birth of a White Nation: The Invention of White People and Its Relevance Today*, London: Routledge, 2021.

14. Linebaugh and Rediker, *The Many-Headed Hydra*.

15. Joseph Douglas Deal III, *Race and Class in Colonial Virginia: Indians, Englishmen, and Africans on the Eastern Shore during the Seventeenth Century*, New York: Garland Press, 1993. See also Linebaugh and Rediker, *The Many-Headed Hydra*.

16. Dabiri, *What White People Can Do Next*.

17. Andrew Marvell, 'Strange News from Virginia; Being a Full and True Account of Life and Death of Nathanial Bacon, Esquire' (London, 1677), cited in Linebaugh and Rediker, *The Many-Headed Hydra*, p. 136.

18. Aphra Behn, 'The Widow Rantero (1690), cited in Linebaugh and Rediker, *The Many-Headed Hydra*.

19. Linebaugh and Rediker, *The Many-Headed Hydra*.

20. Dabiri, *What White People Can Do Next*.

21. Akala, *Natives: Race and Class in the Ruins of Empire*, London: Hodder & Stoughton, 2019. See also Allen, *The Invention of the White Race*.

22. Eric Williams, *Capitalism And Slavery*, 3rd ed., Chapel Hill, NC: University of North Carolina Press, 2021. See also Allen, *The Invention of the White Race*, and Linebaugh and Rediker, *The Many-Headed Hydra*.

23. Williams, *Capitalism and Slavery*.

24. Peter Gessner, Rene Lichtman and Stewart Bird, *Finally Got The News: League Of Revolutionary Black Workers*, Film, 1970.

25. Sarah Kwei, 'Focus E15 mums have fought for the right to a home. This is only the start', *Guardian*, 5 October 2014. www.theguardian.com/commentisfree/2014/oct/05/focus-e15-mums-fight-for-right-to-home. See also 'Focus E15 Campaign', Bishopsgate Institute, 2017. www.bishopsgate.org.uk/collections/focus-e15-campaign

26. 'Carpenters Estate', *Estate Watch*, 2022. www.cstatewatch.london/casestudies/carpenters/

27. Alana Lentin, *Why Race Still Matters*, Cambridge: Polity, 2020.

28. Laybourn, *A History of British Trade Unionism*. See also 'History of the establishment of the London Metropolitan Police', *Drawn Out Thinking*, 2018. https://drawnoutthinking.net/2018/03/02/history-of-the-establishment-of-the-london-metropolitan-police/

29. Tanzil Chowdhury, 'From the colony to the metropole: Race, policing and the colonial boomerang' in Koshka Duff (ed.) *Abolishing The Police*, London: Dog Section Press, 2021.

30. Williams, 'A state of permanent exception'.

31. Palmer, *Police and Protest in England and Ireland, 1780–1850*. See also Robbie McVeigh and Bill Rolston, *Ireland, Colonialism and the Unfinished Revolution*, Belfast: Beyond the Pale Books, 2021, Williams, 'A state of permanent excep-

tion', and James Connolly, *Labour in Irish History*, London: Forgotten Books, 2018.

32. Palmer, *Police and Protest in England and Ireland, 1780–1850*.
33. Williams, 'A state of permanent exception'.
34. Palmer, *Police and Protest in England and Ireland, 1780–1850*.
35. Williams, 'A state of permanent exception'.
36. Robert Brendan McDowell, *Ireland in the Age of Imperialism and Revolution, 1760–1801*, Oxford: Oxford University Press, 1979. Also Williams, 'A state of permanent exception'.
37. David Lloyd, *Nationalism And Minor Literature*, Berkeley: University of California Press, 1988. Also, Chowdhury, 'From the colony to the metropole'.
38. Williams, 'A state of permanent exception'.
39. McVeigh and Rolston, *Ireland, Colonialism and the Unfinished Revolution*.
40. Williams, 'A state of permanent exception'.
41. Chowdhury, 'From the colony to the metropole'.
42. John Lonsdale, David M. Anderson and David Killingray, 'Policing the empire: Government, authority, and control, 1830–1940', *International Journal Of African Historical Studies* 27(2), 1994, p. 374. doi:10.2307/221031
43. Etannibi E.O. Alemika, 'Colonialism, state and policing in Nigeria', *Crime, Law And Social Change* 20(3), 1993, pp. 187–219. doi:10.1007/bf01308450
44. John Moore, 'Protecting the property of slavers: London's first state funded police force', *Abolitionist Futures*, 2022. https://abolitionistfutures.com/latest-news/protecting-the-property-of-slavers-londons-first-state-funded-police-force
45. Linebough, *The London Hanged*. See also fgold1, 'London's New Metropolitan Police Force', *Landmarks In London History*, 1 December 2022. https://landmarks inlondonhistory.wordpress.com/2017/12/01/londons-new-metropolitan-police-force/

46. R.F. Symes and B. Young, 'Minerals of Northern England', Edinburgh and London: Natural History Museum & National Museums Scotland, 2008.
47. Patrick Colquhoun, *Treatise on the Police of the Metropolis*, 1795. Accessed online at: www.gutenberg.org/files/35650/35650-h/35650-h.htm
48. Moore, 'Protecting the property of slavers'.
49. Williams, 'A state of permanent exception'.
50. Moore, 'Protecting the property of slavers'.
51. Michael Brogden, *The Police: Autonomy and Consent*, Kent: Elsevier Science, 2014.
52. James Trafford, *The Empire at Home*, London: Pluto, 2020.
53. Moore, 'Policing by consent'.
54. J.M. Moore, 'Is the Empire coming home?', *Papers from the British Criminology Conference* 14(2014), pp. 31–48. www.britsoccrim.org/new/volume14/pbcc_2014_moore.pdf
55. Henry Schwarz, *Constructing The Criminal Tribe In Colonial India*, Chichester, West Sussex: Wiley-Blackwell, 2010.
56. Trafford, *The Empire at Home*.
57. Jasbinder Nijjar, 'Echoes of empire: Excavating the colonial roots of Britain's "War on Gangs"', *Social Justice* 45(2), 2018, pp. 47–162.
58. Patrick Williams, 'Being Matrixed: the (over)policing of gang suspects in London', *Stopwatch*, 2018. www.stop-watch.org/what-we-do/research/being-matrixed-the-overpolicing-of-gang-suspects-in-london/
59. Matthew Hughes, 'Demobilised soldiers and colonial control: The British Police in Mandate Palestine and after', *Journal Of Modern European History* 13(2), 2015, pp. 268–84. doi:10.17104/1611-8944-2015-2-268
60. George Orwell in his 1934 novel *Burmese Days* and in his 1931 short story tells some of this story of colonial rule, via Hughes, 'Demobilised soldiers and colonial control'.
61. Memoir, 'Fifty Days with a Company in Palestine', 1, 82/24/1, Faviell Papers, IWMD; C. Evans, Lever Arch File 55, Thames TV Material, Imperial War Museum Film Archive,

London (IWMFA); Geoffrey Morton, 12960/6, IWMSA. In Hughes, 'Demobilised soldiers and colonial control'. See also Hughes, 'Demobilised soldiers and colonial control'.

62. Ilan Pappe, *The Ethnic Cleansing of Palestine*, London: One World, 2007.

63. Ronit Lentin, *Traces of Racial Exception: Racializing Israeli Settler Colonialism*. London: Bloomsbury, 2018.

64. Jeff Halper, 'What Do The Israelis Teach Western Police Forces?', *Jewish Socialist*, 28 October 2020. www.jewishsocialist.org.uk/features/item/what-do-the-israelis-teach-western-police-forces

65. Chowdhury, 'From the colony to the metropole'.

66. Ashley Bohrer and Andrés Fabián Henao Castro, 'A global people's history of police exchanges: Settler colonialism, capitalism and the intersectionality of struggles', in Kojo Koram (ed.) *The War on Drugs and the Global Colour Line*, London: Pluto, 2019, pp. 141–55.

67. Jewish Voice for Peace, *Deadly Exchange: The Dangerous Consequences Of American Law Enforcement Trainings In Israel*, Berkeley, CA: Jewish Voice for Peace, 2018.

68. Bohrer and Henao Castro, 'A people's history of police exchanges'.

THESIS 9

1. Natalie Gil, 'Robbed of their futures: How austerity cuts hit young people hardest', *Guardian*, 17 November 2014. www.theguardian.com/education/2014/nov/17/robbed-of-their-futures-how-austerity-cuts-hit-young-people-hardest. See also Sean Coughlan, '"Education, Education, Education"', *BBC News*, 14 May 2007. http://news.bbc.co.uk/1/hi/education/6564933.stm

2. 'Press Release: Monitoring social mobility 2013 To 2020', London: Social Mobility Commission, 2020. See also Patrick Butler, 'Social mobility in decline in Britain, official survey finds', *Guardian*, 21 January 2020. www.theguardian.

com/society/2020/jan/21/social-mobility-decline-britain-official-survey-finds, and Lee Elliot Major and Stephen Machin, 'Covid-19 and social mobility. A series of background briefings on the policy issues arising from the Covid-19 pandemic', London: LSE Centre for Economic Performance, 2022. https://cep.lse.ac.uk/pubs/download/cepcovid-19-004.pdf

3. Patrick Butler, 'Crisis in children's services in England is shocking if not surprising', *Guardian*, 11 August 2021. www.theguardian.com/society/2021/aug/11/crisis-in-childrens-services-in-england-is-shocking-if-not-surprising. See also Sally Weale, 'Young adults most pessimistic on UK social mobility – poll', *Guardian*, 11 December 2018. www.theguardian.com/society/2018/dec/11/young-adults-most-pessimistic-on-uk-social-mobility-poll

4. Juliet Jowit, 'Strivers v shirkers: the language of the welfare debate', *Guardian*, 8 January 2013. www.theguardian.com/politics/2013/jan/08/strivers-shirkers-language-welfare

5. Claire McNeil et al., 'No longer "managing": The rise of working poverty and fixing Britain's broken social settlement', London: Institute for Public Policy Research, 2021.

6. 'Mayor And PCCs call for school "off-rolling" to be outlawed', London Assembly, 2019. www.london.gov.uk/press-releases/mayoral/mayor-and-pccs-call-for-end-to-off-rolling

7. 'The NEU case against academisation', National Education Union (NEU), 2021. https://neu.org.uk/policy/neu-case-against-academisation

8. Jess Staufenberg, '"It takes too long to get support": Alarm over rising primary school exclusions', *Guardian*, 18 September 2021. www.theguardian.com/education/2021/sep/18/alarm-over-rising-primary-school-exclusions-england

9. Jessica Perera, 'How Black working class youth are criminalised and excluded in the English school system'. London: Institute of Race Relations, 2020. See also Jess Staufenberg, 'Number of pupils in private alternative provision soars', *Schools Week*, 2019. https://schoolsweek.

co.uk/investigation-number-of-pupils-in-private-alternative-provision-soars/, and Angela Rayner, 'Number of primary school children in pupil referral units more than doubled since 2011', Labour Party, 2019. https://labour.org.uk/press/number-primary-school-children-pupil-referral-units-doubled-since-2011/

10. '96% of pupils in alternative provision fail GCSEs', *Tes Magazine*, 11 May 2020. www.tes.com/magazine/archive/96-pupils-alternative-provision-fail-gcses

11. '"What about the other 29?" and other faqs', No More Exclusions (NME), 20 January 2022, p. 26. https://nomore-exclusions.com/wp-content/uploads/2022/01/nme.20.01.pdf

12. Kim Williams, Vea Papadopoulou and Natalie Booth, 'Prisoners' childhood and family backgrounds results from the Surveying Prisoner Crime Reduction (SPCR) longitudinal cohort study of prisoners', London: Ministry of Justice, 2012.

13. Aamna Mohdin, '"School-to-prison pipeline": Youth justice services failing black boys', *Guardian*, 21 October 2021. www.theguardian.com/society/2021/oct/21/youth-justice-services-still-failing-black-and-mixed-heritage-boys-finds-report?fr=operanews

14. Janet Murray, 'FE students stand up for their rights', *Guardian*, 15 March 2011. www.theguardian.com/education/2011/mar/15/further-education-students-get-political

15. Myers, *Student Revolt.*

16. Richard Edwards and Tom Whitehead, 'Student tuition fee protest: Scotland Yard expected a march of 5,000 and officers had no riot gear', *Telegraph*, 11 November 2010. www.telegraph.co.uk/education/universityeducation/8124838/Student-tuition-fee-protest-Scotland-Yard-expected-a-march-of-5000-and-officers-had-no-riot-gear.html. See also Paul Lewis et al., 'Student protest over fees turns violent', *Guardian*, 10 November 2010. www.theguardian.com/education/2010/nov/10/student-protest-fees-violent

17. J. Woodcock, 'The trajectory of the 2010 student movement in the UK: From student activism to strikes', in A. Choudry and S. Vally (eds) *The University and Social Justice Struggles Across the Globe*, London: Pluto, 2020, pp. 25–40.

18. Rob Evans and Mustafa Khalili, 'Police tried to spy on Cambridge students, secret footage shows', *Guardian*, 14 November 2013. www.theguardian.com/uk-news/2013/nov/14/police-cambridge-university-secret-footage

19. 'Police use CS spray and taser at Warwick University protest', *Channel4News*, 4 December 2014. www.channel4.com/news/cs-spray-taser-police-warwick-university-student-protest

20. Dulcie Lee and Ben Jackson, 'Thousands of students attend "cops off campus" demo – with police so far nowhere to be seen', *Independent*, 11 December 2013. www.independent.co.uk/student/news/thousands-of-students-attend-cops-off-campus-demo-with-police-so-far-nowhere-to-be-seen-8998440.html

21. Myers, *Student Revolt*.

22. Adam Elliott-Cooper, '"Britain Is Not Innocent": A Netpol report on the policing of Black Lives Matter protests in Britain's towns and cities in 2020', London: Netpol, 2020.

23. Ibid., p. 23.

24. Ibid., p. 4.

25. Damien Gayle, 'Injured boy "stopped and searched" by Met officer he asked for help', *Guardian*, 1 July 2020. www.theguardian.com/world/2020/jul/01/injured-boy-stopped-and-searched-by-met-officer-he-asked-for-help

26. Siham Ali, 'How policing is being sewn into the fabric of British schools', *New Statesman*, July 2021. www.newstatesman.com/politics/2021/07/how-policing-being-sewn-fabric-british-schools

27. Nazia Parveen, Niamh McIntyre and Tobi Thomas, 'UK police forces deploy 683 officers in schools with some poorer areas targeted', *Guardian*, 25 March 2021. www.theguardian.com/education/2021/mar/25/uk-police-forces-deploy-683-officers-in-schools

28. Laura Connelly, Roxy Legane and Remi Joseph-Salisbury, 'Decriminalise the classroom: A community response to police in Greater Manchester's schools', Kids of Colour and Northern Police Monitoring Project, 2020.

29. Jane Dalton, 'Police officer who assaulted autistic boy at special-needs school avoids jail', *Independent*, 9 September 2021. www.independent.co.uk/news/uk/crime/police-officer-assault-autistic-boy-attack-school-b1917378.html

30. Iqbal and Topping, 'The shameful strip search of Child Q'.

31. Owen Bowcott, 'Riots led to 1,400 imprisoned or held on remand, figures show', *Guardian*, 28 June 2012. www.theguardian.com/uk/2012/jun/28/riots-prison-figures

32. Aamna Modhin and Jessica Murray, '"The Mark Duggan case was a catalyst": The 2011 England riots 10 years on', *Guardian*, 30 July 2021. www.theguardian.com/uk-news/2021/jul/30/2011-uk-riots-mark-duggan

33. Myers, *Student Revolt*.

34. Kay, 'Intakes: Communities, commodities and class in the August 2011 riots'.

35. John Drury et al., 'Re-Reading The 2011 English Riots', London: Economic and Social Research Council (ESRC), 2019, pp. 9–10.

36. Paul Lewis et al., 2011. 'Reading the riots: Investigating England's summer of disorder', London: London School of Economics (LSE), 2011, p. 11.

37. Ibid., pp. 5–25.

38. Sadiya Akram, 'Recognizing the 2011 United Kingdom riots as political protest: A theoretical framework based on agency, habitus and the preconscious', *British Journal of Criminology* 54(3), 2014, pp. 375–392. https://doi.org/10.1093/bjc/azu013

39. Office for National Statistics, 'Confidence in the local police'.

40. Alexandra Topping, 'Khadija Saye: Artist on cusp of recognition when she died in Grenfell', *Guardian*, 17 June 2017. www.theguardian.com/uk-news/2017/jun/17/khadija-

saye-artist-was-on-cusp-of-recognition-when-she-died-in-grenfell

41. Ibid.

42. Nadine El-Enany, 'Before Grenfell: British immigration law and production of colonial spaces', in Dan Bulley, Jenny Edkins and Nadine El-Enany (eds), *After Grenfell: Violence, Resistance and Response*, London: Pluto Press, 2019.

43. Aamna Mohdin, '"We couldn't be silent": the new generation behind Britain's anti-racism protests', *Guardian*, 29 July 2020. www.theguardian.com/uk-news/2020/jul/29/new-generation-behind-britain-anti-racism-protests-young-black-activists-equality

44. David Harvey, 'Feral capitalism hits the streets', *Reading Marx's Capital*, 11 August 2011. http://davidharvey.org/2011/08/feral-capitalism-hits-the-streets. See also Ambalavaner Sivanandan, 'This is not the end of rebellion – it is the beginning', *Socialist Worker*, 2011. https://socialistworker.co.uk/comment/a-sivanandan-this-is-not-the-end-of-rebellion-it-is-the-beginning/

45. Jaye Gaskia, 'Understanding Nigeria's #Endsars Movement', *Rs21*, 26 October 2020. www.rs21.org.uk/2020/10/26/understanding-nigerias-endsars-movement/

46. 'Rethinking #Endsars: A revolution postponed?', Podcast, *The Nigerian Scam*, 2021. https://open.spotify.com/episode/5bFkhyLTo1S5ygekxxkueM

47. Ani Kayode Somtochukwu, 'The movement to #Endsars', Podcast. *Millenials Are Killing Capitalism*, 2020. https://podtail.com/podcast/millennials-are-killing-capitalism/the-movement-to-endsars-with-ani-kayode-somtochukw/

48. 'Rethinking #Endsars: A revolution postponed?', Podcast.

49. Saeed Husaini, 'Nigeria's #EndSARS protests aren't just opposing police brutality – they're opposing neoliberalism', *Jacobin*, November 2020. https://jacobinmag.com/2020/11/nigeria-end-sars-protests-police-brutality-neoliberalism

50. Sada Malumfashi, 'Nigeria's SARS: A brief history of the Special Anti-Robbery Squad', *Al Jazeera*, 22 October 2020.

www.aljazeera.com/features/2020/10/22/sars-a-brief-history-of-a-rogue-unit

51. 'SARS: Nigeria "rogue" police unit banned from stop and search', *BBC News*, 4 October 2020. www.bbc.co.uk/news/world-africa-54407397

52. 'In Nigeria police continue to torture with impunity', *Amnesty International*, 26 June 2020. www.amnesty.org/en/latest/news/2020/06/nigeria-horrific-reign-of-impunity-by-sars-makes-mockery-of-anti-torture-law/

53. Somtochukwu, 'The movement To #EndSARS'.

54. Benjamin Maiangwa, 'How the British colonial enterprise wired violence into Nigeria', *Quartz Africa*, 21 October 2020. https://qz.com/africa/1920769/the-british-colonial-enterprise-wired-violence-into-nigeria/

55. Alemika, 'Colonialism, state and policing in Nigeria'.

56. Samuel Fury Childs Daly, 'Nigerians got their abusive SARS police force abolished – but elation soon turned to frustration', *Policing Insight*, 8 January 2021. https://policinginsight.com/features/opinion/nigerians-got-their-abusive-sars-police-force-abolished-but-elation-soon-turned-to-frustration/

57. Somtochukwu, 'The movement To #EndSARS'.

58. Chidi Emenike, '#Endsars protest: Lagos loses N234 million to tollgates closure', *Nairametrics*, 19 October 2020. https://nairametrics.com/2020/10/19/endsars-protest-lagos-loses-n234million-to-tollgates-closure/?amp

59. Emmanuel Akinwoto, '"The lights went out and the shooting started": #Endsars protesters find no justice one year on', *Guardian*, 1 November 2021. www.theguardian.com/global-development/2021/nov/01/nigeria-end-sars-protesters-find-no-justice-one-year-on. See also 'Nigeria: The Lekki Toll Gate massacre – new investigative timeline', *Amnesty International*, 28 October 2020. www.amnesty.org/en/latest/news/2020/10/nigeria-the-lekki-toll-gate-massacre-new-investigative-timeline/

60. Gaskia, 'Understanding Nigeria's #Endsars Movement'.

61. 'Five demands from #Endsars protesters', *Vanguard Nigeria*, 12 October 2020. www.vanguardngr.com/2020/10/five-demands-from-endsars-protesters/

62. Adam Forrest, 'End SARS protests: UK government admits it did train and supply equipment to Nigeria's "brutal" police unit', *Independent*, 30 October 2020. www.independent.co.uk/news/uk/politics/sars-nigeria-police-protests-uk-government-training-equipment-b1424447.html

63. 'SARS ban: Nigeria abolishes loathed federal special police unit', *BBC News*, 11 October 2020. www.bbc.com/news/world-africa-54499497

64. 'End Swat: Nigerians reject police unit replacing hated Sars', *BBC News*, 14 October 2020. www.bbc.com/news/world-africa-54531449

65. Lizzie Dearden, 'New police watchdog launches to replace IPCC and ensure "greater accountability to public"', *Independent*, 8 January 2018. www.independent.co.uk/news/uk/crime/police-watchdog-launch-iopc-replace-ipcc-independent-office-for-police-conduct-uk-public-accountability-a8147696.html

66. Home Office, 'The Police Complaints Procedure: A survey of complainants' views', London: Her Majesty's Stationery Unit, 1987. https://webarchive.nationalarchives.gov.uk/ukgwa/20101208194745/http%3A//rds.homeoffice.gov.uk/rds/pdfs05/hors93.pdf

67. Bernard Dayo, 'Can Nigeria's #EndSARS protests lead to police abolition?', *Al Jazeera*, 23 October 2020. www.aljazeera.com/features/2020/10/23/can-nigerias-endsars-protests-lead-to-abolishing-the-police

68. 'No justice for victims of police brutality one year after #Endsars protests', *Amnesty International*, 20 October 2021. www.amnesty.org/en/latest/news/2021/10/nigeria-no-justice-for-victims-of-police-brutality-one-year-after-endsars-protests/. See also Makua Adimora, 'A year on, women still picking up pieces from #EndSARS protests', *Al Jazeera*, 20 October 2021. www.aljazeera.com/news/

2021/10/20/a-year-on-women-still-picking-up-pieces-from-endsars-protests

69. Tarela Juliet Ike, 'Nigerian police: Why improving public trust has proven difficult', *The Conversation*, 2022. https://theconversation.com/nigerian-police-why-improving-public-trust-has-proven-difficult-163835

70. Dayo, 'Can Nigeria's #EndSARS protests lead to police abolition?'.

71. Donna Murch, 'Watts, Lowndes County, Oakland: The founding of the Black Panther Party for self defense', *Verso Blog*, 15 October 2016. www.versobooks.com/blogs/2882-watts-lowndes-county-oakland-the-founding-of-the-black-panther-party-for-self-defense

72. Elaine Brown, *A Taste of Power: A Black Woman's Story*, New York: Pantheon, 1992.

73. Anonymous, 'Five-nil to the BLM', *LRB Blog*, 15 June 2020. www.lrb.co.uk/blog/2020/june/five-nil-to-the-blm

74. Dan Sabbagh, 'Campaigners fear far-right "defence" of statues such as Churchill's', *Guardian*, 10 June 2020. www.theguardian.com/world/2020/jun/10/far-right-protesters-plan-defence-of-statues-such-as-churchills

75. Ben Quinn, 'Man rescued by UK Black Lives Matter protester is ex-police officer', *Guardian*, 18 June 2020. www.theguardian.com/world/2020/jun/18/man-rescued-by-uk-black-lives-matter-protester-is-ex-police-officer

76. Nosheen Iqbal, 'Interview: Patrick Hutchinson: "My natural instinct is to protect the vulnerable"', *Guardian*, 6 December 2020. www.theguardian.com/world/2020/dec/06/patrick-hutchinson-black-lives-matter-protest-london-faces-2020

THESIS 10

1. Bhattacharyya et al., *Empire's Endgame*.

2. Thomas Volscho, 'The revenge of the capitalist class: Crisis, the legitimacy of capitalism and the restoration of finance

from the 1970s to present', *Critical Sociology* 43(2), 2016, pp. 249–66. doi:10.1177/0896920515589003

3. Nadine El-Enany, *Bordering Britain: Race, Law and Empire*, Manchester: Manchester University Press, 2020.

4. Daniel Trilling, '"Foreign criminals" are just an excuse: The Tories are trying to take away rights from all of us', *Guardian*, 21 December 2021. www.theguardian.com/commentisfree/2021/dec/21/foreign-criminals-tories-human-rights-act. See also Luke De Noronha, 'Deporting "foreign criminals" in the middle of the night doesn't make us safer', *UCL Blog*, August 2021. www.ucl.ac.uk/news/2021/aug/opinion-deporting-foreign-criminals-middle-night-doesnt-make-us-safer

5. Alpa Parmar, 'Arresting (non)citizenship: The policing migration nexus of nationality, race and criminaliza-tion', *Oxford Law Faculty Blog*, March 2020. www.law.ox.ac.uk/research-subject-groups/centre-criminology/centreborder-criminologies/blog/2020/03/arresting

6. Luke De Noronha, *Deporting Black Britons*, Manches-ter: Manchester University Press, 2020, pp. 16–17 and pp. 80–81.

7. Sally Patterson, 'Eight drivers arrested and 22 vehicles seized in Stoke Newington crackdown', *Hackney Gazette*, 25 January 2022. www.hackneygazette.co.uk/news/crime/stoke-newington-moped-drivers-targeted-by-home-of-fice-8644678. See also Ruby Lott-Lavigna, 'UK cops boast of detaining key workers for immigration checks', *Vice.com*, 19 May 2021. www.vice.com/en/article/m7evzy/uk-cops-boast-of-detaining-key-workers-for-immigration-checks

8. Derek Humphry, *Police Power and Black People*, London: Panther Books, 1972, p. 81.

9. Ambalavaner Sivanandan, 'Race, class and the state: The Black experience in Britain', *Race & Class* 17(4), 1976, pp. 347–68. doi:10.1177/030639687601700401

10. El-Enany, *(B)ordering Britain*, pp. 118, 119.

11. John Smith, *Imperialism in the 21st Century: The Globalisation of Production, Super-Exploitation and the Crisis of Capitalism*, New York: Monthly Review Press, 2016.

12. Rikvah Brown, 'Couriers stunt Dalston's gentrification: The police and council want them gone', *Novara Media*, 17 May 2022. https://novaramedia.com/2022/05/17/couriers-stunt-dalstons-gentrification-the-police-and-council-want-them-gone/

13. Ibid.

14. 'IWGB courier's statements on Deliveroo's partnership agreements with GMB', Independent Workers of Great Britain, 2022. https://iwgb.org.uk/en/post/deliveroo-gmb/

15. Matthew Taylor and Robert Booth, 'G4S guards found not guilty of manslaughter of Jimmy Mubenga', *Guardian*, 16 December 2014. www.theguardian.com/uk-news/2014/dec/16/g4s-guards-found-not-guilty-manslaughter-jimmy-mubenga

16. 'Jury rules Jimmy Mubenga was unlawfully killed', *Inquest*, 2013. www.inquest.org.uk/jimmy-mubenga-jury-conclusions

17. Taylor and Booth, 'G4S guards found not guilty of manslaughter of Jimmy Mubenga'.

18. 'What is happening with the Borders Bill?', Joint Council For The Welfare Of Immigrants, 2022. www.jcwi.org.uk/blog/what-is-happening-with-the-borders-bill

THESIS 11

1. Quoted in Davis et al., *Abolition. Feminism. Now.*

2. Ryan and Ward, 'Prison abolition in the UK'.

3. Mick Ryan, *The Acceptable Pressure Group*, Farnborough, Teakfield, 978.

4. R. Totale, 'PROP '72: The history of a UK prisoners' union', 29 September 2019. https://libcom.org/article/prop-72-history-uk-prisoners-union. See also Mike Fitzgerald,

Prisoners in Revolt, Harmondsworth: Penguin, 1977, and Ryan and Ward, 'Prison abolition in the UK'.

5. *Abolitionist Futures*, 'History of UK abolition'.
6. Ramzani Mwamba, '30 years on – A timeline of the events of the Strangeways riots', *Manchester Evening News*, 12 April 2020. www.manchestereveningnews.co.uk/news/gallery/30-years-timeline-events-strangeways-18066166
7. Nicki Jameson and Eric Allison, *Strangeways 1990*, London: Larkin, 1995.
8. Stephen Akpabio-Klementowski, Joe Sim, Eamonn Carrabine and Charlie Weinberg, *After Strangeways: The Past, Present, And Future Of Prisons*, Video, 2021. www.crimeandjustice.org.uk/news/2021-03-01/watch-video-after-strangeways-webinar-2
9. Jameson and Allison, *Strangeways 1990*.
10. Alan Lord and Anita Armstrong, *Life In Strangeways – From Riots To Redemption, My 32 Years Behind Bars*, London: John Blake, 2015.
11. Ruth Wilson Gilmore, *Golden Gulag: Prisons, Surplus, Crisis, and Opposition in Globalizing California*, Berkeley, CA: University of California Press, 2007.
12. Jameson and Allison, *Strangeways 1990*.
13. Donald L. Wasson, 'Plebeians', *World History Encyclopedia*, 8 March 2022. www.worldhistory.org/Plebeians/
14. David Belton, *Strangeways: Britain's Toughest Prison Riot*, Video, London: BBC, 2019.
15. Jameson and Allison, *Strangeways 1990*.
16. Mark Williams, quoted in Jameson and Allison, *Strangeways 1990*. See also Lord and Armstrong, *Life in Strangeways*.
17. Jameson and Allison, *Strangeways 1990*.
18. Imogen Tyler, 'Naked protest: The maternal politics of citizenship and revolt', *Citizenship Studies* 17(2), 2013, pp. 211–26. doi:10.1080/13621025.2013.780742. See also Irene Renny and Tom Kemp, 'Hunger for freedom: Campaigning against detention from inside and outside Yarl's Wood', *Novara Media*, 29 April 2018. https://novaramedia.com/2018/04/29/hunger-for-freedom-campaigning-

against-detention-from-inside-and-outside-yarls-wood/, and Amelia Hill, 'More than 3,000 hunger strikes at immigration centres in UK since 2015', *Guardian*, 15 August 2019. www.theguardian.com/uk-news/2019/aug/15/more-than-3000-hunger-strikes-at-immigration-centres-in-uk-since-2015

19. Harmit Athwal, 'Deaths In immigration detention: 1989–2017', Institute Of Race Relations, 2017. https://irr.org.uk/article/deaths-in-immigration-detention-1989-2017/

20. Press Association, 'Serco apologises after dismissals related to Yarl's Wood allegations', *Guardian*, 24 June 2014. www.theguardian.com/business/2014/jun/24/serco-apologises-dismissals-yarls-wood-allegations

21. Renny and Kemp, 'Hunger for freedom'.

22. 'The hunger strikers' demands', *Detained Voices*, 22 February 2018. https://detainedvoices.com/2018/02/22/the-hunger-strikers-demands/

23. Set up in 2006, the SOAS Detainee Support group is a student-led organisation based at the University of London's School of Oriental and African Studies (SOAS).

24. Damien Gayle, 'Stansted 15: No jail for activists convicted of terror-related offences', *Guardian*, 6 February 2019. www.theguardian.com/global/2019/feb/06/stansted-15-rights-campaigners-urge-judge-to-show-leniency

25. Ambalavaner Sivanandan, *From Resistance to Rebellion: Asian and Afro-Caribbean Struggles in Britain in Catching History on the Wing*, London: Pluto, 2008.

26. SOAS Detainee Support and Sisters Uncut, 'How we chose to be heard': Why the women of Yarl's Wood went on hunger strike, and what's next', *inews*, 3 April 2018. https://inews.co.uk/inews-lifestyle/women/women-yarls-wood-hunger-strike-140743

THESIS 12

1. Home Office, 'FACTSHEET: Prevent and Channel – 2021 – Home Office in the media', *Home Office Media*, 18 October

2021. https://homeofficemedia.blog.gov.uk/2021/10/18/factsheet-prevent-and-channel-2021/. Also, 'Population estimates by ethnic group and religion, England and Wales: 2019', London: Office for National Statistics, 2021.

2. Patrick Wintour, 'Cameron vows to "drain the swamp" creating Islamic extremism', *Guardian*, 3 June 2013. www.theguardian.com/politics/2013/jun/03/cameron-recommendations-islamic-extremism

3. John Holmwood and Layla Aitlhadj, 'The people's review of Prevent', Manchester: *Preventwatch*, February 2022. https://peoplesreviewofprevent.org/wp-content/uploads/2022/02/mainreportlatest.pdf

4. 'Blair on London bombings', *BBC News*, 5 May 2005. www.bbc.co.uk/news/av/uk-13301530

5. Arianne Shahvisi, 'We are all police now: Resisting everyday bordering and the hostile environment', in Koshka Duff (ed.) *Abolishing the Police*, London: Dog Section Press, 2021, p. 43.

6. Wintour, 'Cameron vows to "drain the swamp" creating Islamic extremism'.

7. A transcript of the 1978 *World in Action* interview with Thatcher is available here: www.margaretthatcher.org/document/103485

8. Home Office, 'Revised Prevent Duty Guidance'.

9. Rebecca Ratcliffe, 'Teachers made one-third of referrals to Prevent strategy in 2015', *Guardian*, 12 July 2016. www.theguardian.com/uk-news/2016/jul/12/teachers-made-one-third-of-referrals-to-prevent-strategy-in-2015

10. Hannah Al-Othman, 'Catholic school sought terrorism advice over girl, 6, who wore hijab', *The Times*, 8 August 2021. www.thetimes.co.uk/article/catholic-school-sought-terrorism-advice-over-girl-6-who-wore-hijab-2jw8zbph5

11. Diane Taylor, 'Boy, 11, referred to Prevent for wanting to give "alms to the oppressed"', *Guardian*, 27 June 2021. www.theguardian.com/uk-news/2021/jun/27/boy-11-referred-to-prevent-for-wanting-to-give-alms-to-the-oppressed.

See also Joshua Stein and Mark Townsend, 'Muslim boy, 4, was referred to Prevent over game of Fortnite', *Guardian* , 31 January 2021. www.theguardian.com/uk-news/2021/jan/31/muslim-boy-4-was-referred-to-prevent-over-game-of-fortnite

12. Ben Quinn, 'Nursery "raised fears of radicalisation over boy's cucumber drawing" | UK security and counter-terrorism', *Guardian*, 11 March 2016. www.theguardian.com/uk-news/2016/mar/11/nursery-radicalisation-fears-boys-cucumber-drawing-cooker-bomb

13. Holmwood and Atlhadj, 'The people's review of Prevent'. p.23.

14. Ibid., p. 31.

15. Ibid., p. 58.

16. Nicola Bartlett, 'Police support staff reduced by 23,500 officers due to "brutal" Tory cuts', *Mirror*, 27 December 2019. www.mirror.co.uk/news/politics/police-support-staff-reduced-23500-21172926

17. 'Immigration status checks by the NHS: Guidance for overseas patients', London: Department of Health and Social Care (DHSC), 2019. See also UK Health Security Agency, 'Information sharing with the Home Office for unpaid NHS patient debts: Privacy notice', London: Department of Health and Social Care (DHSC), 2019, and Shahvisi, 'We are all police now', pp. 44–46.

18. Home Office, 'Police awarded £11.3m for programmes to prevent domestic abuse crimes', *gov.uk*, 2022. www.gov.uk/government/news/police-awarded-113m-for-programmes-to-prevent-domestic-abuse-crimes

19. Joseph Timan, 'Council tax hike of £22 to pay for police, buses and fire service', *Manchester Evening News*, 29 January 2022. www.manchestereveningnews.co.uk/news/greater-manchester-news/council-tax-hike-22-pay-22917638

20. Jamie Grierson, 'Environment and animal rights activists being referred to Prevent programme', *Guardian*, 21

February 2020. www.theguardian.com/uk-news/2020/feb/21/prevent-environment-animal-activists-referred-extremism. See also Sally Weale and Steven Morris, 'Universities spark free speech row after halting pro-Palestinian events', *Guardian*, 27 February 2017. www.theguardian.com/world/2017/feb/27/universities-free-speech-row-halting-pro-palestinian-events, and 'Palestine And Prevent Referrals', *Preventwatch*, 2021. www.preventwatch.org/palestine-prevent-referrals/

THESIS 13

1. Steve Swann, 'Drill and rap music on trial', *BBC News*, 13 January 2021. www.bbc.co.uk/news/uk-55617706
2. Joint Enterprise Not Guilty by Association (JENGbA), 'The Law', n.d. https://jointenterprise.co/TheLaw.html
3. Lewis Legane and Regis, 'E155 Roxy Legane: Prison sentences for text messages', *The Surviving Society* podcast, 2022. https://soundcloud.com/user-622675754/e155-roxy-legane-prison-sentences-for-text-messages
4. Robin Bunce and Paul Field, 2010. 'Mangrove Nine: The court challenge against police racism in Notting Hill', *Guardian*, 29 November 2010. www.theguardian.com/law/2010/nov/29/mangrove-nine-40th-anniversary; 'Club owner says police told him to "ban" Jamaican music', *BBC News*, 14 March 2016. www.bbc.co.uk/news/newsbeat-35801841.
5. Will Richards, 'Police cancel Fumez The Engineer's London gig 20 minutes before doors', *NME*, 15 November 2021. www.nme.com/news/music/police-cancel-fumez-the-engineers-london-gig-20-minutes-before-doors-3095793. See also Will Richards, 'Pa Salieu says "authorities" have cancelled his Coventry headline show', *NME*, 21 October 2021. www.nme.com/news/music/pa-salieu-says-authorities-have-cancelled-his-coventry-headline-show-3076084

6. Nadine White, '"Offensive attitudes": Anger as London Assembly Tory leader says "Black community has a crime problem"', *Independent*, 28 February 2022. www.independent.co.uk/news/uk/home-news/susan-hall-london-conservatives-black-crime-b2023783.html

7. Nijjar, *Echoes of Empire*.

8. 'Ethnicity and the Criminal Justice System, 2020', London: Office for National Statistics, 2021. See also 'Research report on population estimates by ethnic group and religion', London: Office for National Statistics, 2019.

9. Ministry of Justice, 'Prison population projections 2021 to 2026'.

10. Ibid., p. 1.

11. T.J. Coati, 'What's wrong with secure schools?', *Abolitionist Futures*, 2021. https://abolitionistfutures.com/latest-news/whats-wrong-with-secure-schools

12. Ministry of Justice, 'Public consultation on plans for a new prison in Chorley', p. 8.

13. 'Business behind bars: Making real work in prison work', London: Howard League for Penal Reform (HLPR), 2016, p. 35. https://howardleague.org/wp-content/uploads/2016/05/Business_behind_bars.pdf

14. Nijjar, *Echoes of Empire*.

15. Jamie Grierson and Pamela Duncan, 'Private jails more violent than public ones, data analysis shows', *Guardian*, 13 May 2019. www.theguardian.com/society/2019/may/13/private-jails-more-violent-than-public-prisons-england-wales-data-analysis

16. 'Liberty challenges Met Police's discriminatory gangs matrix', *Liberty*, 1 February 2022. www.libertyhumanrights.org.uk/issue/liberty-challenges-met-polices-discriminatory-gangs-matrix/

17. Patrick Williams and Becky Clarke, 'Dangerous associations: Joint enterprise, gangs and racism', London: Centre for Crime and Justice Studies, 2016. www.crimeandjustice.

org.uk/publications/dangerous-associations-joint-enterprise-gangs-and-racism

18. 'The gangs matrix', *Stopwatch*, 2022. www.stop-watch.org/what-we-do/projects/the-gangs-matrix/

19. David Cameron, 'PM's speech on the fightback after the riots', *gov.uk*, 15 August 2011. www.gov.uk/government/speeches/pms-speech-on-the-fightback-after-the-riots

20. Jessica Perera, 'The London Clearances: Race, housing and policing', London: Institute of Race Relations, 2019. https://irr.org.uk/wp-content/uploads/2020/09/The-London-Clearances-Race-Housing-and-Policing-1.pdf

21. Patrick Williams, 'Being Matrixed – The (over)policing of gang suspects in London', *StopWatch*, 2018. https://tinyurl.com/mup3hf5u

22. David Cameron, 'I've put the bulldozing of sink estates at the heart of turnaround Britain', *The Times*, 10 January 2016. www.thetimes.co.uk/article/ive-put-the-bulldozing-of-sink-estates-at-the-heart-of-turnaround-britain-rtcgg2gnb6h

23. R. Sharma, 'One step forward, two steps back: A decade of social housing decline', *Shelter*, July 2021. https://blog.shelter.org.uk/2021/07/one-step-forward-two-steps-back-a-decade-of-social-housing-decline/. See also P. Butler and H. Saddique, 'The bedroom tax explained', *Guardian*, 27 January 2016. www.theguardian.com/society/2016/jan/27/the-bedroom-tax-explained

24. L. Lees and H. White, 'The social cleansing of London council estates: everyday experiences of "accumulative dispossession"', *Housing Studies*, 35(10), 2020, pp. 1701–22, doi: 10.1080/02673037.2019.1680814

25. 'Trapped in the gangs matrix', London: Amnesty International, 2018.

26. Dawn Foster, 'Evicting gang members' families punishes the innocent'. *Guardian*, 26 June 2018. www.theguardian.com/commentisfree/2018/jun/26/gang-members-families-evicting

27. Stafford Scott, 'Broadwater Farm revisited', *Tottenham Rights*, 6 March 2014. www.tottenhamrights.org/blog/broadwater-farm-revisited

28. Paul Bond, 'UK: Haringey development vehicle scheme scrapped, but social cleansing threat remains', *World Socialist Web Site*, 8 August 2018. www.wsws.org/en/articles/2018/08/08/hari-a08.html

29. 'Broadwater Farm – compulsory purchase order', Haringey Council, September 2021. www.haringey.gov.uk/housing/broadwater-farm.

30. Home Office, 'Serious Violence Duty factsheet'.

THESIS 14

1. George Monbiot, 'The UK is heading towards authoritarianism: Just look at this attack on a minority', *Guardian*, 12 January 2022. www.theguardian.com/commentisfree/2022/jan/12/uk-authoritarianism-minority-policing-bill-roma-gypsy-traveller

2. Donald Kenrick and Grattan Puxon, *The Destiny of Europe's Gypsies*, London: Basic Books, 1972. See also Derek Hawes and Barbara Perez, *The Gypsy and the State: The Ethnic Cleansing of British Society*, Bristol: Polity Press, 1996, and Leanne Weber and Benjamin Bowling, 'Valiant beggars and global vagabonds', *Theoretical Criminology* 12(3), 2008, pp. 355–75. doi:10.1177/1362480608093311

3. Hickel, *The Divide*.

4. Palmer, *Police and Protest in England and Ireland 1780–1850*.

5. Neocleous, *A Critical Theory of Police Power*.

6. Gypsies at this time were called Egyptians due to a misunderstanding of where they had migrated from.

7. Laura Soréna Tittel, 'Racial and social dimensions of antiziganism: The representation of "Gypsies" in political theory', *On Culture: The Open Journal for the Study of Culture*, 2020, p. 10. http://geb.uni-giessen.de/geb/volltexte/2021/16025/

8. John O'Sullivan, 'Britain's 1970s retread', *Economist*, 15 November 2017. www.economist.com/buttonwoods-notebook/2017/11/15/britains-1970s-retread

9. John Moore, 'Oh Angela! Policing the crisis will never solve the economic or policing crisis', *Abolitionist Futures*, 2021. https://abolitionistfutures.com/latest-news/oh-angela-policing-the-crisis-will-never-solve-the-economic-or-policing-crisis. See also Hall et al., *Policing the Crisis*, and Elliott-Cooper, *Black Resistance to British Policing*.

10. Dan Allen and Victoria Hamnett, 'Gypsy, Roma and Traveller children in child welfare services in England', *British Journal Of Social Work*, 7 January 2022. doi:10.1093/bjsw/bcab265.

11. C. Goddard, 'Review: Gypsy Roma Traveller Children in child welfare services in England'. *Children and Young People Now*, 1 March 2022. www.cypnow.co.uk/research/article/gypsy-roma-and-traveller-children-in-child-welfare-services-in-england

12. 'Adopted and looked-after children', London: Department for Education (DFE), 2021. www.ethnicity-facts-figures.service.gov.uk/health/social-care/adopted-and-looked-after-children/latest#by-ethnicity-looked-after-and-adopted-children

13. Perera, 'How Black working class youth are criminalised and excluded in the English school system'.

14. John Boughton, *The Rise and Fall of Council Housing*, London: Verso, 2019.

15. David Harvey, *The New Imperialism*, Oxford: Oxford University Press, 2003.

16. Katharine Quarmby, *No Place to Call Home: Inside the Real Lives of Gypsies and Travellers*, London: Oneworld Publications, 2013.

17. 'Public Order Bill: factsheet', London: Home Office, 2022.

18. 'Count of Traveller caravans, July 2021 England', London: Department for Levelling Up, Housing and Communities (DfLUHC), 2021. https://assets.publishing.service.gov.uk/

government/uploads/system/uploads/attachment_data/
file/1040638/TCC_July_2021_count.pdf

19. Blyth Brentnall, 'UK Traveller communities fear "cultural annihilation" over upcoming trespass laws', *Open Democracy*, 25 January 2022. www.opendemocracy.net/en/opendemocracyuk/police-bill-travellers-gypsy-roma-trespass-laws-cultural-annihilation/

20. More on this written in Quarmby, *No Place to Call Home*.

THESIS 15

1. 'Brian Douglas', *4Front*, 2022. www.4frontproject.org/brian-douglas; 'Christopher Alder', *4Front*, 2022. www.4frontproject.org/christopher-alder; 'Sean Rigg', *4Front*, 2022. www.4frontproject.org/sean-rigg; 'Jermaine Baker', *4Front*, 2022. https://www.4frontproject.org/jermaine-baker; 'Rashan Charles', *4Front*, 2022. https://www.4frontproject.org/rashan-charles

2. Gary Younge and Caelainn Barr, 'How Scotland reduced knife deaths among young people', *Guardian*. 3 December 2017. www.theguardian.com/membership/2017/dec/03/how-scotland-reduced-knife-deaths-among-young-people

3. Barr and Topping, 'Fewer than one in 60 rape cases lead to charge in England and Wales'.

4. 'Deaths in police custody', *Inquest*, 2022. www.inquest.org.uk/deaths-in-police-custody

5. Nationally: 'Crime and income deprivation', *Trust For London*, 2022. www.trustforlondon.org.uk/data/crime-and-income-deprivation. Internationally: 'Crime', *Equalitytrust.Org.Uk*, 2022. https://equalitytrust.org.uk/crime

6. Vikram Dodd, 'Tackle and inequality to reduce crime, says police chief', *Guardian*, 18 April 2021. www.theguardian.com/uk-news/2021/apr/18/tackle-poverty-and-inequality-to-reduce-says-police-chief

7. Vikram Dodd, 'Dalian Atkinson's family tell of agony over footballer's Taser death', *Guardian*, 17 November 2016. www.

theguardian.com/world/2016/nov/17/dalian-atkinsons-family-tell-of-agony-over-footballers-taser-death; 'Mouayed Bashir's brother says it is like "Torture" waiting for answers about his death', *ITV News*, 21 March 2022. www.itv.com/news/wales/2022-03-21/mouayed-bashirs-brother-says-its-torture-waiting-for-answers-about-his-death; 'Kingsley Burrell', *4Front*, 2022. www.4frontproject.org/kingsley-burrell

8. Sam Francis, Tarah Welsh and Zack Adesina, 'Met Police "four times more likely" to use force on black people', *BBC News*, 30 July 2020. www.bbc.co.uk/news/uk-england-london-53407560

9. 'BAME deaths in police custody', *Inquest*, 2022. www.inquest.org.uk/bame-deaths-in-police-custody

10. Tristan Cork, 'More than 60 people said they were injured by police in the first three "Kill the Bill" protests', *Bristol Post*, 20 April 2021. www.bristolpost.co.uk/news/bristol-news/62-people-said-were-injured-5317757

11. Steven Morris, 'Bristol police chief accepts force was slow to correct protest injury claims', *Guardian*, 2 April 2021. www.theguardian.com/uk-news/2021/apr/02/bristol-police-chief-accepts-force-was-slow-to-correct-protest-injury-claims

12. 'Defund the police: Reformist reforms vs abolitionist steps for UK policing', *Abolitionist Futures*, 2020. https://abolitionistfutures.com/defund-the-police

THESIS 16

1. Dhoruba Bin Wahad, 'The last of the loud', 2021. https://millennialsarekillingcapitalism.libsyn.com/the-last-of-the-loud-dhoruba-bin-wahad-philosopher-of-the-whirlwind

2. Novara Media, *'Defeat Was Snatched From The Jaws Of Victory'* – *Remembering The Grunwick Strike*, Video, 2016. www.youtube.com/watch?v=oIrr5e2mHzI

3. Mar Townsend, 'Rashan Charles family accuses Metropolitan police of "disdain"', *Guardian*, 8 October 2017.

www.theguardian.com/uk-news/2017/oct/08/rashan-charles-police-custody-death

4. Beth Mann, 'More Britons now unconfident than confident in the police to deal with crime locally', *YouGov*, 2021. https://yougov.co.uk/topics/politics/articles-reports/2021/10/06/more-britons-now-unconfident-confident-police-deal

5. 'Find your local CopWatch group', The Network for Police Monitoring (Netpol), 2022. https://netpol.org/2022/04/06/find-your-local-copwatch-group/

6. Rosa Luxemburg, 'The mass strike', 1906. www.marxists.org/archive/luxemburg/1906/mass-strike/ch04.htm

Index

Virginia colony 101, 102

Wahad, Dhoruba bin 197, 199
war: language of 156, 158–9
'war on terror' 156
Weinstein, Harvey 30
welfare state 135–6
white people: confidence in
    police force of 61–2
Windrush scandal 11, 134–5, 139
women 78–88, 214–5
    criminalisation and imprison-
        ment of 25, 28, 86
    violence against 60, 78–9
Women Against Rape (organisa-
    tion) 24
women police officers 61

women workers 83–4
women's liberation movement
    80–1, 84
women's refuges 76, 80, 81–2
working class 59, 68, 71–2, 140
    criminalising of 109–10,
        130–1
    racism in 104–5

X, Michael 11

Yarl's Wood detention centre 23,
    24, 146, 151–3, 154–5
young people 221–3
    police violence against 121–2
    protests by 119–21, 123–6
youth work 221–3

Thanks to our Patreon subscribers:

Andrew Perry
Ciaran Kane

Who have shown generosity and
comradeship in support of our publishing.

Check out the other perks you get by subscribing
to our Patreon – visit patreon.com/plutopress.
Subscriptions start from £3 a month.